Working with

DIFFICULT
PEOPLE

Muriel Solomon

PRENTICE HALL
Englewood Cliffs, New Jersey 07632

Prentice-Hall International (UK) Limited, *London*
Prentice-Hall of Australia Pty. Limited, *Sydney*
Prentice-Hall Canada, Inc., *Toronto*
Prentice-Hall Hispanoamericana, S.A., *Mexico*
Prentice-Hall of India Private Limited, *New Delhi*
Prentice-Hall of Japan, Inc., *Tokyo*
Simon & Schuster Asia Pte. Ltd., *Singapore*
Editora Prentice-Hall do Brasil, Ltda., *Rio de Janeiro*

© 1990 *by*

Muriel Solomon

Library of Congress Cataloging-in-Publication Data

Solomon, Muriel.
   Working with difficult people / by Muriel Solomon.
      p.   cm.
   Includes index.
   ISBN 0-13-957382-8 (case). — ISBN 0-13-957390-9 (pbk.)
   1. Conflict management.   2. Interpersonal relations.
3. Interpersonal conflict.   I. Title.
HD42.S65   1990
650.1'3—dc20   90-7467
                                                         CIP

ISBN 0-13-957382-8

ISBN 0-13-957390-9 (pbk)

PRENTICE HALL
BUSINESS & PROFESSIONAL DIVISION
A division of Simon & Schuster
Englewood Cliffs, New Jersey 07632

Printed in the United States of America

BOMC offers recordings and compact discs, cassettes
and records. For information and catalog write to
BOMR, Camp Hill, PA 17012.

to Susan Solomon Cooper and
Nancy and Bernard Goldberg,
always incisive, supportive sounding boards

HOW TO USE THIS GUIDEBOOK

The 100 people you'll meet on these pages should be founding members of E.O.O.—Equal Opportunity Offenders. They show no bias. They are as obnoxious to their bosses as they are to their book-keepers. And while you have every right to feel affronted by them, you're not their prime target. You just happen to be in the way—or provide the way—for them to get what they're after. You are caught in their web and it's up to you to free yourself.

Here's the key. This book is designed as an instant reference tool. Look up a workable strategy as easily as you look up a correct spelling. From Blame Shifters, Hotheads, Snipers to Zealots, you wrestle with them everyday, so keep your guidebook in a handy spot. You'll find a quick sketch of your particular "problem" boss, peer, or worker in the Table of Contents, with additional help from the index in locating your subject.

Parts One through Ten divide difficult people into ten basic types. Each type is discussed in three separate chapters because you're after different results when dealing with people you work for, people you work with, and people who work for you. You have to tailor your tactics to the outcome you desire. Then, within each chapter you'll find the most frequent culprits.

No matter how bright you are, being angry, hurt, or disappointed blocks your good judgment. The purpose of this book is to provide you logical action instead of emotional reaction. For each exasperating personality, we look first at what's upsetting you, then what might be going through the mind of that difficult person. While you're cooling off, bone up on the tested strategy and review the exact phrases you can say to carry out the suggested tactics.

This guidebook is about communicating effectively on the job. But in case the Fox description fits your sly Uncle Fred, and the Battering Ram sounds like your overpowering next door neighbor, or Forked Tongue is your friend who speaks out of both sides of his mouth, remember people don't shed their vexing ways because the office clock strikes five. Maybe you'll pick up some hints for dealing with these types off the job as well. *Working with Difficult People* offers a practical way to help you turn a bad situation to your advantage.

Muriel Solomon

CONTENTS

PART SEVEN—DEALING WITH PROCRASTINATING/ VACILLATING PEOPLE • 171

PART EIGHT—DEALING WITH RIGID/OBSTINATE PEOPLE • 201

AUTHOR'S NOTE: In recent years, the role of women in business has expanded beyond the traditional assistant roles. It is not uncommon for women to supervise men as well as women. Therefore, I hope it will be understood that when I use the personal pronouns "he," "his," and "him," I am referring to women and men alike.

ALSO BY MURIEL SOLOMON:

"What Do I Say When . . . ": A Guidebook for Getting Your Way with People on the Job (Prentice Hall, 1988)

PART ONE

DEALING WITH HOSTILE/ANGRY PEOPLE

What do people with personal problems do when they go to work? They pack up their troubles in an old attache case and growl, growl, growl.

Some are chronic belligerents who take out their anger on you. They are so weighted down by jealousy, rage or resentment that only by throwing stones at others do they get the lift they need to go on. To overcome their inferiority and anxiety, they act in a superior and aggressive way. They actually *need* to intimidate and deflate you and treat you as a nonperson in order to bolster their feeling of self worth.

Whether you are their boss, colleague, or subordinate, they'll find your vulnerable area and zing you right in your Achilles' heel.

And what do you do when that happens? You get angry, too, and keep thinking how badly you've been treated. As long as you sit there licking your wounds, you're not focusing on how to deal with these belligerents to get the results you want.

CHAPTER 1

WHEN YOUR BOSS IS BELLIGERENT

1.1 Tyrants
1.2 Bullies
1.3 Sadists
1.4 Time Bombs

First, let's admit it. We've all pulled bonehead maneuvers and, frankly, we deserved it when the boss lit into us about the fiascoes. Managers correct mistakes. That's their right.

But no one can give a boss the right to call you an ignoramus, especially in front of an audience. Somehow you have to reduce the abuse dished out by tyrannical, bullying, sadistic or exploding villains. Telling them off and storming out in a huff won't help. The fleeting satisfaction you receive from landing a verbal punch is a luxury you can't afford.

We're going to look at a better way. A method for letting go of the hurt and going after what's *really* important to you, getting ahead in your job. You'll choose different strategies, depending on whether or not the boss is intentionally hostile. Either way, you can't *assume* you know what the boss wants from you until he himself tells you what's on his mind.

However, you can't reason with the enraged. Wait until the boss calms down, then talk it over and, at least, agree on objectives. You listen hard, you plot your strategy, and you think before you speak up. That's how to handle a hostile boss.

1.1 TYRANTS

Tyrants treat you in a high-handed, harsh, and dictatorial manner.

These abusive, abrasive bosses are gluttons for power. They're even reluctant to delegate tasks because that means they can't hog all the control.

Tyrants tend to rule arbitrarily, as despots, cruelly imposing their will. Their need to feel omnipotent isn't met until they can demean you and trample upon your ego. A favorite tactic is to interrupt you in the middle of what you're saying, assassinating your character as they tear apart your remarks.

They have deluded themselves to believe that they, uniquely, know the right answers. If you criticize them, you'll escalate their attacks. You have to assert yourself with utmost tact if you are going to survive their reign.

What You're Thinking

All I did was make a decision that was part of my job to make. The boss gets jealous if any of his staff people gets recognition. He rants at me whenever his every wish isn't carried out. My stomach is in knots working with this dictator. Some day I'll get even with the ogre for humiliating me in front of my staff, my peers, and my clients.

A Tyrant's Thoughts

I'm still not getting the proper respect around here. Everyone has always tried to put me down, but now I have the authority and I'll show them who's boss. I've got a great system worked out. This is the structure they need. Why aren't they cooperating? Why do they have to argue with me over every assignment? It's tough enough running this outfit without getting flak from disrespectful workers. As if I don't have enough trouble at home. Well, I don't care what they think, they had just better do what I say.

Strategy

Your goal is to get your boss to treat you in a civil, courteous manner and to stop being so overbearing. To accomplish this:

(1) *Prepare to act.* Stop accepting the situation. If you do nothing, the sharp stabs will fester until you finally blow up or break down.

(2) *Appear firm, strong and unemotional.* If you reveal that you're weak and angry, the Tyrant tries harder to dominate you. Let him rage. You must appear serene and not threaten his majesty's self image.

(3) *Use tact to get his attention and respect.* Telling him he's wrong will make him seek revenge. Instead ask questions that show you want to talk. He may actually be starving for approval and affection but trying to get it the wrong way. Even a Tyrant needs a friend.

Tactical Talk

Boss: "THIS WHOLE OFFICE WOULD BE IN COMPLETE CHAOS IF I ALLOWED EACH OF YOU DUMBHEADS TO DO WHATEVER YOU WANT. YOU DO IT MY WAY AND DON'T EVEN THINK ABOUT COMING BACK HERE UNTIL THAT CONTRACT IS SIGNED."

You: "BOSS, I UNDERSTAND WHAT YOU'RE TRYING TO ACCOMPLISH, BUT WHEN YOU SAY INSULTING THINGS LIKE THAT, HOW DO YOU THINK THAT MAKES US FEEL?

"I REALIZE HOW IMPORTANT THIS CONTRACT IS TO YOU AND THE COMPANY. HAVE YOU CONSIDERED THAT WE MIGHT HAVE A BETTER CHANCE OF CLOSING THE DEAL IF WE ADDED ANOTHER ...?"

Tip: Don't grieve—leave. Bosses who seem as tyrannical as Attila the Hun are often quite bright. Learn all you can from them. Then, if you can't change the climate and your boss is solidly entrenched, to keep your sanity, think about working someplace else.

1.2 BULLIES

Bullies are habitually cruel, threatening your present and future.

While Tyrants believe they were ordained to rule, Bullies believe they can control if they use hate and fear as weapons.

Bullies appear self-confident and strong because they intimidate weaker people. If you vacillate and submit, or act afraid, or react with rage, that proves to them that you are inferior and deserve to be disparaged.

When Bully bosses belittle you, crushing your self-confidence with their authoritarian threats, your best defense is an offense. You have to stand up to the bully.

What You're Thinking

My boss tortures me with emotional blackmail. If I don't do exactly what he wants when he wants, I'll never get a raise or move up, or he could make me lose my job. I can't afford to upset him, so I hide my anger. But I'm always tense and on edge.

A Bully's Thoughts

These people make me mad. They're so weak and stupid. They can't think anything through. Well, I told them the right way to handle it. Yes, it *was* the right way. At any rate, the matter is not negotiable. I must prove I am right. If I frighten them and show them how weak they are, they will see how strong I am.

Strategy

Your aim is to protect your job by redeeming your self-esteem and, thereby, gaining the Bully's respect. To fight back, arm yourself with friendliness and self-confidence and avoid a clash of wills:

(1) *Let the Bully vent his anger without attempting to stop him.* In a pleasant tone, pose questions to get him to disclose what's really bugging him. He may be a Bully, but he's human, so don't be surprised if he reacts positively when you show concern for his feelings.

(2) *Deal with the problem without criticizing his thinking or actions.* If you agree with part of what he says, say so while indicating that some other points confuse you. If you totally disagree, show respect for his authority as you ask him to consider another possibility.

(3) *Be wary about ganging up to make a complaint.* Unless this is very carefully orchestrated, if a group of you marches into his office, your boss will feel threatened. Then he'll clamp down harder. And going to the boss's boss will probably backfire, too. Your boss may be hailed in the upper echelons as an achiever deserving their total support.

Tactical Talk

Boss: "YOU ARE WRONG. SHUT UP AND LISTEN AND THEN DO AS YOU'RE TOLD OR ELSE YOU CAN EMPTY OUT YOUR DESK AND YOU ARE HISTORY."

You: "OK, BOSS, I CAN SEE YOU DON'T AGREE. OF COURSE YOU HAVE THE FINAL SAY AND I'LL DO MY DARNDEST TO CARRY OUT YOUR DECISION, BUT IT WOULD SEEM THAT—" *(boss interrupts, but you continue, interrupting the interrupter)*

You: "EXCUSE ME, I'M NOT THROUGH. GIVE ME 30 SECONDS TO FINISH THIS POINT. IF XYZ CAUSES THE PROBLEM, WHAT WOULD HAPPEN IF WE SHIFTED THE..."

Tip: Bullies lose their power if you don't cower. Deep down, they doubt they deserve your respect. They admire your speaking with self assurance and confidence. So when they bombard, don't counterpunch. Best the Bully with your strong, firm, courteous demeanor.

1.3 SADISTS

Sadists take pleasure in causing you difficulty.

Sadistic bosses also are hostile, but their joy is in catching you in a mistake and making you squirm. With an "Aha, gotcha!" look, they get their kicks out of attacking you or threatening to fire you, and its more delightful for them if their reprimand is given in front of your colleagues or customers.

These Sadists demand blind obedience, but keep changing the rules to fit their whims. They berate you for errors they initiated and then not only deny any responsibility, but also fail to show you a better way.

With no letup, Sadists are deliberately mean. You can't disagree with them without making matters worse. You have to find a way to keep them from sapping your spirit and all but eradicating your ego.

What You're Thinking

My boss just isn't happy unless he's degrading his staff. He purposely tries to make me look foolish or inept. I am particularly upset because he asked me to talk frankly with him when I had any problems with my department, but when I did, he used my voluntary information to give me a low evaluation. He humiliates me for mistakes and punishes me for problems! I've started covering up instead of talking to him because I think he's making me a scapegoat to protect his position.

A Sadist's Thoughts

I've got to shake my people out of their complacency. If I embarrass them some more, I can motivate them to work faster. But this is cutting into the time I'd planned to use for developing the new system. I guess I'll have to push a little harder. So what if I have to break a few company regulations in the process? It's coming out ahead of my colleagues and keeping in tight with the head honchos that count.

Strategy

Your immediate goal is to reduce your daily stress on the job. You can move along two tracks simultaneously:

(1) *Try a shock treatment.* Stand up for yourself by asking your boss to please sit down, look him in the eye without blinking, and calmly state that you wish to be treated with the respect due another human being. Your unexpected action may get him to see you as a person instead of a punching bag.

(2) *Learn the recourse you have in your company.* Your personnel director knows the transfer openings and can explain if there are any grievance procedures. If your boss thinks his behavior may be tagged "unprofessional," he'll want to do something to avoid the hearing process. He very well may let up a little.

If the torture continues and you're becoming a physical or emotional wreck, consider moving out while you're still able to work at all.

Tactical Talk

Boss: "YOU STUPID FOOL. CAN'T YOU FOLLOW THE SIMPLEST ORDERS? HOW CAN I RUN A DIVISION WHEN THEY GIVE ME INCOMPETENTS LIKE YOU!"

You: "YES, BOSS, BUT WHICH ORDER DO YOU WANT ME TO FOLLOW—THE EXECUTIVE ORDER IN THE MANUAL OR THE ONE YOU ARE TELLING ME ABOUT NOW? IF I MADE A MISTAKE TELL ME. I'M GLAD TO DO WHATEVER YOU THINK BEST. BUT THERE'S NO NEED TO CALL ME NAMES."

Tip: With Sadists, an anonymous letter may be better. If you have no grievance procedure, write the top boss. Point to high turnover, low morale, or other pervasive problems.

Recommend better supervisory training. Request that an ombudsman hear employees' fears and resolve their complaints. Propose a formalized system that enables workers to make suggestions to managers positioned above their immediate supervisors.

1.4 TIME BOMBS

Time Bombs—their anger unexpectedly erupts in tantrums.

Time Bombs differ from other hostile bosses in that their actions aren't planned. Their frenzy leaves you feeling both confused and frightened because you are witnessing someone out of control.

These are adults who throw childish tantrums. They learned early in life that exploding in anger is a defense against fear and frustration.

Time Bombs can't tolerate opposing opinions. When you disagree, they believe you are criticizing them on a personal level. During a quiet discussion, if your statement happens to touch a sensitive spot, it's snap, crackle, pop. They suddenly erupt in a rage, shouting tirades, blaming you for everything. Your mind shifts into shock.

What You're Thinking

I never know when to expect my overemotional boss to explode. At times he acts like I'm the enemy. He's super touchy and I can't figure out how to talk over a problem without triggering an explosion. Sometimes I'm scared that when he starts throwing ash trays at me, I won't be able to duck in time.

A Time Bomb's Thoughts

I mustn't let my workers see me so angry. I have to prove that what I am saying is in their own best interest and that they are unable to comprehend the complexity of the problem. They are implying that I am confused—imagine that! I am the only one who can see the situation clearly. But they are fighting me. Maybe they are after my job. Maybe they're trying to advance by stepping all over me.

Strategy

Your immediate aim is to defuse the Time Bomb and then to gain his trust:

(1) *Protect yourself.* While the Time Bomb is having his tantrum, if you think he may become violent, leave instantly saying you'll talk later.

(2) *Be patient.* Wait for the exploder to run down and regain some self-control. Especially don't mention the "explosive" issue. Get his attention after a few minutes by repeatedly shouting his name ("John, John, John, listen, listen"). Keep a friendly tone to avoid a screaming duet.

(3) *Tactfully resume talking if he calms down.* Acknowledge his thinking. Show you understand how important the issue is to him. Reassure him that you're on his side. You're not questioning his authority, you're merely offering a suggestion.

Tactical Talk

"JOHN, YOU KNOW I RESPECT YOUR DECISIONS AND I'VE ALWAYS BEEN A TEAM PLAYER. I REALIZE HOW IMPORTANT IT IS TO HAVE ALL THE BASES COVERED.

"I JUST WANTED YOU TO CONSIDER HOW I FEEL WHEN I HAVE TO WORK WEEKENDS BECAUSE I'M UNMARRIED AND YOU DON'T ASK MARY OR PETER BECAUSE THEY HAVE FAMILIES. I FEEL I'M BEING PUNISHED AND TREATED UNFAIRLY, JOHN, AND I WANTED YOU TO SEE THIS FROM ANOTHER ANGLE."

Tip: If Mt. Vesuvius starts erupting in an open area, usher your boss to a quiet spot. Try to save him from embarrassing himself. Exploders need your support and understanding to help them cope with their fears. Be respectful and concerned as you gingerly attempt to disarm the Time Bomb.

There are many varieties of belligerent bosses. When a hostile boss attacks you, bottling up your feelings can make you ill. But you don't have to mask those feelings beneath a smile or go to the other extreme and storm out of the room. Take a cue from one of our most assertive First Ladies, Eleanor Roosevelt, who wrote, "Nobody can make you feel inferior without your consent." Learn to stand up for yourself and express your anger in a positive way. That's good for you and for your boss.

CHAPTER 2

WHEN YOUR COLLEAGUES ARE BELLIGERENT

2.1 Tacklers

2.2 Enviers

2.3 Intimidators

It's normal to react angrily when a colleague is hostile to you, or is even aggressive without obvious hostility. That's OK. Now you have a choice. How are you going to use this anger when you have to deal with Tacklers, Enviers and Intimidators?

If you do nothing but cry about it, your brain will rust. But if you admit to yourself how you're feeling, you begin to put the anger to work. You start dreaming up ways to dispose of your resentment.

After eliminating the tactics of physically punching the aggressor and "accidentally" anointing his head with hot coffee, you free your mind to focus on achieving the objectives that *are* in your best interest.

2.1 TACKLERS

Tacklers attack you personally while arguing an issue. These colleagues are so determined to score points with the boss that they block whatever you toss out for consideration and tackle you instead of the problem. They twist everything you say so that you become the opponent who has to be brought down and overcome.

When they tackle you, you know you've been hit. They don't hold back with their attack. You feel hurt, but are more concerned with the consequences. Your credibility is being kicked around like a football. How can you keep the Tacklers from injuring your career?

What You're Thinking

Vicky can't debate an issue on its merits. It's somehow my fault that I don't go along with her conclusions. After the boss asked me to head the study group, we divided the jobs and all the other members came through. Vicky didn't do the work and then blamed me for picking on her when I asked for her assignments. I have to dodge her attacks while Vicky gets away with goofing off. If she keeps this up, the others could lose confidence in my leadership ability.

A Tackler's Thoughts

If she wasn't so stupid she'd see that another approach would get the job done a lot faster without putting forth so much effort. She just wants to show me up, but I'll beat her to it. I'll make sure the whole group sees how incompetent she is.

Strategy

Your goal is to maintain your professionalism as you carry out your assignments, while minimizing any damage Tacklers can do to your standing:

(1) *Continue your game plan.* Don't be sidelined by a groveling match. Instead, question the Tackler to show that you are determined to do the job without stooping to his level. Elevate the discussion by moving the emphasis away from individuals back to the issue at hand.

(2) *Talk to him privately if he continues to tackle you.* Say that you'd like to have a better relationship and ask how he thinks you might be able to resolve your differences.

(3) *Learn where you can—and can't—expect support.* Determine through the grapevine if the Tackler has company friends in high places. If so, an ongoing feud could hurt your chance to advance. It's not worth the fuss. Concentrate on doing your job and making more friends.

Tactical Talk

You: "VICKY, WHEN WE DIVIDED THE WORK YOU SAID YOU'D LIKE THE RESEARCH JOB. IF THAT'S A PROBLEM, WE STILL HAVE OPENINGS IN THREE OTHER AREAS—"

Vicky: "YOU REALLY HAVE IT IN FOR ME, DON'T YOU? WHY ARE YOU BEING SO MEAN TO ME? YOU LOVE TO LORD IT OVER EVERYONE THAT YOU'RE CHAIRING THIS STUDY GROUP AND—"

You: "VICKY, OBVIOUSLY YOU'VE MISCONSTRUED MY ROLE. NOW THE THREE AREAS IN WHICH WE NEED MORE CONCENTRATION ARE (1)... (2)...AND (3)... WHICH DO YOU PREFER?"

Tip: You're not after 100 percent harmony. You and your Tackler will seldom sing the same tune. You just need to come to some understanding that lets you get on with your work. To arrange a truce, handle the conflict with direct, clear, face-to-face confrontation instead of memos or phone calls which may tend to muddy the waters.

2.2 ENVIERS

Enviers jealously begrudge you the praises you receive. These peers are resentful. They want what you have. More than that, they believe they *should have* what you have. Keep in mind that a whole company can't be fooled for long. Most of the time, sooner or later, we all get what's coming to us.

The worst part about envy is that it erodes the spirit and eats up energy that could have been put to better use. But until the Envier can let go of his jealousy and anger over your having what is "rightfully" his, he can become consumed with getting revenge. You may be totally innocent and find yourself the victim of spiteful, childish behavior.

What You're Thinking

I worked night and day for four weeks on that project to make it a success and everybody's been slapping me on the back and telling me what a great job I did. Except for Ben. He's too self-centered to be happy for me. He said "Congratulations," but I can feel his hostility and his envy. I don't know why he seems to consider me an adversary. My instincts tell me to be on guard for a disguised attack.

An Envier's Thoughts

I can't understand why everyone's making such a fuss over him. I could have done it better if only I'd been given that assignment. I don't think it was just luck that landed him that project. I wonder what he did to get it. I'll have to dig up the dirt about him because I'm sure he told some lies about me or else I'd have been handed that plum. But I'll get even and he'll never know what hit him.

Strategy

Your goal is to protect yourself and, if possible, help your colleague think more positively:

(1) *Keep your talks on a high and friendly level.* Don't let the Envier get you into an argument, especially not with others present.

(2) *Convey that each person's effort is judged on its own merit.* It isn't good because another's is bad or valuable because another's is not valuable. One's work stands good or bad by itself.

(3) *Encourage the Envier.* Help him define his personal goals and develop his own special skills and expertise. This will bolster his sense of self worth.

Tactical Talk

"C'MON, BEN, I DON'T WANT TO ARGUE ABOUT THAT. WE CAN BE CIVIL TO EACH OTHER. IF YOU CAN'T TALK ABOUT THIS NOW, LET'S TALK ABOUT IT LATER." (*and leave*)

"BEN, YOU HAVE A REAL TALENT FOR FINANCIAL ANALYSIS. HAVE YOU CONSIDERED ASKING THE BOSS TO SEND YOU TO ONE OF THOSE SPECIAL TRAINING COURSES HE WAS TALKING ABOUT LAST WEEK?"

Tip: Disarm the Envier with an honest compliment. Just when he's all set to hate you, make him like you. Express admiration for whatever he does well, talk about his interests and offer helpful suggestions for him to mull over that may not have occurred to him before.

2.3 INTIMIDATORS

Intimidators gain support by implying they can hurt or embarrass you.

These hostile colleagues don't come right out and threaten you, but you still hear their warning loud and clear. You know you are in for some form of pain or punishment if you don't go along with whatever they want from you.

An intimidating boss who can fire you has real power over you; an intimidating colleague has *perceived* power. Nevertheless, this too can be a dangerous threat. With every contact, watch for the blinking yellow caution lights.

What You're Thinking

He makes me feel inferior even though I know I do the job as well or better than he does. But I've been going along with all his ideas because I'm afraid if I don't, he'll turn the others against me.

An Intimidator's Thoughts

I've got to shut up this pip-squeak. Whenever Iris comes up with her bright ideas at staff meetings, the boss is all ears. She's a threat. When Carl leaves next year and the assistant director's job is open, I want to be the natural choice. Until then, I've got to keep Iris from winning over everybody on the team. I'd better squash her before she gets the job I want.

Strategy

Your goal is to keep control of yourself, not allowing the Intimidator to push you into doing or not doing anything you don't want to:

(1) *Rehearse retorts at home.* Unharried, you can come up with quick responses you'll say the next time your Intimidator strikes. Remember, you never have to give an instant answer. You can take your time or pick only the part of his remarks that you care to reply to. Role play with a trusted friend ("If he says this..., I'll say that...").

(2) *Force yourself to appear poised and calm.* Pretend you are unruffled even if you are momentarily intimidated. You can't do anything about the thoughts that the Intimidator has, but you can decide which thoughts you will let yourself dwell on. Practice with a tape recorder and act in front of a mirror. Say the words out loud to listen to how you sound.

(3) *Psych yourself.* Put emotional space between the Intimidator's threats and your replies; for example, imagine yourself encased in protective plastic that won't permit any verbal attacks to penetrate. Until you learn to do this, put as much physical space as you can between yourself and the offender.

(4) *Know when to laugh it off.* If you are new on the job and several coworkers are hazing you, ask a friendly colleague if this behavior is par for the course. If so,

though the pranks may be obnoxious, they're harmless, simply meant as a fraternity initiation to see if you can "pass the test."

Tactical Talk

A few quick replies to the Intimidator:

(*laughing it off*) "YOU'RE NOT REALLY SERIOUS, ARE YOU?"

(*buying time*) "DON'T RUSH ME. I'M WEIGHING WHAT YOU SAID."

(*being selective*) "I DON'T FEEL TOTALLY COMFORTABLE WITH THAT."

Tip: Break the cycle—anger begets anger, and retaliation begets retaliation. Concentrate on your desired outcome to reinforce your resolve. You can be firm, forceful and assertive without sounding mad. Allow yourself to feel friendly and to smile. Ask yourself: What am I afraid of? How can this colleague hurt me? How can I stand up to him and at the same time convert him to be my friend?

When colleagues act hostile, don't let their anger become contagious and infect your good judgment. Your peers are having a problem with negative feelings—frustration, fear, jealousy, inadequacy, and so on. Perhaps you can find out why. You can say that they seem upset and appear to be annoyed at you. In a calm discussion, if you both will identify potential options, you will both feel better because the two of you will then be exercising control.

CHAPTER 3

WHEN YOUR SUBORDINATES ARE BELLIGERENT

3.1 Hotheads
3.2 Revengers
3.3 Snipers

The authority you have over your workers may seem to give you unlimited power, but since your job is to get work done *through* your subordinates, they also wield power over you. For things to run smoothly, you are every bit as dependent on them as they are on you. So if you've been acting like an army general, remember that your noncoms have feelings too, just as you do. And if they seem aggressive, they may be angry because they think somebody made them feel inferior, inadequate or insecure.

Even when you *are* sensitive to your subordinates' feelings, a few may become hostile, spreading tension among the rest. Some pick fights among their peers. Some try to sabotage your operation if they think you did them wrong. Some use humor or sarcasm to try to discredit you. And then there are some subordinates, who like children, try to get you to referee their fights.

3.1 HOTHEADS

Hotheads are scrappers who start arguments among your workers.

When Hotheads can't figure out how to cope with pressure, they can become belligerent. They provoke quarrels among their colleagues, but may not be angry at them. You may be seeing signs of their frustration because they have had to suppress their hostility. They may really be angry with you and are afraid to confront you.

Instructing them to stop worrying, or to relax, or that they ought to feel any given way doesn't diminish their hostility. It would help to get them to discuss their anger, but only if they trust you and believe they can talk to you about their feelings without risking their jobs.

What You're Thinking

Wayne has a short fuse. He's an excellent worker if only he could learn to control his temper. His actions are becoming too disruptive to put up with anymore. If I can't get him to tone down his anger, I'll have to dismiss him.

A Hothead's Thoughts

They all stop talking when I join them. They obviously don't trust me. Well, who needs teacher's pets? When Margo takes extra time off, she gets called in for coffee with the boss. When Mike messed up that order, he and the boss went out to lunch to straighten it out. I keep plugging away, doing my work, and nobody notices me. I guess you have to act up before you can get recognized around here.

Strategy

Your objective is to keep your team from being disrupted. Help Hotheads articulate their anger and deal with it constructively so that they can become more productive:

(1) *Review your management style.* Be sure you aren't rewarding nonperformance. When subordinates feel they are treated unfairly, great animosity can result. Establish your rules and periodically check yourself to see that you treat all your workers the same.

(2) *Wait to discuss the problem.* Until your Hothead cools down, don't take a stand, just talk about the anger he's feeling. Then when he's able to tell you how he thinks he's being exploited, you can shift to solutions.

(3) *Work together to resolve the issue.* Ask what he thinks would salve his injured feelings. Listen carefully, without interrupting. Nod agreement whenever you honestly can. When you disagree, ask more questions.

(4) *Refuse to be a referee.* When two squabbling workers look to you to side with his case, decide if the problem is in the system and something you can correct. If, for instance, others are putting too much pressure on them, monitor the work flow and route complaints through your desk. If there's a personality clash, insist they function as part of the team. Be firm that you won't tolerate interference with your standards and warn them that if the disturbances continue, they'll both be gone.

Tactical Talk

You: "YOU'RE OBVIOUSLY UPSET."

Wayne: "I'M SO MAD I COULD SPIT!"

You: "YES, I CAN SEE THAT YOU'RE MAD."

Wayne: "NO ONE HAS ANY REGARD FOR MY FEELINGS!"

You: "YOU THINK WE'RE ALL CALLOUS?"

Wayne: "I SURE DO. THE ONLY WAY TO GET ANY NO-
          TICE IN THIS COMPANY IS TO GOOF UP. I GET
          MY WORK DONE EARLY, SO I'M LOADED DOWN
          WITH THEIRS. IT'S NOT FAIR."

You: "I CAN UNDERSTAND YOUR REACTION. WHAT
          DO YOU SUGGEST WE DO TO MAKE THE WORK-
          LOAD MORE EQUITABLE?"

Tip: Sometimes you have to talk tough. If a subordinate threatens to quit unless you meet his demands, refuse the ultimatum and tell him you believe he's putting his interest above the company's and you can no longer bank on his loyalty. Usually, however, you can take a soft approach that will protect your Hothead's self image and help him deal effectively with his hostility.

3.2 REVENGERS

Revengers deeply resent how they believe you mistreated them.

They are soreheads who feel cheated or neglected. Sometimes they misread your comments or mannerisms and mistakenly feel you are disappointed in them. Without checking out their perception, they hang on to the grudge.

Sometimes workers who are transferred because of company reorganization are resentful and balk at *any* assignment. True or not, they may *feel* that you and their new colleagues are belittling them and this results in an escalating spiral of hostility.

Also, there are workers who get agitated when you say the status quo must go. Unless you've done careful advance planning, they not only resist the change but become angry and search for ways to get back at you.

What You're Thinking

I had to turn down Megan's request. I thought I explained my reasons, but she's obviously harboring some grudge against me. I can feel her resentment and hostility, and I sense she's plotting some revenge. She's probably about to make some deliberate mistake for which I'll have to take the rap. She could cost me my career. Why did the chief make me hire her—I told him I needed a trainer, not an analyst.

A Revenger's Thoughts

I don't know why the boss won't give me a chance to head up the new division. This is the perfect time, while they're reorganizing the department. I've certainly earned the right. The proposal I presented shows a carefully thought out plan that can't miss. The boss must be waiting for someone with more clout in the company. He thinks I don't know enough of the "right" people. Well, I'll have to show him what can happen when I drop certain pieces of information to the "right" people. He'll be sorry he turned me down.

Strategy

Your goal is to get Revengers to behave more cooperatively by teaching them that speaking out honestly rather than showing resentment is the way to get what they want:

(1) *Clear up misconceptions.* No matter how brilliantly you reason, an agitated person can't "hear" you while he's highly emotional. Begin with probing questions to learn what the subordinate is thinking and, if he's feeling revengeful, why. Work with your subordinates to identify alternative ways to handle touchy situations. Get him to express the likely consequences of each option.

(2) *Give honest, more frequent recognition.* Explain how important your workers are to the company and how their individual roles fit into the total picture. Get teammates to help each other. Tell workers how *they benefit* by reaching your short-term goals. Monitor progress, praising good work while redirecting aggressors.

(3) *Express your appreciation immediately.* As soon as the job is done, tell your worker you *noticed* how much he improved. Don't wait until you have time to write him a memo or present him with an achievement award.

(4) *Plan ahead when changes will disrupt your workers.* Before resentment has a chance to mushroom, take your people into your confidence, ask them what problems they anticipate and what suggestions they have for handling them.

Tactical Talk

You: "MEGAN, YOU'RE USUALLY SO ANIMATED ABOUT YOUR ASSIGNMENTS. BUT YOU'VE BEEN AWFULLY QUIET THIS PAST WEEK, ESPECIALLY WHEN I STOP BY YOUR DESK. ARE YOU AN-

NOYED AT SOMETHING I'VE DONE? I REALLY
WISH YOU'D TELL ME."

Megan: "WELL FRANKLY, BOSS, I'M FEELING VERY DIS-
APPOINTED THAT I WASN'T ALLOWED TO
HEAD UP THE NEW DIVISION."

You: "I KNOW YOU WERE DISAPPOINTED, BUT AS I
EXPLAINED TO YOU WE'RE GOING TO HAVE TO
HOLD OFF FORMING THAT DIVISION. IT MAY
TAKE ANOTHER YEAR. IN THE MEANTIME, YOU
COULD BE OF TREMENDOUS HELP TO US BY..."

Megan: "OH, I DIDN'T REALIZE YOU HAD OTHER PLANS
FOR ME ..."

Tip: If you let your workers share more in the planning, you'll
reduce the panning. When you sense subordinates are spiteful,
be certain they clearly understand what's happening. If Revengers are hostile, instead of firing knee-jerk responses, allow
them to release their anger. Now you both can deal with the
root cause.

3.3 SNIPERS

Snipers attack you under some cover, often disguising their
jabs with jokes.

Snipers wait to assail you until they are safely surrounded,
for example, by an audience of cohorts in the middle of a
meeting. For these public potshots, they often don the cloak
of a comedian, pretending their barbs are meant as humor.
Rather than be regarded as having no sense of humor, everyone else laughs uneasily. Whether you accept the attack and
join the laughter or reject it by snapping back, you'll be de-
graded in front of your troops. That's what the Sniper hopes
to accomplish.

Unless they tell you, there's no way to know why these
subordinates have this negative attitude toward you. It could
stem from something as simple as feeling neglected, unappre-
ciated, or unrecognized.

What You're Thinking

That was supposed to be a joke, but I felt the sharp edge of that cutting remark. Why is Gil attacking me in this fashion? Why doesn't he just say what's bothering him? There's more to this than what appears on the surface.

A Sniper's Thoughts

The boss thinks she's so smart. She claims her master plan is making this division come out on top. But where would she be now if I wasn't such a good budget director? If I jab at her weak fiscal background, I can take her down a few pegs.

Strategy

Your objectives are to maintain your leadership stance, restore any damage the Snipers have done to your standing, and prevent future attacks.

(1) *Show you won't stand for being put down.* Calmly and dispassionately indicate that you're glad to discuss any legitimate criticism.

(2) *Keep your tone light and your message crystal clear:* Snipers, you can't hide your hostility with humor. Then turn the tables and needle the Snipers by asking them to be a little more specific, and after that, a little more clarification please. Reply factually without getting defensive.

(3) *Confront the Snipers in private.* Try to get at the root of their hostility. If they won't tell you, then let them know that *you* know they've been attacking you and ask them to stop. Use a friendly but no-nonsense tone.

Tactical Talk

You: "MAYBE IT'S MY IMAGINATION, GIL, BUT IT SEEMS TO ME THAT SOME OF YOUR REMARKS AT THE MEETING THIS MORNING WERE SARCASTIC. IS THERE SOMETHING I'VE DONE THAT'S OFFENDED YOU?"

Gil: "AW, C'MON, BOSS, WHERE'S YOUR SENSE OF
         HUMOR?"

You: "GIL, I ENJOY A JOKE AS MUCH AS ANYONE
         ELSE, BUT CUTTING REMARKS AREN'T FUNNY.
         I REALIZE YOU DIDN'T MEAN TO OFFEND ME,
         BUT YOU DID, AND I'D APPRECIATE YOUR NOT
         DOING THAT ANYMORE. THANK YOU."

Tip: Stop the sniping with firmness and good humor. If the
Sniper is willing to disclose to you what's really bothering
him, you can discuss the problem and probably resolve the
matter.

You need your subordinates as much as they need you.
When they act hostile, learn why. Actions don't always reveal
real feelings. A subordinate may feel trapped because he's
afraid to tell you why he's angry at you.

At times, the system is at fault and your workers will
gladly suggest changes. Most of the time misunderstandings
can be cleared up if you send this message: We're in this
together—what can we do to make it better?

PART TWO

DEALING WITH PUSHY/PRESUMPTUOUS PEOPLE

They don't mean to be mean, yet they come at you with such force and determination that you feel you're under seige. You may not be the enemy, but you're still being attacked. They bombard you with their beliefs, they steal your thunder, they assault your sensitivities. Pushy people are resolved to do things their way.

Boss, peer, or worker, they share a common arrogance. Bursting with unwarranted self-importance, they barge in and try to take over while you're left wondering if you should surrender or salute.

These people long to be liked. They need to feel accepted. But they can't seem to express themselves without offending you with their embarrassing gestures, barking commands, and intolerant views. Consequently, they don't have many friends. The more they reach out, the more they're rejected; the more they're rejected, the pushier they get. They *have* to dominate everyone and every situation. They are so afraid of losing control that being in control becomes their prime objective. Pushy/presumptuous types must run the show and may not realize they've also run over your feelings.

CHAPTER 4

WHEN YOUR BOSS IS ARROGANT

4.1 Fame Claimers
4.2 Blockers
4.3 Hagglers

There's a story that President Calvin Coolidge, upon waking from a midday nap, jokingly asked his aide, "Is the country still here?" Some bosses really believe the company can't breathe without their incessant checking and frequent commandeering of your job.

If the plan isn't theirs, it can't be any good. They interfere with your work by constantly bickering about petty points. If they let you proceed, they steal credit for your efforts. These bosses don't intentionally want to hurt you by coming on too strong, but you still feel intimidated.

To continue the relationship, you need to stay alert and plan carefully. When your pushy/presumptuous boss is aggressive and quick, it doesn't mean he's not listening to you. He's probably moving at a fast clip himself and you may have to trot to keep up with him. Also, it's easy to misconstrue as rejection a comment that was meant merely as caution. Instead of jumping to the wrong conclusion, ask the boss if his statement was intended as a final call. Don't take the boss's arrogance personally. He's the one with the problem, but you can both come out ahead.

4.1 FAME CLAIMERS

Fame Claimers haughtily assume credit for your work.

To them, this isn't stealing. They're just taking what they believe to be rightfully theirs. Sure, you did the work and you're not getting the recognition you deserve, but the boss believes he earned the credit.

These Fame Claimers are pumped up with pride they are unwilling to share. Their haughty air of self-importance advertises their belief that they alone are responsible for results because they are totally in control. If you tactfully accuse them of stealing your credit, they'll promise to arrange some recognition for you. Don't hold your breath. People who are so hungry to get credit are usually extremely touchy if you criticize them.

What You're Thinking

My project was a smashing success, and my boss is grabbing all the glory. I worked darn hard to pull it off. It was my precise planning and coordination that made it click. He hasn't acknowledged any of my contributions—what an ingrate!

A Fame Claimer's Thoughts

I taught him well. I really deserve the accolades on this one. I cleared the path with the other departments so that he'd have the support he needed to get the job done. He did just what I told him and the result was even better than I expected. Wow! These figures will look great in my report.

Strategy

There's more involved here than satisfying your ego. Getting acclaimed as an idea person and a good implementer is important for your career advancement. Your objective is clear. You need to gain recognition for your achievements:

(1) *Share the credit and gain a friend.* Be willing to dole out some of the acclaim. Instead of complaining that you

didn't get recognition, acknowledge to the boss and everyone else around whatever you can legitimately say the boss taught you. Win over the boss by getting him to think of the two of you as a team.

(2) *Share problems and how you're handling them.* Be considerate of the boss's time as you plot ways to become more visible to him on the important matters. You can ask his opinion without seeking his permission.

(3) *Document your procedures and accomplishments.* Send progress reports to your boss and copies to anyone else who might possibly benefit from reading them. This written evidence has a double benefit. Many people become aware of your efforts, you get the credit you deserve, and in addition, having this record will help you recall your feats during future negotiations.

Tactical Talk

"BOSS, I APPRECIATE HOW MUCH I'VE LEARNED FROM YOU. THAT TECHNIQUE YOU TAUGHT ME TO PROCESS THE REPORTS FASTER REALLY HAS HELPED ME CUT THROUGH..."

"BOSS, I WANT TO MAKE SURE I'M PROCEEDING THE WAY YOU WANT. HOW DOES THIS LOOK TO YOU? WHAT DO YOU THINK ABOUT...?"

Tip: To convert your boss from stealing your praises to singing your praises, keep telling him how much he is helping you. Your boss needs an extra boost to satisfy his greed and need for recognition, but neither of you could accomplish the success alone. Both of you deserve to paste up the gold stars.

4.2 BLOCKERS

Blockers advance their ideas and obstruct the ones they don't originate.

If it's their idea, it has enormous potential; if it's someone else's, they slash it to shreds. Blocker bosses are unreasonable in the way they disagree or oppose what you're suggesting. They don't want to delegate the act of thinking to anyone else in the department. If you dare to suggest an original thought, you'll feel the tag "Troublemaker" being pinned to your lapel.

You wish your boss would plan with you, not for you. If the procedures to improve the operation are so obvious to you, why doesn't the boss want to hear any of your suggestions? You get the feeling that he resents your interference. He does.

What You're Thinking

I've checked and double-checked my figures. I know this is a fantastic idea. Why can't he see that? Why is he so possessive about keeping the old procedure? Nothing can fly around here unless the boss introduces it.

A Blocker's Thoughts

These pinheads think they know it all. They have no idea how chaotic it was here before I got everything organized. I spent months perfecting that procedure and now they're trying to undo all my good work.

Strategy

Your goal is to get your ideas considered objectively without antagonizing your boss. This is a good time to review the way in which you are telling the boss your recommendations. Here's a short checklist. How well do you score?

CHECKLIST FOR OFFERING UNSOLICITED IDEAS/PROPOSALS

( ) *Are you offering suggestions for the boss to consider rather than demanding changes?* All you can hope for is that your idea be considered; the boss's role is to determine the value of the suggestion.

( ) *Do you make the boss feel that he had a part in the development of your idea?* Mention that this is an outgrowth of something he said last week or that the idea came to you this morning when the boss was discussing the need to increase productivity. You get him to hear you by claiming to have heard him.

( ) *Before plunging in, do you first ask the boss if he has a few minutes to talk to you?* Otherwise, you might catch him at a bad time. If you know you can garner peer support, and if the atmosphere at staff meetings is free and open, throw the question to the rest of the group.

( ) *Before you talk do you reduce your thoughts to paper?* If you ramble, you're wasting the boss's time. Be crystal-clear and sharpen the main points that need to be brought out.

( ) *Do you deal with drawbacks as well as benefits?* This is especially important when it comes to spending time, money, and other resources. When preparing a proposal, pay close attention to whatever the boss is saying on this subject, question him, get him to restate his position. Expand your idea with ways to implement it.

( ) *Can you defend your plan if it's torn apart?* As the boss is talking, make note of what you consider to be his legitimate objections. When you speak again, first answer the valid criticism, ignore the rest, and then continue with other positive points.

( ) *Did you do your homework? Is it possible this fantastic idea of yours was already considered and rejected?* Is the regulation you want to change one that was initiated by your boss? Protect yourself. Ask the boss what experience he has had with this sort of thing. If he started the regulation, ask how he believes the conditions have changed since then and what might be needed now to meet these changes.

( ) *Are you sure what you're saying is in sync with the aggressive style in which the boss paints himself?* If one of his favorite sayings is, "You have to get them before they get you," beware of suggestions the boss might resent because he should have come up with the idea himself and didn't.

( ) *Do you ask the boss how long before he might have a decision?* Leave the door open by getting him to tell you when to check back with him.

( ) *Do you give a new boss time to size up the operation?* He may be refusing all suggestions from you and your colleagues in an effort to appear confident when he doesn't feel like he's in command. Don't say anything yet. You may no longer have a problem with him once he gets his bearings.

Tactical Talk

"BOSS, I THINK I UNDERSTAND HOW YOU FEEL. YOU'RE SAYING THAT IF WE WERE TO ADOPT THE PLAN, IT WOULD MEAN THAT...I JUST WANT TO POINT OUT, HOWEVER, THAT..."

"HOW WOULD THAT WORK IN THE CASE OF...?"

"HOW DOES THAT COMPARE WITH THE STUDY REPORTED IN LAST MONTH'S JOURNAL THAT CLAIMS...?"

"BOSS, MAYBE YOU'VE ALREADY THOUGHT ABOUT USING A MORE FLEXIBLE MEASURE..."

"I'D APPRECIATE YOUR THINKING ABOUT AN IDEA THAT CAME TO ME ON IMPROVING THE FLOW. WHAT WOULD HAPPEN IF WE SHIFTED...?"

"BOSS, NOW THAT WE HAVE THE AUTOMATIC RECORDER, DO WE STILL NEED THE...?"

Tip: Without kowtowing, you can build up the boss instead of tearing him down. If he's in good standing with the company, ask yourself why he remains there. He must be doing something top management likes. Learn what it is. Gain strength by exercising your tact and feeding his ego.

4.3 HAGGLERS

Hagglers make their point in a petty, noisy, angry manner.

If you were your boss's boss, you'd fire him instantly for insolence. You're not troubled as much by being pushed, as by being pushed in such a picayune and inflammatory fashion. You can count on your boss to furnish a skirmish over every minor misunderstanding while manifesting no dignity in the way he disagrees.

Hagglers are argumentative and wrangling and often raise their voices as they find fault and pick fights. You're not only drowning in a sea of advice, you're also choking on incessant, irritating, and unwanted assistance. The petty person doesn't realize as you do that his thinking is small. It's up to you to spell out the larger aspects.

What You're Thinking

Why won't he get off my back? He picks up on these insignificant details and makes sure everyone around us can hear his bickering. It must make him feel like a big shot.

A Haggler's Thoughts

They don't appreciate all I do for them. They just look for ways to load their work back to me. I held down most of those jobs before I moved up to supervisor. I know the best way to get them done, but they close their minds when I'm talking. I have to shout to be heard.

Strategy

Your objective is to help your Haggler boss see the larger picture and stop hounding you about the trivial:

(1) *Carefully shed some insight.* Summarize what's been said. Point up the bigger problem at stake.

(2) *Think big and act big.* Refuse to "hear" petty insults and insinuations and keep talking issues.

Tactical Talk

"FROM WHAT YOU'RE SAYING, BOSS, THE SIT-UATION SEEMS TO BE THAT...IS THAT COR-RECT?"

"OF THE THREE OPTIONS WE DISCUSSED, WHICH DO YOU THINK IS THE BEST WAY TO HANDLE THE OBJECTION?"

Tip: Learn to tune out your boss's negative outbursts. Tune in to what is useful to you and stay on the same wave length.

When arrogant bosses are all puffed up, you can gradually let the air out of their balloons without their even realizing it. Work with them, don't fight them. As you and your boss experience more successes together, the boss will gain more confidence in himself and in you. There will be less need for bluster or hogging the credit or holding on to outdated procedures.

CHAPTER 5

WHEN YOUR COLLEAGUES ARE ARROGANT

5.1 Battering Rams
5.2 Believers
5.3 Zealots
5.4 Competitors

These pushy/presumptuous colleagues share with their counterpart bosses a prideful, unearned arrogance. If it didn't affect your work you could ignore them or avoid them.

But their behavior does interfere because in some way they are trying to get a measure of control over you and the friction causes sparks to fly. They dominate group discussions drowning out better potential solutions. They nag you about improving the way you run your own unit. They create a constant us-against-them tension. When they try to take over the situation, their poor manners embarrass you in front of friends, strangers, and clients.

5.1 BATTERING RAMS

Battering Rams crush opposition, forcing their views on you.

They are so convinced that their way is the better way that they are bound and determined to push it through whatever the cost. You're supposed to be playing on the same team, but if you get in their way, you pay the price. They'll try to destroy you. They'll trespass upon your turf with a driving, forceful crush.

Sometimes a poor *system* enables Battering Rams to get away with their attempts at encroachment. Perhaps assignments weren't made clear and each worker believes his prerogatives have been usurped. Or, occasionally you're caught in a bind when, in formulating a project, your boss divides the decision-making authority equally between two assistants. Unless you and your partner are truly simpatico, expect that you two princes will be each wanting to crown the other.

What You're Thinking

Ever since Erin was appointed chairman of the athletic tournament our company is sponsoring, she's become so difficult. I wanted to get together with her to kick around some ideas, but she has already decided that she's going to do her job and mine too. I can't allow this because she'll botch up my responsibility and I'll get the blame. On the other hand, it would make me appear weak if I have to ask the boss to run interference.

A Battering Ram's Thoughts

I'm the tournament director and therefore I should make the final decision on every aspect of the event. I can't have that communications director handling the publicity. She doesn't understand what I want to achieve. She won't make this a top priority. I've got to get her out of my way.

Strategy

Your goal is to carry out your responsibilities, putting out the brush fire before everyone is inflamed.

(1) *Tactfully, but assertively, put your foot down when anyone attempts to walk all over you.* You can't survive being trampled. Without divulging any emotion, stand up for yourself while showing the Battering Ram how you can help him get what he really wants.

(2) *When the fault is at least partially with the system, point this out to your boss.* Suggest how restructuring might help. When you and a few cohorts each have your own turf but have to work on a joint activity where the responsibility and authority seem to overlap, suggest that a higher-level administrator direct the project.

Tactical Talk

"ERIN, THE BOSS ASKED US BOTH TO WORK ON THIS TOURNAMENT AND I KNOW WE BOTH WANT IT TO BE SUCCESSFUL. SO LET'S BE CLEAR ABOUT WHAT WE'RE DOING. AS I SEE IT, IT'S YOUR JOB AS PROJECT CHAIRMAN TO DECIDE WHAT INFORMATION SHOULD BE GIVEN THE MEDIA. RIGHT?

"AND IT'S MY JOB TO HELP YOU GET OUT THE MESSAGES YOU WANT BY CONTACTING MY MEDIA SOURCES AND ARRANGING FOR IN-TERVIEWS, STORIES, AND SO ON. I ALSO HAVE TO KEEP YOU UPDATED AND COORDINATE WITH YOUR CALENDAR. RIGHT? SUPPOSE YOU START FILLING ME IN NOW ON HOW THIS EVENT..."

Tip: When the Battering Ram tries to force through a procedure that jeopardizes your position, you can't afford to let your authority be sheared, but you'd probably lose if you locked horns. Stay calm as you observe his rule-or-ruin mentality. Then, coolly and cooperatively, suggest the professional approach. This is no time to be sheepish.

5.2 BELIEVERS

They alone are right; they unreasonably expect your agreement.

Believers, like their Battering Ram cohorts, also act out of belief. The difference is that if you get in the way of the rams, they'll ruin you. With Believers, if you disagree with them, they'll wear you down.

Believers are enormously opinionated, with absolute conviction that they know the only way to proceed, and these highly charged dynamos won't stop their propagandizing until they've converted you. They have the faith and they're spreading the gospel. After a while, you don't have the energy to talk any further. Not only can't you change their minds, you can't even get them to open their minds a little crack to consider another view. Exhausting as it may be to deal with Believers, they serve an important purpose. They force you to rethink the issue. Then you either alter your original opinion or feel reinforced that you were "right" all along.

What You're Thinking

What is with Diane? She's promoting that policy like she's on some kind of holy mission. If she'd listen, I could tell her we tried something almost like that a few years back. But we can't get her to respond to any of the valid points we're making. I'm afraid the group is going to go along with her just to shut her up.

A Believer's Thoughts

They may have been here longer than me, but this process worked so well in my last job I know it can turn things around here. I checked out what they did before. This is different. I can't give up on this. A success here is what I need to make a place for myself with this company. This is good for me and for the organization. I must convince all of them that I have the best answer.

Strategy

Your goal is to act objectively and not be swayed by your personal and emotional reactions to the Believers.

(1) *Re-evaluate your position.* The Believer sees the situation differently from the way you perceive it and is tenaciously hanging on to his perceptions. How valid is that viewpoint?

Is the Believer trying to impose impossible standards on the rest of you? Go back over your stand noting both pros and cons. Prepare yourself to be clear and specific in presenting your views.

(2) *Examine how the Believer would be affected by this action.* Does the Believer alone stand to benefit? Are there any potentially harmful consequences that might interfere with his personal career ambitions that you would want to mention to him?

(3) *Be as firm in expressing your conviction as the Believer is in expressing his.* In the absence of absolute proof that a plan or procedure is going to work, we can only rely on the evidence we're able to amass, our reasoning, and our intuition. And, of course, our faith.

Tactical Talk

"DIANE, YOUR ENTHUSIASM IS REFRESHING AND WE ALL APPRECIATE YOUR DEDICATION. THESE RECORDS, HOWEVER, SUGGEST THAT WE SHOULD MOVE CAUTIOUSLY IN THAT AREA BE- CAUSE OF THE DEEP SWINGS IN..."

Tip: If you don't want to sell your soul, you have to fight fire with fire and faith with faith. Fortify your stand, and then be as strong in your conviction as the Believer is in his.

5.3 ZEALOTS

Zealots are fanatics who commit themselves without weighing all considerations.

Zealots are your pushy/presumptuous colleagues who let their intense enthusiasm overcome their reason. They get so excited about an idea, they become full of fervor, passionately extolling its merits. Unfortunately, they are also knee-jerkers. They spout their vigorous support without knowing exactly what they hope to achieve and, consequently, have no clear sense of direction. Overpowered by their own zeal, they are unrealistically positive because they react without thinking through the consequences. Their certainty that they are right has become such a compelling emotion that it's difficult to bring them back to reality.

What You're Thinking

Josh is a master at doing all the talking, always sounding off and monopolizing every discussion. He's wasting the team's time and energy. His animated, but unreasonable, speeches are moving us away from our objectives. But we all sit around like dunces, absorbing what he says, even though we don't agree with him. We've tried subtle digs and they don't deter him. I doubt if outright insults would silence him. What else can we try?

A Zealot's Thoughts

The new system I'm proposing will put our department out in front. I bet they'll write us up with a big feature in the newsletter, and then that will be picked up by Business News, and who knows where else that will lead. We can be the new leaders in this area, and heaven knows, our industry is crying for a better, workable system.

Strategy

Your objective is to redirect the Zealot so that you can get your discussions back on an even keel:

(1) *You and your colleagues have to stand up and speak out.* Without being insulting, in a calm, pleasant, nonaggressive manner, take turns at asking the Zealot to interpret what he's saying and to explain in greater detail what, specifically, would be accomplished.

(2) *Press the Zealot for details such as how his position compares with another's.* Without attacking his opinions, force him to defend his views.

Tactical Talk

> *An unrelenting barrage:* "JOSH, WHICH COMPA-
> NIES DID YOU SAY HAD A SUCCESSFUL EXPE-
> RIENCE WITH IT?"
>
> "WHAT SPECIFIC KINDS OF NEW INFORMATION
> WERE THEY ABLE TO SECURE?"
>
> "WHAT WERE THE EXACT COSTS OF THE INI-
> TIAL SIX-MONTH PERIOD?"
>
> "BESIDES THE TRAINING DELAY, WHAT OTHER
> PROBLEMS DID THEY RUN INTO?"

Tip: If you all get together and decide to stop buying what the Zealot is selling, you'll force him to be better prepared for his next attempt.

5.4 COMPETITORS

Competitors must surpass you, making the simplest contest into a rivalry.

Some pushy/presumptuous colleagues push competition beyond its intended purpose. Not only must they win standard organized matches such as sales contests, they also attempt to turn most other tasks into a clash purely for the "prize" of coming out ahead. You can be brainstorming for a solution, everybody offering possibilities, and only the Competitor takes it as a personal rejection when his idea isn't accepted. By denying him the applause he seeks, you become his enemy.

You aren't aware you're in a contest while Competitors feel compelled to keep winning at whatever they do with you, regardless of what it costs them. Deep down, they are afraid they don't really excel, and so they feel forced to prove to themselves and to you that they are superior. They are saddled with an unnecessary load—the fear that they may not continue being the best.

Competitors are on top of the world when they win; dejected when they don't. All this subjects you to a perpetually tense situation.

What You're Thinking

We should be pooling our ideas to evolve a faster procedure. I like to match wits with Lynn because she makes me justify my reasoning, but she's making this into some sort of rivalry to make herself shine. She's trying to get me to say I'm wrong because I don't do things her way. She must lie awake at night dreaming up schemes to come out looking better than the rest of us.

A Competitor's Thoughts

Why did I have to embarrass myself like that? If only I'd worked a little longer, I could have devised a winning plan. I know I can outthink them, but they keep putting me down because they won't admit I'm smarter than they are. My co-workers pretend to be my friends, but they are standing in the way of my promotion. I have to try harder to wipe them out.

Strategy

Your goal is to help restore a friendly climate. To enjoy your work without feeling the hot breath of hostility:

(1) *Be professional and gracious.* Give Competitors the respect and recognition they desperately seek. In a professional manner, show them you want to be friends even though they rebuff you. Allow them to feel important so that they won't have to run you down in order to uplift their self-esteem.

(2) *Explain the value of synthesizing.* The whole (the resulting outcome) is greater than the sum of the parts because when you share your thinking and extract the best thoughts from each of you, you form a new and more valuable combination.

(3) *Be honorable in taking and giving credit.* You want credit for your work, and Competitors should get credit for theirs. Don't allow anyone to claim as *his* achievement your efforts or joint efforts. Concentrate on running your own race—no seeking revenge with dirty tricks or back-stabbing.

(4) *Be up front.* Inform your colleague if you're going to compete for a job opening or assignment that you know he's hoping to get. It will get back to him anyway if you talk, for example, to the personnel director. Expect it to be common knowledge around the office before you get back to your desk. And when the competition is over, regardless of who won, take steps to mend any rift. You can remain friendly rivals. Neither of you needs bitter enemies.

Tactical Talk

"GEE, THAT'S A GOOD POINT WE HAVEN'T CONSIDERED. I CAN SEE WHERE IT MIGHT BE APPLICABLE. WHAT IF WE COMBINED YOUR SUGGESTION WITH FRED'S, WOULDN'T WE HAVE A STRONGER FORCE TO ...?"

"I DON'T MIND MEETING TO DEBATE OUR DIF-FERENCES ..."

"YOU RAN A GOOD RACE. I HOPE YOU GET IT NEXT TIME. LET ME KNOW HOW I CAN HELP."

"CONGRATULATIONS. I KNOW YOU'LL DO A GREAT JOB."

Tip: If your own ego is intact, you can afford to be generous. You can give your Competitor-cohort the reassurance he needs while you are spurred on to greater creativity, matching wits with someone else who's reaching for a better way.

With pushy/presumptuous colleagues, it's not their pride you're trying to puncture, just their influence. You don't have to deflate these types, but you do have to help redirect them if you want to restore a healthy atmosphere at the office.

CHAPTER 6

WHEN YOUR SUBORDINATES ARE ARROGANT

6.1 Rule Benders
6.2 Clansmen
6.3 Commandants

Managing pushy/presumptuous workers—subordinates who are just short of being insubordinate—can be difficult. They may be overeager and don't care how they run roughshod over everyone else. Or they may be looking for something you're not giving them enough of—a chance to voice their thinking on matters that concern their work. Even though it is your right and responsibility to make the decisions, you help build group spirit if you ask for their suggestions.

Consider, too, that bold and outspoken workers may be voicing what restrained workers are thinking and don't dare to say. Maybe you need regularly scheduled staff meetings in which all your people are encouraged to speak up about vital issues. Maybe you have to relax and give these meetings back to the members of the group.

On the other hand, you may be moving in a fine motivational direction and still have to deal with individual troublemakers. These are pushy, presumptuous, arrogant people who ignore procedures and precedents and whose aim it is to wield power either alone or through small cliques.

6.1 RULE BENDERS

Rule Benders cut corners, skirting the borders of acceptability.

You don't need a search warrant to find these rebels. They're in plain sight. In their enthusiasm to get something done, these subordinates bend the rules almost to the breaking point or take unauthorized action and make their own rules as they go along. It doesn't matter whose turf they stomp on. They can be equally offensive to bosses and colleagues.

Some of them threaten you, demanding that you change your procedures or they won't produce what you desperately want. You find your spirit and self respect being held hostage as you try to get them to understand the importance of following your directives and getting along with others.

What You're Thinking

I know Dick gets good results, but we've established these regulations for good reasons. If I ignore them for Dick, I'll have problems with the boss as well as the others on my staff. I have to know and approve what Dick is going to do before he takes action, not after the fact. I also can't allow Dick to destroy morale among my other workers. How can I bring him into line?

A Rule Bender's Thoughts

I can't be hog-tied with their stupid restrictions. If I wait for approval, we'll miss this golden opportunity. And when the boss finds out, what's he going to do—fire me? Heck no, he needs me too much. He'll be jumping for joy with the outcome. I know what has to be done. It's the only way this can work. I'll deal with those stupid restrictions later.

Strategy

Your objectives are to get the Rule Benders to obtain permission before they attempt any unauthorized acts and, whenever possible, to maintain the go-getters' enthusiasm and productivity:

(1) *Re-establish universal rules and stick to them.* If you play the game with different sets of rules for certain players, you're inviting poor morale, possible sabotage, and even outright mutiny.

(2) *Talk face-to-face with the Rule Bender.* Emphasize that (a) noncompliance is a serious problem for him, spelling out the serious consequences; (b) complying is the Rule Bender's responsibility, getting him to tell you the exact steps he'll take to change his pattern; (c) his behavior is the focus of the discussion—what's acceptable and unacceptable. Praise what he does well, but don't let him off the hook with a claim that his ends justified his means.

(3) *Follow up with feedback.* Be specific with your suggestions. Hopefully, you'll be able to tell him how well he's doing, acknowledging *any* improvement, and offering further suggestions.

Tactical Talk

You: "DICK, I KNOW THE DEALS YOU'VE BEEN MAKING HAVE ALLOWED US TO EXPAND THE OPERATION, BUT WE HAVE A BIDDING PROCEDURE THAT IS REQUIRED BY LAW. IF YOU DON'T FOLLOW IT, YOU FACE MAJOR TROUBLE; SPECIFICALLY...HOW DO YOU INTEND TO PROCEED SO THAT YOU CAN AVOID ANY FUTURE PROBLEMS?"

Dick: "BOSS, DO YOU REALIZE WHERE THIS ORGANIZATION WOULD BE TODAY IF I HADN'T OK'D THE CONTRACTS WITH—"

You: "THAT'S NOT THE POINT, DICK. WE ARE DISCUSSING YOUR FAILURE TO FOLLOW A PRESCRIBED PROCEDURE. THAT COULD GET US ALL IN A LOT OF TROUBLE. IF YOU CONTINUE IN THIS MANNER—NO MATTER HOW WONDERFUL YOUR RESULTS—WE CAN NO LONGER AFFORD TO KEEP YOU. I AM TELLING YOU FLATLY THAT YOUR JOB IS IN JEOPARDY. NOW, WHAT DO YOU INTEND TO DO TO KEEP YOUR JOB?"

Tip: Be consistent in applying your regulations and in expecting adherence. If procedures need to be modified, change them. But if you give Rule Benders special privileges, you can expect other workers to feel there's no use in trying. Any semblance of team spirit will evaporate.

6.2 CLANSMEN

Clansmen exert power by banding together in a clique.

These are not workers who simply enjoy each other's company and seem to prefer being part of the same cluster. We're not talking about people who like to sit with each other at meetings or always go to lunch together. Some apparently need the comfort of a group to bolster their individual weak self images. Let them be. They pose no threat to you.

Clansmen, on the other hand, are workers who flock together to ruffle your feathers and try to subvert the chain of command. They push for what they want (or what the leader of their band tells them they want) not based on the merit of the issue, but on the power they perceive they can wield. When they believe they can influence or threaten your decisions by the sheer weight of their numbers, the gang is ganging up on you.

What You're Thinking

This group could spell major trouble. They're leaning on me to change my mind, but I'm the one who is held responsible and I've got to be free to make final decisions. I've got to do something to minimize their influence, but if they sense that I'm trying to break them up, that will only reinforce their resolve. I have to talk to their leader, Clyde.

A Clansman's Thoughts

We've got the boss right where we want him. He'll have to go along with what we want now because he doesn't know how we'll strike back.

Strategy

Your goal is to maintain control of your organization. A direct frontal attack will solidify their defense. Your tactics have to be more conciliatory:

(1) *Win over the ringleader.* Ask for his help in very specific ways and then be extremely appreciative of such efforts. The more that he feels he has your support, the less he needs to plan with his clan.

(2) *Strengthen the individual clansmen.* Improve your internal communications. Provide your workers with frequent and rewarding opportunities to speak out and bolster individual confidence. Coach those who need help or encouragement.

(3) *Dissolve threatening cliques without mentioning it.* Reassign members to unrelated tasks, more suited to individual capabilities and preferably requiring that the work be done in different locations. Have them report for work and take lunch at different times.

(4) *Utilize cliques on projects requiring the joint effort of several people who work well together.* This is especially helpful when you have to meet an urgent deadline.

Tactical Talk

"CLYDE, I'VE RUN INTO A LITTLE PROBLEM AND I NEED YOUR HELP. COULD YOU ROUND UP FOUR MORE PEOPLE TO MEET IN MY OFFICE IN A HALF HOUR. WE'VE JUST BEEN ASKED TO COMPILE SOME NEW STATS BY THE END OF THE DAY."

"JANE, I'M REASSIGNING YOU TO THE CENTER OFFICE. THEY NEED SOMEONE WITH YOUR CO-ORDINATING SKILL..."

Tip: Don't clobber the clique. Utilize it if you can. If not, dissolve it in a quiet, professional manner.

6.3 COMMANDANTS

Commandants are very bossy; without authority, they order their peers around.

It's bad enough when these pushy/presumptuous subordinates try to take over your job, but in overstepping their limits, they step on everyone's toes with dictatorial boots. Using their desks as command posts from which to direct operations, Commandants can't be part of the troop, they have to issue the orders.

Although they perform very well, Commandants are offensively impatient with those who move at a slower pace. You've watched their condescending attitude when talking to or about their colleagues. They are aggressive in criticizing their coworkers, putting down their efforts or telling them how they ought to be handling assignments. No wonder negative body language surfaces whenever Commandants' names come up during discussions.

What You're Thinking

What am I going to do about Clay? His own work is excellent and he's quick—maybe too quick for the rest of us. He's as domineering as a fascist general. His overbearing ways are antagonizing everyone. I've got to slow him down and teach him some tact before we have a major morale problem. Clay has so much talent we can use if only I can help him handle his aggression.

A Commandant's Thoughts

I did a fantastic job. Must have set some kind of time record. Boy, did Ed jump when I told him it didn't matter how many people had orders in before me, I needed mine now. I've got places to go and I'm not going to let my dull-witted colleagues hold me up.

Strategy

Your objective is to salvage the Commandants' high level of talent, energy, and productivity and yet teach them to get along better with their peers. They have to understand that learning people skills is essential for them to succeed and that you want to help them:

(1) *Give them the recognition they're due.* Publicly acknowledge their good work and privately point out specific ways to improve.

(2) *Give these rising stars every chance to shine.* Assign them challenging jobs that look good on resumes. Encourage them to tell you their ideas for special projects they want to develop.

(3) *Coach them on how to talk to people so that their words are well received.* Spell out the difference between being insultingly offensive and expressing enthusiasm in a positive way that gets others excited too.

(4) *Enlist help from those complaining about a Commandant's behavior.* Suggest they use staff meetings to nail down as a group problem unclear lines of authority. Without anyone pointing a finger directly at the accused, the Commandant, too, will have his say, but will definitely feel the group pressure. Your role will be to keep the fight polite.

Tactical Talk

"CLAY, I THOUGHT YOUR REPORT WAS SO GOOD, I HAD IT CIRCULATED FOR THE OTHER DIVISION DIRECTORS TO CONSIDER. YOU ARE VERY CLEAR ON YOUR WORK OBJECTIVES, BUT YOU NEED TO ADD ANOTHER GOAL IF YOU WANT TO MAKE IT TO THE TOP—GETTING THE COOPERATION OF YOUR PEERS AND STAFF.

"LET'S MAP OUT A PLAN AND TIME TABLE, THE WAY WE'D DO FOR ANY MANAGEMENT OBJECTIVE. ...I'LL CHECK BACK WITH YOU IN A FEW WEEKS AND I'M CONFIDENT YOU'LL BE ABLE TO REPORT SOME IMPORTANT CHANGES."

Tip: Don't be surprised how quickly your Commandants become good soldiers. These are bright, eager people who learn fast and are probably overachievers needing a challenge. Once you treat the "people" problem the same way you set out the business problem (clearly stated, measurable objectives broken down into steps and time frames) they can't wait to beat their own calendar.

Many of the subordinates who are being pushy and presumptuous, infringing on your territory, are trying to get your attention. You can regain control maintaining their good attributes (energy, enthusiasm, efficiency, productivity) while showing them how to go by your rules or be kinder to their cohorts.

If workers are aggressive in volunteering unasked-for proposals, thank them for their interest. You don't want to pass up a potential gold mine when all you have to do is consider the matter and get back to them. If you reject the idea, do so kindly and positively: "Ted, you made some good points, but it's not quite what we need at this time. Maybe you can come up with a way that would decrease our costs..." And when Ted finally does hit on a solution to your liking, thank him for being so clever.

PART THREE

DEALING WITH DECEITFUL/UNDERHANDED PEOPLE

These are people you believe deliberately lie, cheat, double-cross, deceive, misrepresent, and mislead you. To get what they want, they use any means to achieve their ends and then justify their underhanded actions to themselves.

Many of them distort the situation. They delude you into making mistakes. They dupe you in areas where you are inexperienced or naive. Deceivers don't necessarily mean to harm you, but their welfare, not yours, is their prime concern.

Some of them put their principles into practice by telling you only half-truths. Their talk is purposely unclear. Or they try to hoodwink, bamboozle, or bluff you. It's persuasion by deception—a coward's way out.

CHAPTER 7

WHEN YOUR BOSS IS DECEPTIVE

7.1 Hypocrites

7.2 Renegers

7.3 Forked Tongues

Meeting quotas, reducing costs, balancing budgets—whatever the objective to be reached, deceitful bosses move with a one-track mind. Reach the goal no matter what it takes.

In the process, if your feelings get hurt because they mislead you or if you feel angry because they cheated you, it's somehow "your fault." They rationalize that you must have misunderstood them.

That leaves you forced to deal with intentionally foggy directives from gutless supervisors who won't behave responsibly.

7.1 HYPOCRITES

Hypocrites are two-faced double-dealers who purposely misrepresent or mislead you.

Hypocrite bosses are sneaky. You can't trust them. They pretend to be your good buddy, but you have to find out from a reporter, seeking your reaction, that the program you direct has been cut out of next year's budget. Or the boss cons you into confiding in him and then uses the information against you. Another favorite tactic of Hypocrites is to take facts and figures out of context or to quote nonexistent studies and authorities. Led astray, you draw incorrect conclusions.

The only thing you can depend on from Hypocrite bosses is that they will actually do the opposite of what they pretend to be doing.

What You're Thinking

I trusted the boss. I can't believe she's out to get me demoted. But she said one thing to me about a new unit when we reorganized the division and then took a diametrically contrary position when she spoke to Marsha. And from what I can make of this memo, it looks like Marsha's version was right. I can draw only one conclusion: the boss is a chicken-hearted, dastardly hypocrite.

A Hypocrite's Thoughts

Why is Hank acting so upset? He knew we were going to reorganize the division. I told him that. He made the decision years ago to become a specialist instead of a generalist. That's his problem. I have now reached a conclusion about what should be done with the division. I'm sure I need a generalist to head the new unit. I'll make it up to Hank some other way.

Strategy

Your goal is to get a straight answer from your boss so that you know where you stand and can plan accordingly. Before you assume that the boss is out to get you, you need to find out what's making him act that way.

(1) *Ask questions that require direct answers.* The boss probably doesn't realize that he has wronged you or hurt you. He may have been thinking out loud when he spoke to you. It may have sounded definite to you and inconclusive to him. But as a result the great expectations he built you up for led to a letdown. Although he was proceeding along a direct route, he was indeed insensitive to your feelings.

(2) *Protect yourself in the future.* Don't accept anything your boss tells you at face value until it's confirmed in writing or announced before other people. If he asks you to keep a plan secret, honor this request but ask when you may inquire if the plan will be enacted. Once you are convinced that the boss has made a definite deal with you, publicize it, involving other people, so that he will have difficulty backing out. You can, for example, prepare a memo stating your understanding of what is to occur. Give the original to the boss, keep a copy for yourself, and send copies to others who in *any* way will be involved.

Tactical Talk

You: "BOSS, WHEN WE TALKED A COUPLE OF WEEKS AGO, I THOUGHT IT WAS DEFINITE THAT I'D BE HEADING THE NEW UNIT WHEN THE DIVISION REORGANIZED. IS THAT STILL YOUR PLAN?"

Boss: "HANK, I THOUGHT YOU UNDERSTOOD I WAS GOING OVER ALL THE OPTIONS..."

You: "OH, I DIDN'T REALIZE THAT CONVERSATION WAS JUST EXPLORATORY. EVEN IF I'M NOT GOING TO HEAD THE NEW UNIT, I'VE GIVEN A LOT OF THOUGHT TO IT AND I HAVE SEVERAL IDEAS YOU MIGHT WANT TO CONSIDER." (You lost this round. Be gracious and set yourself up to get back in the ring.)

Tip: Find some goals on which you agree. The boss you see as a hypocritical snake in the grass may actually be a fraidy cat who has a tiger by the tail. He pussyfoots, lacking courage to tell you face to face that he decided on changes because a situation became more difficult than anticipated. You're not the only one who's been victimized by such behavior. Even some presidents of the United States were reputed to be similarly gutless when communicating bad news to subordinates. Understand your boss's flaw and work around it.

7.2 RENEGERS

Renegers go back on promises they never intended to keep.

While Hypocrite bosses mislead you because they are too cowardly to face you, Reneger bosses mislead you by breaking promises they hadn't planned to keep in the first place. And you're left to deal with immature, irresponsible behavior from someone who wields considerable power over your career.

For instance, the boss gives you the assignment you asked for, but he doesn't back up the responsibility with the necessary authority, resources, and other support. He might tell himself that he kept his promise, but he never really wanted you to succeed because, at least subconsciously, he had no intention of giving up any control. In reality, he reneged. He backed out of the deal.

What You're Thinking

The boss has undermined my assignment. He didn't make any sort of announcement or even tell the crew that I was in charge. I had to tell them myself that I was their new supervisor. It would have gone a lot smoother if the boss had backed me up the way he promised. He also said that as long as I kept within the company regulations, I had a clear field to run with my decisions. Then why is he listening to gripes from my staff? He's breaking the chain of command by not referring them back to me. First he breaks his promise to support me, then he knocks the props out from under me. That's a pretty underhanded way to run an organization.

A Reneger's Thoughts

Maybe I made a mistake in assigning Ted. I thought he could handle his staff. Some of his new regulations seem a little off the wall. I guess if I want anything done right, I just have to do it myself. If Ted doesn't shape up, I'm going to have to replace him.

Strategy

Your goal is to get the boss to keep his promise and stop blaming you for the impossible situations he creates.

(1) *Talk about the problems as his, not yours.* Discuss your mutual goals and what is of most importance to your company, department, and unit. Remind him of the benefits *he* receives if he carries through on what he promised.

(2) *Make it easy for the boss to keep his promise.* Assess what is needed and spell it out. Be considerate of your boss's time and make as many of the preliminary arrangements as you can.

Tactical Talk

"BOSS, YOU TOLD ME INITIALLY THAT YOU HAD TO HAVE A 25% INCREASE IN THE SHIPMENT SPEED WITHIN TWO MONTHS IF YOU WERE GOING TO BE RECOGNIZED AS AN INNOVATIVE MANAGER...I KNOW WE CAN MEET THAT GOAL IF WE ADD..."

"BOSS, I'VE PREPARED THIS ANNOUNCEMENT FOR YOUR SIGNATURE. AND I'VE SCHEDULED A PEP MEETING WITH MY STAFF ON MONDAY AT 10 AM. THEY NEED TO HEAR ABOUT THE IMPORTANCE OF THE WORK DIRECTLY FROM YOU AND THAT YOU STAND BEHIND MY DECISIONS. THEY RESPECT YOU AND MUST KNOW THAT WE'RE ALL WORKING AS A TEAM WITHIN THE CHAIN OF COMMAND."

Tip: Tactfully reassure Reneger bosses that you're going to help them get where they want to go. They often have a problem letting go of anything under their control, believing if they themselves were handling it, they could do it better.

7.3 FORKED TONGUES

Forked tongues send you ambiguous, deliberately unclear, mixed messages.

Dealing with Forked Tongues is extremely frustrating because with these misleading bosses you feel that you're on a perpetual roller coaster. The boss tells you he likes your work and the next time you do it that way, he tears into you. He says he's not blaming you for some error that occurred, but it's your report he's going over word-by-word, and he's scowling as he utters the "reassurance." Should you believe the words or the body language? Another cause for confusion is when the boss is praising your excellent performance and then asks, "Why can't you do this all the time?" Where do you stand with the boss? Which signals should you accept?

While you may be constantly under stress, bosses who speak ambiguously are often surprised to hear they appear to be talking out of both sides of their mouths.

What You're Thinking

I'm never sure what I'm supposed to do because I can't follow my boss's muddied, mixed-up directions. Asking for clarification just results in more of his doubletalk. He hedges, evading a straightforward answer. I really believe he does this purposely. Then when something goes wrong, he can put the blame on me for not following orders.

A Forked Tongue's Thoughts

Why doesn't Gina perform better? She looked so promising when I hired her. I've tried to motivate her by praising what she does well, but she can't follow the simplest directions without screwing up. I'll have to discuss lack of motivation at her next evaluation conference.

Strategy

Your goal is to clear up muddied messages and open up good two-way communication. Forget the boss's motive and focus on helping yourself.

(1) *Act as though the problem is with the system.* Even if you think the whole project is so iffy that the boss is staying vague so as not to have to take all the heat, give him the benefit of the doubt. Or, let him play his little games. Either way, you still need to help establish some communicating ground rules.

(2) *Speak up now.* Bottled frustration eventually explodes in an untimely outburst. Prepare your case and rehearse your talk from key word reminders. Pick a good time for an appointment with your boss "to discuss something important."

(3) *Keep your talk friendly and impersonal.* No accusations. Discuss your mutual concern for the company and offer procedural suggestions for the boss's consideration.

Tactical Talk

"BOSS, WITH OUR DIVISION HAVING TROUBLE MEETING THIS MONTH'S QUOTA, I HAVE A FEW IDEAS THAT MIGHT HELP US." *(Talk his language. He needs to meet the quota. You just declared yourself on his team.)*

"THERE SEEMS TO BE A PROBLEM WITH OUR UNDERSTANDING DIRECTIONS..." *(No blame or pain from an ungarnished fact. Then skip the cause and jump to the solution.)*

"WHAT WOULD YOU THINK ABOUT A CHECKLIST SOMETHING LIKE THIS? I'VE MARKED POINTS I THINK ARE TROUBLE SPOTS, SUCH AS WHOM TO NOTIFY IF THERE'S A MISTAKE." or "COULD WE DISCUSS INSTRUCTIONS FACE TO FACE TO AVOID ANY INCORRECT INTERPRETATION? YOU KNOW HOW SOMETIMES THE SAME WORD MEANS DIFFERENT THINGS TO DIFFERENT PEOPLE."

Tip: When you think your boss speaks with a Forked Tongue, instead of trying to make him eat his words, feed him some ground rules for improved communication.

You think your boss is being deliberately deceitful and underhanded. Maybe you're right. But chances are the boss doesn't see any problem with the way he's acting and you're not going to change his personality. Again, get back to basics and go after your desired result. First you have to let go of your anger. Use whatever venting system works for you. Now your head is clear so that you can be in control when you speak up, ask direct and specific questions, and make appropriate suggestions. Keep in mind that you can always blame the system for the confusion—which certainly beats blaming the boss.

CHAPTER 8

WHEN YOUR COLLEAGUES ARE DECEPTIVE

8.1 Brainpickers

8.2 Back-stabbers

8.3 Underminers

Your boss has a certain amount of power over you as you do over your subordinates, but it's supposed to be different with your peers. You're supposed to be on the same level. You're supposed to pull together as a team and help each other. In the real world, some colleagues just pretend to do this.

These cohorts are so concerned with getting ahead and looking good, they don't want to admit that some of their acts can make you look bad. Sometimes they misinterpret your actions, believing that you're looking down at them, and move to get back at you. Others, knowingly and unknowingly, use your brainpower to generate their copycat proposals.

For the time being, you're stuck with the daily headache of dealing with deceitful colleagues. Your concern is keeping their underhanded behavior from interfering with your career.

8.1 BRAINPICKERS

Brainpickers exploit your ideas, stealing credit for and profiting from them.

Brainpickers are phony office friends who pretend to care about you, but only care about information they can extract from you. Instead of suggesting that you team up and brainstorm some idea or activity to which you both contribute and claim credit, they probe your mind with delicately worded questions. Then they take your brainchild and adopt it or adapt it as their own.

You thought once you left the street and entered the office you were safe from thieves? Just as pickpockets steal your wallet, Brainpickers steal your ideas. Because these con artists don't use guns, you didn't even know you were being robbed.

What You're Thinking

It wasn't just my imagination. Larry pumped me for information about the best way to organize the program so that we'd have the cooperation of all the agencies under the umbrella. Now I find my ideas in this memo from the boss, lauding Larry for coming up with the plan that can help the department achieve better coordination. I can't decide whether to quietly punch Larry or loudly expose him for the thief that he is. But how can I prove that the ideas were really mine and not Larry's?

A Brainpicker's Thoughts

Boy that was a great memo that the boss sent out praising me for my coordinating ideas. I'll add this to my list when it's time to hit the boss for a raise.

Strategy

Obviously, you won't gain anything from a confrontation. The Brainpicker has already convinced himself that your ideas came to him as divine inspiration. Learn from your mistake. Your objective now is to separate your concepts into those you want to present as your own proposals and those that need the collective wisdom of a group to be properly developed. Then direct the flow of your ideas.

(1) *Plug the leak.* Once you've fingered the folks who want to drain your brain, be polite but tight-lipped. Just stop supplying the information.

(2) *Welcome discussion when concepts affect other units.* You don't want to work in a vacuum, not when you need the cooperation of your cohorts. But don't limit yourself to a one-brainpicker audience. Enlarge the group. Call over other colleagues or bring up these matters at lunch or at staff meetings.

Tactical Talk

(tight-lipped) "YES, LARRY, THAT REALLY WILL BE A PROBLEM, BUT I HAVEN'T THOUGHT IT THROUGH YET. WHY DON'T YOU BRING IT UP AT THE NEXT MEETING?"

(group discussion) "YOU KNOW, GUYS, THE BOSS HAS REQUESTED THAT WE MEASURE THE CHANGE IN....I WONDER IF THIS AP-PROACH COULD WORK IN EACH OF OUR UNITS. WHAT IF WE WERE TO..."

Tip: OK, you were snookered by the Brainpicker. Be glad this happened to you now. You'll be wiser in the future when you come up with a really brilliant gem. Then you'll know how to nourish, protect, and present your prize-win-ning idea.

8.2 BACK-STABBERS

Back-Stabbers are nice to your face, but very critical of you behind your back.

These colleagues stab you in absentia. They are bad-mouth-ers, telling lies or being critical about you when you're not there. When you're with them, they act like they're your friends. But out of sight, the phonies betray your trust, re-vealing some disclosure you confided about your personal life or opposing some action you've taken.

They keep trying to outwit you or get some measure of control over you. Maybe they misinterpreted your action. Maybe you did something that angered them, but you can't imagine what it was. You're scratching your head while you're pulling the blade out of your back.

What You're Thinking

I still find it hard to accept that Kate would say anything bad about me behind my back. But three people heard the same thing, so it must have really happened. I guess in an office you can't have any really close friends because the competition is too keen. From now on I'll keep details about my private life to myself. But how do I stop Kate from bad-mouthing me again? And what made her do it in the first place?

A Back-Stabber's Thoughts

Diane was bragging so much about the progress her staff had made. She's making the rest of us look like a bunch of loafers. I'm really sick and tired of everyone thinking she's perfect and using her work as the standard we should all follow.

Strategy

Your objective is to stop the back-stabbing. If criticism made about your work is legitimate, that has to be aired and resolved.

(1) *Confront Back-Stabbers.* But simply report what you heard. Don't start swinging. Ask them to spell out specifically whatever accusations they allegedly made. Speak up firmly, without showing any anger or voicing any blame.

(2) *If the mistake was yours, apologize immediately.* Sometimes you become a victim of Back-Stabbers if they perceive you were insensitive to their feelings. If, for example, they believe that you meant to put them down by elevating yourself, you could have made them feel insecure and want to strike back at you.

(3) *Provide a graceful way out.* If Back-Stabbers accuse you unjustly and then deny having made the reported statements, let them off the hook. Once they know that you know they've attacked your reputation and you won't sit still for such immature behavior, Back-Stabbers will back off. But if you create an emotional scene, a tip-off that they got a rise out of you, they may keep it up.

Tactical Talk

"KATE, I'D APPRECIATE YOUR CLEARING UP SOME CONFUSION. I'VE BEEN TOLD THAT YOU SAID I DID....DID YOU MAKE THAT STATEMENT, AND, IF SO, I'D REALLY LIKE YOU TO EXPLAIN TO ME..."

"WELL, I'M GLAD TO HEAR WHAT WAS REPORTED TO ME WAS AN EXAGGERATION AND THAT YOU DIDN'T INTEND IT AS CRITICISM."

"KATE, I HAD NO IDEA YOU FELT THAT WAY. IF I HURT YOUR FEELINGS, I'M SORRY. I CERTAINLY DIDN'T MEAN TO IMPLY..."

Tip: If you allow the back-stabbing to persist, it can eventually harm your reputation. Such actions are childish and it takes your calm, no-nonsense demeanor to make the culprits behave as adults.

8.3 UNDERMINERS

Underminers undercut your efforts and set you up to fail.

Undermining colleagues take back-stabbing a step further. They weaken your position by clever, crafty means. They lie in wait to make a sneak attack. When the ambush occurs you are completely surprised. Their maneuver is more serious than the Back-Stabbers' because it can result

in sapping support and enthusiasm and reducing the impact
of your efforts.

Sometimes Underminers hurt your work by subtle means
such as purposely being late with needed information or
supplying you with flawed data. Or, agreeing to go along
with a proposal until they sense no support, and then backing out to leave you holding the bag.

They often level a charge when there's no opportunity
for you to defend yourself. When you do, the damage is
already done. Maybe they didn't mean to make you fall flat
on your face, but they certainly are grandstanding at your
expense.

What You're Thinking

Why is Danny doing this to me? He sends a memo to
the manager stating that my program is not hiring minorities
in accordance with company policy. First of all, he has distorted the facts by giving an inaccurate account. Secondly,
he never bothered to check with me before writing that
attack. What is his game? Why is he undermining my program? And what can I do to counteract this?

An Underminer's Thoughts

I'll send copies of this memo to all the minority groups.
That will show them that I'm really in there fighting for them
and I may be able to milk some publicity from it. Then the
manager will see how hard I'm working, that I'm right on
top of things, actually visiting the sites of our programs to
observe for myself conformance to policy.

Strategy

Your Underminer is playing politics and, unfortunately,
you are the butt of dirty tricks. You were probably selected
as the target because you appeared weak and vulnerable. If
you stay still, you're dead, and can go no where but down
or out of the organization. You must launch a counteroffensive.

(1) *Prepare a crisp outline of the real facts.* Go over it again
and again to strike all the inflammatory, emotional words

describing the despicable, treacherous act. What you do with this depends on the situation. If the damage wasn't too serious, sending the correction to your boss, and copies to the Underminer and everyone else involved, may be sufficient to clear your good name.

(2) *When it's serious, pay a visit to all the people you know with clout.* If you have mentors, this is the time to get help. Hand each one copies of both the offensive evidence and the rebuttal you prepared. Ask their advice and get their help. Powerful people who work well behind the scenes generally know the diplomatic language to use that results in correcting misinformation. Whether or not you have other mentors, go in to see your boss.

Tactical Talk

Don't add fuel to the flames:

Not this: "IF HE HAD BOTHERED TO CHECK, HE WOULD HAVE KNOWN THAT..."

But this: "WHEN THE FACTS ARE CHECKED, IT WILL BE-COME APPARENT THAT..."

A sneak has trouble handling a face to face encounter:

You: "DANNY, I DON'T KNOW WHY YOU SENT THIS MEMO, BUT THE INFORMATION IS INACCU-RATE. THIS PAPER WILL GIVE YOU THE FACTS THAT YOU NEED. I KNOW I CAN DEPEND ON YOU TO CORRECT A FALSE IMPRESSION."

Your boss is responsible for your work. He must be kept informed:

"BOSS, THERE HAS BEEN SOME MISLEADING, DAMAGING, AND INACCURATE INFORMATION CIRCULATED ABOUT MY PROGRAM. I'VE COME TO ASK YOUR HELP IN SETTING THE RECORD STRAIGHT. HERE ARE BOTH THE TROUBLESOME MEMO AND MY RESPONSE..."

Tip: When you have been sandbagged by a colleague, it knocks the wind out of you. Take a few deep breaths, then realize the Underminer's intention wasn't to squash you but to inflate himself. Regardless of motive, you still have to clear the muddied record and prevent future sneak attacks.

Deceptive colleagues use various means to step on you in order to make themselves appear taller. You have to protect yourself because their pouncing weakens your prospects of career advancement. Responses you can choose to use range from zipping your lips, settling legitimate criticism, confronting your accuser, to launching a counteroffensive.

CHAPTER 9

WHEN YOUR SUBORDINATES ARE DECEPTIVE

9.1 Foxes
9.2 Bluffers
9.3 Instigators

With a few exceptions, you believe that you and your workers get along well. You're meeting your schedules. Morale seems to be good. But there are a few unhappy subordinates who are afraid to, or don't know how to, take a direct approach to resolving their complaints. They resort to underhanded tactics to get what they want. They concoct devious schemes to relieve their boredom, receive due credit, untangle red tape, and pump for information.

These discontented subordinates have a strong need to get your attention and they meet this need with inappropriate, deceptive behavior. Some try to confuse or outwit you or get away with stalling or faking answers. Others stir up trouble among their peers to create a bit of excitement or as an act of revenge or rebellion.

Whatever their reasons for being deceptive, it's giving you a headache. You can get relief by taking a closer look at areas where your methods may be demotivating, if not demoralizing, them.

9.1 FOXES

Foxes are sly, cunning wheeler-dealers, out to outsmart you.

You wonder why they're so evasive, shifty, or crafty. Workers you perceive as sly may really be shy, reluctant to ask you for better assignments or for more responsibility. They'd rather be clever than pushy. They may feel left out, ignored, not a part of what's going on. They do what's asked, but realize their opinions don't count in a massive, faceless superstructure. Some are ingenious in creating problems for the sole purpose of being praised for their brilliance in solving them.

What You're Thinking

Scott is clever, his work is great, but I have to wonder if he's resorting to deception. This morning was a good example. How did that contract with the client get so twisted that Scott had to jump in to straighten it out? He may be trying to outwit me. I'm going to have to have a frank talk with him to find out what he's thinking.

A Fox's Thoughts

Well, I guess I'm not getting anywhere in this organization. The juicy jobs are still going to the old-timers. Good work isn't enough to get noticed. Where can I spark a little calamity so the boss can see for himself how handy I am when it comes to resolving difficulties?

Strategy

Foxes are clever. Your goal is to put their quick thinking and shrewdness to work for you, not against you. This requires:

(1) *More discussion when you give feedback.* Throw them a challenge to find and fill gaps in the process. Say you'll grade performance on this as well as on assigned work.

(2) *Establishing a better recognition system.* Give them the credit they've earned. Consider giving awards to entire units instead of to individuals. You may need more frequent rewards, made after each step. Or to tie accomplishments to financial incentives and profit-sharing plans.

(3) *Helping workers move out of their one-specialty rut.* Tie training to personal goals and ambitions. Give more time for creative work by unshackling them from unnecessary paper work.

(4) *Keeping your people informed.* Tell them what other departments are doing. Explain how their work fits into the total picture, and why their efforts make a difference.

Tactical Talk

"HOW DO YOU FEEL ABOUT THE COMMENTS I'VE MADE ABOUT YOUR WORK?"

"YES, I SEE WHERE THAT CAUSES DIFFICULTY. YOU KNOW I REALLY DEPEND ON YOU. HOW DO YOU THINK YOU SHOULD SOLVE THE PROBLEM?"

"TAKING INTO ACCOUNT A NORMAL ATTRITION RATE, EACH DIVISION IS CONCENTRATING ON REDUCED TURNOVER. YOUR PROJECT IS ESPECIALLY VITAL TO US IN ACHIEVING THIS OBJECTIVE..."

Tip: People who try to outsmart you often feel like outsiders. Bridge the gap. They'll stop playing tricks if you invite them in and let them be part of what's going on.

9.2 BLUFFERS

Bluffers are misleading fakers. They don't know and won't check it out.

They conceal the truth or outright lie while giving you incomplete or wrong information. They palm off one thing as another, present data as accurate without bothering to verify, or assure you they've taken care of a matter when they have yet to lift a finger.

It may surprise you that some of these subordinates who lie, cheat, and snooker you are actually obsessive worriers who fear they can't handle the task and keep putting it off. Some Bluffers use stalling tactics because they're afraid if they do what they're supposed to, they'd be trespassing on a cohort's turf.

Other Bluffers are lazy and irresponsible. A quirk in their personality makes them lie to get out of work. Some, out for revenge, invent work. They rip you off by creating problems that will require their working overtime, and thereby receiving overtime pay.

If you're being plagued by Bluffers, you probably have trouble "hearing" each other.

What You're Thinking

Jack told me the computer training workshop was all taken care of when it wasn't. Now his team is scrambling to adjust their schedules to fit the newly announced times. His staff people are having a deadline anxiety attack. Why couldn't he just tell me he was having trouble and we could have made other arrangements?

A Bluffer's Thoughts

My boss forgets I'm a person and feeds me directions as though I'm a robot. He doesn't listen or even care about what I'm saying. How frustrating, a stiff-as-starch style and unclear instructions. I never really understand exactly what he wants me to do. If I guess wrong, I have to fib about having done something until I can get back to it and straighten it out.

Strategy

Your goal is to have everyone tuned into the same channel. Adjust the wavelength by:

(1) *Clarifying instructions.* You can eliminate a lot of the bluffing/stalling by asking workers to restate assignments in their own words to be sure they understand. Talk about any concerns they may have. Shorten reporting periods with *segmented* deadlines. Assure Bluffers who are also perfectionists that they'll have time later to polish their masterpieces.

(2) *Devising a better feedback plan.* It should be more frequent, more specific, more helpful and less threatening. With those you regard as irresponsible, keep the tone constructive instead of critical by concentrating on consequences rather than on threats.

(3) *Linking individual performance to team spirit.* Act as though they've already developed a potential capability you've detected. Talk in terms of the value of their work to the whole unit.

Tactical Talk

"WHY DO YOU THINK YOU WERE UNABLE TO DO WHAT YOU PROMISED?...WHAT DO YOU SUGGEST WE DO ABOUT THAT?"

"WHAT DO YOU THINK WOULD HAPPEN TO OUR DEPARTMENT IF EVERYONE ACTED LIKE THAT? ...DO YOU KNOW WHAT WILL HAPPEN IF YOU CONTINUE TO...WHAT STEPS WILL YOU TAKE TO CORRECT THIS?"

"YOUR QUICK ACTION WAS REALLY HELPFUL TO OUR UNIT. BUT WHY DO YOU THINK WE FOUND OURSELVES IN THAT CRISIS? HOW CAN WE PREVENT A REPETITION...?"

Tip: Subordinates bluff for many reasons. More direct face-to-face communication will help allay their fears, have them believe you're on their side, and accept responsibility for their own actions.

9.3 INSTIGATORS

Instigators are troublemakers. They stir up your workers and provoke action.

These subordinates say nasty things, twisting the truth to goad other workers, fomenting unnecessary problems. While they don't steal equipment or supplies, they are guilty of stealing your time. You have to keep putting out the brush fires their prodding has initiated.

Some troublemakers are bored, unchallenged, underutilized high achievers. It could be a mismatch of job and worker. Or, they see no reason for assignments they find unexciting and unimportant and know they're capable of doing a lot more.

Some Instigators are expressing their resentment of your management style. If you keep stressing what they do wrong, they may be pleading for personal growth opportunities. Or they want to get back at you for chewing them out, throwing cold water on their hot ideas, or making it impossible for them to penetrate a tight circle of select employees. Also, they might be having personal problems and are taking out their hostility on you.

Other Instigators rebel against the red tape that stifles any initiative. Some have been disillusioned by phoniness and resent compromises that occur in the work place. They've been hurt and want to expose acts they consider unfair or unethical because they still care deeply about integrity.

What You're Thinking

Jerry reminds me of the kid in the schoolroom who's always giving the teacher a hard time. He's too bright to stay with the group, gets bored, and gets into trouble. I certainly give him enough attention and recognition. I need to channel his energy into a new challenge.

An Instigator's Thoughts

This organization is so bogged down in overlapping rules and policies nobody can breathe. It starts from the day you get hired and go through their protracted orientation sessions.

I suggested ways to improve it to the boss, but he didn't pay any attention. What if I goad our group into pressuring the boss to change a lot of their ridiculous procedures? Even if we don't get them changed, I can stir up some action and at least add a little excitement to the daily grind.

Strategy

Your goal is to turn troublemakers around and help re-shape their destructive efforts into productive ones.

(1) *Add excitement to reduce the mischief.* Change jobs if workers are mismatched with their jobs by inflating, rather than crushing, the ego. When feasible, rotate jobs for the joy and value of learning something new. Start competition among your units with meaningful prizes. Discover the one thing a low achiever desires (everyone wants something) and encourage him to go after it.

(2) *Offer empathy to show your understanding.* Let workers know you feel some affinity for their position because you were once in their shoes. Explore without trying to trap. Suggest training courses that could help them achieve personal goals. Enlarge the circle of people you listen to. Show your confidence in them by planning meetings, workshops, and informal sessions to garner their ideas. Double-check your personnel policies to assure fair and equal treatment.

(3) *Give them more control over their own work.* Eliminate overly restrictive rules requiring ten signatures before they can act. Explain why the company is moving in a given direction, then give them a chance to buy into your ideas. Let rebels become creative by designing a plan and implementing it once it has your approval. Share, delegate, and eliminate excessive superstructure.

Tactical Talk

"JERRY, I CAN SEE YOU'RE A NATURAL LEADER AND THIS JOB DOESN'T ALLOW YOU TO DE-VELOP YOUR LEADERSHIP SKILLS. I'M MOVING

YOU TO THE PERSONNEL UNIT AND I'M COUNT-
ING ON YOU TO INSPIRE THE NEW WORKERS..."

"BETTY, I KNOW HOW YOU FEEL BECAUSE I
HAD TO WORK MY WAY UP, TOO. LET'S TALK
ABOUT YOUR FUTURE AND HOW YOU CAN
PROGRESS. WHERE WOULD YOU LIKE TO BE
TWO YEARS FROM NOW?"

Tip: Instigators are causing you trouble because they feel
bored, bitter, or restricted. Review your rules, policies, and
procedures to add excitement, understanding, and opportunity. Especially, eliminate the extraneous to make room for
the spontaneous.

When employees' actions are deceptive and underhanded,
instead of trying to psychoanalyze their behavior, focus on the
results you want to achieve and move them in that direction.
Some studies show that boredom is the top complaint among
workers. If that's true in your arena, it's up to you to help your
subordinates understand their value and the importance of their
work. Having underutilized subordinates with great potential
is like having money in the bank, except that their interest won't
grow if you save them. Give bored workers the chance and the
challenge to develop and contribute.

PART FOUR

DEALING WITH SHREWD/MANIPULATIVE PEOPLE

When we try to influence others, we call it persuasion. When other people try to influence us, we call it manipulation. To some extent, we're all bent on trying to grab control to get what we want, but the shrewd/manipulative bosses, colleagues, and subordinates we're discussing here go beyond the normal attempts at convincing.

These people have *no respect* for a differing point of view. Because of their need to keep the upper hand, they can't enjoy competition. They don't stop to think how they're affecting you. They simply don't care because they're consumed with achieving a goal no matter the means. To them, people are pawns—objects to be pushed around and promised anything. They are imposers who praise and promote, taking advantage of your good nature.

In order to gain control, in guises that range from arrogant to sycophant, exploiters habitually hide their true feelings. Suffering from a shortage of scruples or sensitivity, they are free to infringe and encroach on your time and talent. Their keen insight enables them to make quick decisions in touchy situations, swerving past roadblocks with roundabout routes. They can't risk being forthright, so their body language becomes particularly important for you to observe. It may take a while to register that you are being victimized by clever exploiters.

CHAPTER 10

WHEN YOUR BOSS IS EXPLOITATIVE

10.1 Connivers
10.2 Camouflagers
10.3 Flatterers
10.4 Slave Drivers

Sometimes you may wonder how certain bosses are able to advance as far as they have within the organization. You know that you're swifter with the facts and figures. Maybe so, but they are probably head of the class in office politics. Perhaps they're slick about avoiding blame and quick about grabbing applause, especially for work done by peers or subordinates. They may spend most of their time making friends and making deals, promising anything and everything. They can be charming in the way they pump you up in preparation for dumping on you projects no one else wants. Or, they may be insensitive when they ask you to put in an unreasonable amount of time or effort.

Whatever the particular manner may be, you're convinced that these exploitive bosses are using you. Because of their position and power, you feel that they've got you over a barrel and it's no barrel of fun to accept this kind of treatment.

10.1 CONNIVERS

Connivers imply consent and blame you when the wrongful act backfires.

The bottom line is that conniving bosses won't gamble on their own ability. Taking a risk means accepting a situation as beyond your control and manipulators *have* to feel in control. Therefore, Connivers maintain command by hiding behind a powerful position.

They want everyone to believe they had no knowledge of what went wrong. They're usually careful not to leave telltale fingerprints on clues that could point back to them. Although you and the boss discussed the proposed action before proceeding, rather than share any responsibility for the fiasco, he leaves you out on a limb. If it's necessary to save their own hides, Connivers even saw off the branch. Either way, you become a victim.

What You're Thinking

A few months ago the boss said we had to seek additional funding. I checked the crucial points with the boss while preparing one of the proposals to a potential source. Unfortunately, the proposal was rejected. All of a sudden it became "Keith's proposal," as though the boss had nothing whatsoever to do with it. He played a big part in calling the shots and, of course, he had to sign off on the application. I may have picked up a reputation as a loser and I sure hate being the fall guy, but how can I buck the boss?

A Conniver's Thoughts

It's a shame that proposal Keith prepared didn't get funded. I thought it had a pretty good chance. But at least the one Carole wrote did come through. So, as far as the big boss is concerned, my department and I are still looking good.

Strategy

Your goal is not to buck the boss, but to stop feeling victimized. Keep in mind that if the boss acts the same with the rest of the staff, his troublesome behavior is not directed at you exclusively. Your aim is to secure his support instead of being his shield.

(1) *Appeal to his sense of fairness.* Your boss hasn't been losing any sleep thinking about you or how you are affected. He's worried about protecting himself. Utilize questions to reveal to him the true situation. Ask questions that penetrate to the core of the problem. If the discussion is not going the way you want, change the direction by asking more questions.

(2) *Make suggestions that will strengthen his position.* It's obviously very important to him that he be well regarded by his peers and superiors. Try harder to dig up information and refine it for his immediate use and offer it tactfully. Help the boss become what he'd like everyone to believe he already is.

Tactical Talk

"BOSS, I'VE ALWAYS REGARDED YOU AS A FAIR-MINDED PERSON, SO I DON'T THINK YOU REALIZE THE POSITION I'M IN. DID YOU MEAN TO IMPLY THAT I ALONE WAS RESPONSIBLE FOR THE REJECTED PROPOSAL? I FEEL LIKE I WAS LEFT TWISTING IN THE WIND. THAT WASN'T WHAT YOU INTENDED, WAS IT?"

"BOSS, ANALYZING THESE REPORTED EVENTS, THERE'S A DEFINITE PATTERN EMERGING THAT YOU MIGHT WANT TO ACT ON BEFORE EVERYONE ELSE JUMPS ON THE BANDWAGON. EVEN IF WE DON'T REACH THE PROJECTED AMOUNTS, YOUR APPROACH WILL BE RECOGNIZED AS INNOVATIVE AND WILL HELP MOVE THE ORGANIZATION IN A GOOD DIRECTION."

Tip: While driving you up the wall, Conniver bosses are similar to backseat drivers who refuse to take the wheel. Because they can't tolerate being regarded as inept, they protect their self-image, probably unaware that they habitually blame others for making a wrong turn. Point out the benefits as you gently steer them toward accepting a challenge.

10.2 CAMOUFLAGERS

Camouflagers have hidden agendas, telling half-truths and omitting necessary facts.

Whereas Connivers hide so that no one will think they're ineffective, Camouflagers hide so that no one will learn their true personal goals. These bosses won't level with you, always masking the real reason for their request. They are pleasant, nonthreatening, pretending they are as concerned about you as they are about getting the job done. They make deals: "If you do this for me, I'll do that for you."

Camouflagers constantly maneuver and manipulate. They're so busy trading favors they're barely able to make their deadlines. And they really believe they can outthink you. How could you learn that what they're suggesting wasn't meant to help you but to bail themselves out of some self-inflicted difficulty? You do as they ask, and find yourself repeatedly disappointed and frustrated.

What You're Thinking

I don't understand the boss. Why did he have to wait until the last minute to worry about that report that is due tomorrow? He said if I burn the midnight oil and finish it by 10 AM, he'll remember my cooperation next time raises are being considered. He forgot, that's what he promised me six months ago. Budget time came and went along with another broken promise. Then when I tried to ask him about it, he was suddenly too busy to talk to me. I wonder how I can ever trust him again.

A Camouflager's Thoughts

Boy, I really slipped up on that Liberty Bell report and it's due at tomorrow's 11 AM meeting. I've got to talk Reena into doing it for me and getting it done tonight. I could tell her that I'll mention her name to the board and then I'll dangle a possible raise. That should do it.

Strategy

To the guideline of doing whatever the boss asks as long as it's not illegal, immoral, or unethical, add another qualification—unreasonable. When you can't do what is requested, your goal is to escape without incurring the boss's wrath or vengeance.

(1) *Forget long-range deals and broken promises.* The leopard won't change his spots. Any agreement on advancement that you reach with the Camouflager has to be in writing and preferably witnessed. Don't do what he asks because you expect the promised prize. Do it if you can because you want to be regarded as a reasonable, cooperative, and dependable worker.

(2) *Suggest an alternative to your doing the task.* Maybe a rush job can be divided among a few of you or perhaps there's a way to get an extension. Maybe by teaching someone else to do a technical task, you could be unchained from your desk.

(3) *Sound like a team player even though you're not playing his game.* Don't get angry, or threaten or remind the boss that you've heard that song before. Play it cool, cheerful, and helpful. A pro pitches in without making deals whether acting as doer, mobilizer, or encourager.

Tactical Talk

(accepting) "BOSS, I'D BE GLAD TO WORK ALL NIGHT ON THE REPORT BECAUSE I KNOW HOW IMPORTANT IT IS TO OUR DIVISION. WE CAN DISCUSS RECOGNITION AND RAISES LATER. THAT'S NOT WHY I'M DOING THIS. BUT I WILL

NEED A LITTLE HELP WITH MY ROUTINE TASKS TOMORROW. DO YOU THINK CLARK COULD TAKE OVER A FEW OF THEM FOR ME?"

(rejecting or hedging) "BOSS, I'D BE GLAD TO WORK ALL NIGHT ON THE REPORT BECAUSE I KNOW HOW IMPORTANT IT IS TO OUR DIVISION. BUT WE'RE RUNNING TOO GREAT A RISK THAT I MAY NOT BE ABLE TO FINISH IT ON TIME FOR YOUR MEETING. HOW ABOUT DIVIDING THE FOUR SEGMENTS AMONG CLARK, DAN, MAR-LENE, AND ME?"

Tip: Act professionally even when your boss seems to have forgotten how. If your boss is a wheeler-dealer, that's his problem, not yours. You can be above the shenanigans by changing the scenario. Also, it would help you to find a mentor other than your boss.

10.3 FLATTERERS

Flatterers insincerely give you excessive praise in order to use you.

These bosses believe if they constantly say things designed to please you, greatly exaggerating reality, they are pouring on personal charm and charisma. ("This project would have been an absolute flop without you.") They want you to like them on a personal level in order to win your support and loyalty. They're afraid their plan, procedure, policy, or assignment can't stand on its own merit. So they employ unwarranted praise to gain your acceptance of them and their request *as one package.* Inflating your ego and promising rewards of success to make you want to join in does work for awhile. There's nothing we enjoy more than hearing the boss give praise we honestly believe we earned. And, conversely, nothing makes us more suspicious than a boss heaping elaborate compliments we regard as undeserved and phony. This method of motivating their workers can boomerang for Flatterers when their plans can't stand up and you begin to lose faith in the leader you're following.

What You're Thinking

What's going on? The boss tells me everything I do is great. The results of the last meeting were great, but the previous ones were nothing to brag about because I didn't have time to make them better. Does she know the difference between mediocre and quality, and would she know how to give excellent work widespread distribution? Or, does she have some ulterior motive, buttering me up with lavish praise to get me to do something I might ordinarily object to?

A Flatterer's Thoughts

You can't show too much attention too often to win over your employees. Nothing gets them to strive for excellence every time like compliments. Besides, after you compliment them, it's easier to tell them something they won't want to hear. They're going to have to put in a lot of extra hours to get our department the extra support we need. I must make all of them team players, totally loyal to me.

Strategy

Your goal is to get ahead, preferably with your boss's help, but without buying into a phony plan. The harm caused by Flatterer bosses is that they leave you disillusioned because you sense a leadership vacuum. However, this may be your opportunity. You may be able to fill at least some of the void.

(1) *Maintain your objectivity.* Take the saccharine remarks with a grain of salt. If you're being praised for a task that fell short, be gracious and appreciative, and then speak up on what is needed for improvement. If your relationship is cordial enough, make a joke out of the flattery and tease the Flatterer.

(2) *Get clear statements of desired results and individual roles.* Research useful data the boss can employ in

deciding policy. Encourage group discussions from which better strategies and clear blueprints can emerge. A team that has a part in the planning is automatically more interested in the outcome. You can raise the spirits of your group without being the boss.

Tactical Talk

"I APPRECIATE THE KIND REMARKS, BOSS, BUT I KNOW YOU'D LIKE IT TO BE EVEN BETTER. IT SEEMS TO ME THAT IF WE COULD ALLOT A LITTLE MORE STAFF TIME AND EQUIPMENT, WE COULD MORE THAN DOUBLE..."

"OK, BOSS, THIS FLATTERY WILL GET YOU WHATEVER YOU WANT."

"DON'T YOU THINK WE NEED A TIGHTER PLAN TO MAKE THIS SUCCEED? IT SEEMS TO ME WE HAVE TO BREAK DOWN THE STAGES INTO..."

Tip: A Flatterer boss gives you the chance to enhance your own leadership skills. Help your boss plan to stand on firmer ground so that he won't have to rely on phony compliments to motivate the team.

10.4 SLAVE DRIVERS

Slave Drivers are overly ambitious and demand unreasonable pace or overtime.

You may indeed be working for cruel Simon Legree but, before we get into that, consider two other possibilities:

One, the boss keeps piling on work without a peep of protest out of you. He hasn't the foggiest notion how you feel and assumes you are prioritizing your assignments and putting off the less important until you have time to catch up. You're afraid to speak up lest you jeopardize your job. So you keep being overburdened because you never say no. The pain is self-induced and the remedy is self-help.

Two, the boss keeps piling on work because of pressure imposed on him from top management. You're in a relay race without the fun and prizes. The system is poorly coordinated or the signals are crossed. Again, if you remain mute, you remain on the whirling merry-go-round.

On the other hand, a genuine Slave Driver boss, afraid to make decisions, may habitually slide these matters from his desk to yours. He may abdicate his responsibility because he feels inadequate, lacking some necessary skill for his present post. He could resent your potential and keep you overloaded to maintain his control, or maybe he demands excellence without allotting the time it takes to hone your product. It's time to negotiate the preposterous workload your boss is demanding.

What You're Thinking

Why is the boss so mean to me? What a hassle getting stuck with that lousy tri-county committee one more time. It means traveling an extra 25 miles back and forth twice a week to attend late evening meetings and dragging myself in exhausted the next morning. But I don't dare complain. If I do, the boss will get back at me and give that promised appointment to someone else. I'm trapped.

A Slave Driver's Thoughts

That was a good move delegating Ron again as my representative on the tri-county committee. He's a very skillful debater. He'll argue our position well and I won't have to make any quick decisions. He didn't seem too pleased to be going, but he's really the only one I can depend on. He's a good sport. He'll get over it.

Strategy

Your goal is to be treated fairly and to be compensated appropriately when you're asked to put in additional hours.

(1) *Determine if you are really being overworked.* Were you asked to work extra hours or are you being a compulsive performer who can't let go of the work until it's "perfect"?

(2) *Determine if the burdensome assignment could be divided among your colleagues or done by one of them.* If it's a one-person job, consider that what you think of as a drag, your peer may envision as an opportunity to become more visible. That person may be delighted to learn the procedure from you.

(3) *Negotiate better terms with your boss.* Query your boss on why you're being drowned in extra work. Decide what the boss needs most and how you can help him get it. And just as important, decide what you need most (e.g., more time for the job or more time off, more money, more staff, modified objectives) so that you can articulate this after expressing your concerns about being overburdened. Don't reveal your anger and don't attack the boss's motives. Appear calm and cooperative as you suggest ways to change the situation.

(4) *Gang up on the boss with very gentle pressure.* Sometimes if all the staff join in some good natured teasing, it can slow down a dynamo.

Tactical Talk

"BOSS, DON'T YOU THINK IT'D BE A GOOD IDEA FOR US TO HAVE A BACKUP PERSON FOR THE COMMITTEE? MAYBE IF ALLISON CAME ALONG AS AN OBSERVER, WE COULD BE TRAINING HER..."

"BOSS, I REALIZE THE SIGNIFICANCE OF OUR FORMING AN ALLIANCE, BUT I NEED YOUR HELP IN FIGURING OUT HOW TO HANDLE MY OTHER FOUR MAJOR ASSIGNMENTS...SPECIFIC-ALLY, I HAVE TO UNDERSTAND YOUR PRIORI-TIES SO THAT WE AGREE ON A TIME SCHEDULE..."

"BOSS, I KNOW HOW IMPORTANT THE NEW SYS-
TEM IS, BUT FOR THE PAST MONTH SINCE WE
PUT IT IN, I'VE BEEN ASKED TO WORK SEVERAL
EXTRA HOURS A WEEK WITHOUT BEING COM-
PENSATED. IF THAT'S GOING TO CONTINUE, IT
DOESN'T SEEM FAIR TO ME. HOW DO YOU FEEL
ABOUT IT?"

Tip: You can't assume the boss knows what you're feeling if
you keep still. Without groping or griping or putting the boss
on the defensive, you can learn to refuse or reshuffle assignments. Focus the discussion on the Slave Driver's desire to
get the work accomplished when and how he wants.

Some bosses deliberately drain every last ounce of work
out of you, or cover up their real reasons for their requests,
or blame you in order to protect themselves. More often, exploitative bosses act like that because they are preoccupied
or insensitive, unaware that they appear to be tricky. You're
only ensnared when you're too scared to speak up. There are
always other options to suggest. You can be cooperative without becoming the fly who steps into the spider's parlor.

CHAPTER 11

WHEN YOUR COLLEAGUES ARE EXPLOITATIVE

11.1 Plotters

11.2 Imposers

11.3 Duck and Divers

11.4 Operators

Many colleagues who take advantage of you don't intentionally practice Machiavellian methods. More likely, they've put their personal feelings about you aside as they analyze what is needed to accomplish their ends. To them, how they feel about you is quite beside the point. This absence of emotion, which you perceive as deceitful, rude, or insensitive, allows them to use you to get what they're after. They play their hands with finesse, knowing how you will most probably react and planning ahead their countermoves if you should present an obstacle.

When you feel that you're being tricked or exploited, you'd like to give in to your rage and attack the manipulators. However, all that does is show everyone else that you've lost control.

You have to stop dead in your tracks until you figure out what your cohort is trying to get away with. Only then can you respond accordingly in a logical and positive fashion.

11.1 PLOTTERS

Plotters conspire secretly and clam up when you join them.

Your anxiety increases when you feel you're being put down or ganged up on by a couple of colleagues, or when one of them has the ear of your boss. As soon as the discussion starts, a warning bell rings in your brain. You sense the conspirators have schemed something that will affect your ability to perform. By the time the hidden agenda is revealed, you may already have been pushed aside.

Plotters scheme their every act as a step toward moving up. The problem is that they don't care that their gains are at your expense.

What You're Thinking

Uh-oh, the boss and Arthur have made some sort of pact. They're relocating my office down the hall and moving Arthur closer to the boss. It's not the inconvenience or even the loss of prestige that's bothering me. I'm also losing out on my essential support staff who will now be reporting directly to Arthur. It was hard enough before. With less help, how will I ever get my reports out on time? What a lousy deal!

A Plotter's Thoughts

The boss finally sees me as a real rising star. He knows I have really good contacts and good instincts, and I think I've convinced him that I can do us a lot of good. My objective is to work closely with him. The first step is to get him to move my office closer to his and to give me the additional staff I asked for. I could suggest that David and I switch offices. From a results standpoint, David doesn't need to consult frequently with the boss or require as much staff as I do.

Strategy

When you've been pushed aside by a plotting and manipulative colleague, you've obviously lost some ground. Your goal is to recover as much as you can.

(1) *Be still or stall the action until you regain your composure.* Don't let them see that you're angry or you can count yourself out of the game. Digest what has just been discussed, calculating how you're affected and what you'll need to compensate.

(2) *Support, on the surface, the Plotter's proposal.* You've lost this round no matter what you say. It's to your advantage to appear cooperative.

(3) *Negotiate by linking what they want to what you want.* Sound unemotional and very factual. ("In order to do this, we have to do that.") Ask how they think that result might be accomplished.

Tactical Talk

(if you have to stall for time) "WOULD YOU PLEASE EXCUSE ME? I'LL BE BACK IN A COUPLE OF MINUTES."

(to appear supportive) "I CAN UNDERSTAND WHY YOU FEEL IT'S IMPORTANT FOR ARTHUR TO BE GIVEN EXTRA STAFF."

(to negotiate) "BUT IF ARTHUR IS GOING TO SUCCEED WITH THESE CONTACTS, HE'S GOING TO NEED THE REPORTS I DEVELOP. AFTER I PREPARE THE DRAFTS, WOULD HIS PEOPLE BE ABLE TO FINALIZE THEM, OR DO YOU HAVE SOME OTHER THOUGHTS ON HOW TO HANDLE THAT SEGMENT OF THE WORK?"

Tip: When you're caught in their plot, don't get hot under the collar. Take a few deep breaths so you won't react to implications which you regard as putting you down or edging you out. State your understanding of their needs. Then explain how responding to your needs will help them accomplish their desired result.

11.2 IMPOSERS

Imposers take unfair advantage of your time, talent, and good nature.

Colleagues such as these are just plain self-centered and inconsiderate of others. You certainly don't mind doing a favor every once in a while and you're glad to pitch in during an emergency, but Imposers make a habit of exploiting you. They are so wound up in whatever they want to do that they are oblivious to anyone else's feelings or needs. They promise to return the favor and never do, but you're not looking for favors. You want them to leave you alone and stop saying that you ought to help them "because that's what friends are for." No friend would be that unfeeling and presumptuous.

Some Imposers put on a helpless act. These poor dependent souls aren't helpless at all, just crafty in getting you to do their work while they use company time for personal business.

You know what they're doing is wrong. You hate being a part of it, but you don't want to hurt their feelings. You have great difficulty saying no to Imposers.

What You're Thinking

I'm so mad at myself for letting Melissa put me in this position. I'm getting behind in my own work while I'm answering the requests she's supposed to handle. I thought she just needed an hour or so, but she's been on the phone every day this week with her attorney or witnesses for her trial. I tried to tell her I didn't want to do this any more. She was so insistent, I couldn't get out of it.

An Imposer's Thoughts

I sure hope the boss doesn't catch me on the phone so much, but I really don't have a choice. I have to take care of personal business and the only time I can reach these people is during office hours.

Strategy

Your goal is to free yourself from doing something you don't want to do. This is especially important if you also believe what you've been asked to do is wrong and you feel torn between helping a colleague and obeying company policy.

(1) *Remember that you really don't need a reason to refuse a request.* Expressing your regret is sufficient. But if that sticks in your soft-hearted throat, sandwich your refusal between two compliments or helpful comments.

(2) *Practice firm responses at home.* Listen to yourself on a recorder. Or role play rejections so that they roll off your tongue in a calm and polite manner. Just because you think your colleague is being lazy or inconsiderate, that doesn't give you the right to be rude.

(3) *Suggest more appropriate ways to deal with the problem.* Consider how else the needs of the Imposer might be met in a more responsible fashion. Place that responsibility back where it belongs—on the Imposer—without showing signs of hostility or sarcasm.

Tactical Talk

"I'M SORRY, MELISSA, I CAN'T HELP YOU TODAY."

"GEE, MELISSA, I CAN SEE YOU'RE REALLY IN A BIND, BUT I CAN'T HELP OUT BECAUSE I'M SO FAR BEHIND IN MY OWN WORK. MAYBE RALPH ISN'T TOO BUSY, WHY NOT ASK HIM?"

"MELISSA, YOU REALLY DO NEED SOME HELP ON TWO COUNTS: THE ONLY TIME YOU CAN MAKE THE PERSONAL CALLS IS DURING OFFICE HOURS WHICH IS STRICTLY VERBOTEN. IF YOU GET CAUGHT, YOU'RE IN BIG TROUBLE. BUT THERE IS AN ANSWER. DISCUSS THE PROBLEM WITH THE BOSS. ARRANGE FOR A FEW HOURS OFF TO TAKE CARE OF A PERSONAL EMER-

GENCY AND OFFER TO MAKE UP THE TIME
LATER ON."

Tip: Refuse to be used. You're not really helping dependent
people by supplying the crutch instead of making them face
their responsibilities. And you're not helping yourself by remaining silent when you're being unreasonably imposed
upon. If you're meek and don't speak, you won't like yourself.
The anger within you builds and sometimes explodes, and
then you find yourself apologizing to peers, friends, and family. Speak up!

11.3 DUCK AND DIVERS

Duck and Divers plan with you, then leave you holding
the bag to face the consequences.

These colleagues are cowards. They support you as long
as they think the issue is popular, then they cut and run,
leaving you alone to take the responsibility. You thought they
were your friends, and that hurts.

While there's no excusing people who encourage you to
go out on a limb and then saw it off, you do have to face the
fact than an office friend differs from a social friend. Selfish
interests may get in the way, for example, when you both go
after the same top assignment or promotion. So, as long as it
seems safe, the office friends agree with you on what should
be done. Then the boss opposes the idea, or it doesn't meet
group approval, and your colleagues start ducking and diving
before you even know what hit you. You feel pretty foolish
being out there by yourself when you claimed to be speaking
for "a few of us" who had this brainstorm.

What You're Thinking

I'm going to find a way to get even with Ava and Glen
for setting me up. When we talked about presenting a leadership workshop for our supervisors they were all for it and
promised to back me up if I presented the plan at the management meeting. Then when the boss started frowning and

the others started complaining about the costs and time away from work, Ava and Glen joined the chorus. I felt like an idiot, but I'll get back at them.

A Duck and Diver's Thoughts

Robert has no antenna working for him. He should have sensed from the boss's expression that this was no time to bring up a proposal that would cost unbudgeted money. He never knows when to back off. The timing was wrong. There was no way I was going to stick my neck out.

Strategy

If you put your finger on a hot stove you get burned. But you still have to use the stove and so the next time you put on a mitt. Similarly, you still have to work with the Duck and Divers. Getting even with your colleagues won't help. Your goal is to protect your feelings from any such future injuries by better preparation.

(1) *Plan to negotiate.* Decide in advance where you perceive the power lies among your peers and how much influence each of you has. What is it that you want and what are you willing to exchange for something they want?

(2) *Stay in control.* When you want your concept to be presented as a joint effort, act rather than react. Put an outlined plan in writing with all of you signing on. Decide how each of you will participate. If you alone are doing the speaking, introduce your fellow planners before you start your talk. That way no one can back out of the commitment.

Tactical Talk

"AVA AND GLEN, I'M GLAD YOU LIKE THIS IDEA BECAUSE I THINK YOUR OPINIONS CARRY WEIGHT IN INFLUENCING THE OTHERS. YOU'VE ADDED SOME GOOD TOUCHES AND I'D

LIKE TO PRESENT THIS AS A JOINT PROPOSAL TO RECOGNIZE THE PART YOU'VE PLAYED IN MAKING IT SALEABLE."

"I'VE INCORPORATED YOUR THINKING INTO THIS OUTLINE WE CAN SUBMIT ALONG WITH THE PRESENTATION..."

Tip: Don't float a shaky idea until you've organized a raft of support. Before presenting a joint proposal, prepare it in written form with each participant's signature.

11.4 OPERATORS

Operators, with charming gift of gab, convince you to do their bidding.

These colleagues are so smooth, you don't realize you've been duped by a con artist. Operators are glib, slick, and crafty. Their reasons are so compelling, you readily agree to do what they ask. Sometimes they've violated company policy and want you to make some phone calls or to intercede with the boss on their behalf. Sometimes they see a potential career advantage and pump you for information that is supposed to be kept confidential. Whatever they're after, you go along because you believe you're serving some good purpose. You tell yourself the end result excuses the questionable method.

After a time, it dawns on you that you feel downright uncomfortable being mixed up in somebody else's wheeling and dealing.

What You're Thinking

Frank is asking me to tell the boss that there were extenuating circumstances that led him to violate the policy. I can see where Frank might have thought he was justified, and I know I need Frank to help me with my projects. I sure hate being in the middle of his muddle, but how can I refuse?

An Operator's Thoughts

When the boss spelled out our company's objectives, he did say that we should stay clear of certain contacts. But I don't think he understood the true picture. If it had worked out, I'd be a hero today. I've got to scrounge up some support from cohorts the boss respects, especially people whose work benefits from my talent.

Strategy

Your goal is to avoid being drawn into an Operator's shrewd and perhaps unscrupulous schemes.

(1) *Ask a lot of questions.* While Operators are clever and quick-witted, they'd rather deal with colleagues who don't require protracted explanations. If your initial gut feeling is that the request might be improper or unethical, it probably is.

(2) *Offer the proper kind of assistance.* Don't take on somebody else's work or problem as your own. Ask more questions to focus the Operator's attention on acceptable alternatives that are available.

(3) *Refuse future favors from Operators.* The price you pay may be eternal kowtowing or worse.

Tactical Talk

"FRANK, DID THE BOSS SPECIFICALLY TELL YOU NOT TO MAKE THESE CONTACTS?...HOW MANY DID YOU MAKE?...WHAT EXACTLY WERE YOU TRYING TO ACCOMPLISH?...WHY DID YOU FEEL YOU COULDN'T GO THROUGH REGULAR CHANNELS?..."

"WHAT OTHER OPTIONS DO YOU THINK MIGHT BE OPEN?...HAVE YOU CONSIDERED MAKING A FORMAL REQUEST?...ARE THERE OTHERS IN THE GROUP WHO FEEL AS YOU DO? HAVE YOU TRIED BRAINSTORMING WITH THEM...?"

"LISA, WHY DO YOU NEED THIS INFORMATION? ...HOW ARE YOU GOING TO USE IT?...I THINK BOTH OF US WOULD GET INTO A LOT OF TROUBLE IF I OPENED THE FILES, AND YOU DON'T WANT THAT TO HAPPEN, DO YOU?"

Tip: Dispel the spell that Operators cast over you. By asking pointed questions, you'll find the sorcerer's black magic takes on a new and revealing light.

Counteracting shrewd and manipulative colleagues requires honesty and candor. Some people lock themselves into stressful situations by keeping still, believing, as Cervantes wrote, "a closed mouth catches no flies." That may be so, but a closed mouth also offers no relief from people who take advantage of you.

Stop worrying about hurting the feelings of colleagues who exploit you. You won't. You can refuse without being rude. You may be able to show them a better way. If they don't want to listen, they'll just try to trick the next person into doing what they want done.

CHAPTER 12

WHEN YOUR SUBORDINATES ARE EXPLOITATIVE

12.1 Bootlickers
12.2 Snitchers
12.3 Rumor Mongers

Some workers try to manipulate bosses much the way children try to manage their parents. Among the more popular tactics is currying favor by flattery in order to be assigned a certain task or to get out of doing one.

Other subordinates take advantage of your need to know what's going on by telling tales on their cohorts. Some workers will purposely spread rumors to make themselves seem more important. While you oppose snitching and personal gossiping, just by being there you are enmeshed in office politics, whether or not you want to be part of the political process.

You're faced with having to differentiate between views colored by manipulating maneuvers and news that's valid business information you should be tuned in on.

12.1 BOOTLICKERS

Bootlickers fawn over you, seek favors, and say what you want to hear.

Sycophant subordinates will say anything to get your attention and win your support. They use insincere compliments to try to get you to like them. They cling like parasites, getting others to do their work. They're not lazy or helpless, but they are manipulative.

They want to get noticed and are using the wrong means to catch your eyes and your ears. If you think these workers have potential worth developing, help them build up their confidence by reducing their dependency.

What You're Thinking

Bobbie keeps saying how happy she is to be working for me, what a wonderful boss I am, how much she's learning from me, how my leadership has put our division far ahead of the others. OK, I admit that's what I want to believe. Her flattery sure sounds good and I'm being taken in. She has managed to twist me around her finger, slipping and sliding out of tasks I assigned to her. Like when I asked her to go with Jeff to see Hamilton, she begged off claiming she needed more time to work on the annual report. She'd bristle if I forced her to go, so I conceded. I think she's managing me more than I'm managing her. How can I get her to do what I want without creating animosity?

A Bootlicker's Thoughts

The boss really fell for that line about his leadership style and the way I tied that into our annual report. I had to say something because I'll be darned if I'll go to another meeting with Hamilton. The boss really is good, but he's a soft touch. I certainly want to remain in his good favor and move up the ladder as he advances with the company.

Strategy

Your goal is to regain control of your unit.

(1) *Ask yourself the right questions, not nonquestions.* Stop going around in circles wondering what to do to avoid resentment. Ask questions for which there are answers such as "What traits should we be helping our employees

develop?" Cooperativeness and dependability are two of them.

(2) *Be firm and resolute when making assignments.* Get to the point, without a preamble. As long as you're polite and reasonable, subordinates understand their survival depends upon doing what the boss asks. If, for instance, you need someone's expertise at a given time, you make the decision based on a broader picture than the worker has. If the subordinate's response is unexpected and you want to modify your request, instead of an instant reply, say you'll get back to him a little later.

(3) *Build the Bootlickers' confidence.* Provide opportunities for them to develop in areas where they've experienced success. Encourage discussion. Be there, but let them solve their own work problems. Give frequent feedback, sharing your view of how they come across and how they can improve and why they'd want to.

(4) *Teach Bootlickers the proper way to praise.* Show by your own example how to compliment someone's work, saying something specific about the performance rather than a general comment about the person, and why you believe what he did was important. Develop a system for acknowledging good work both publicly and privately.

(5) *Be constructive when criticizing.* Accent the positive, avoiding threats, bribes, and comparisons with coworkers. Talk about why something angers you rather than accusing them of deliberately jeopardizing your operation.

Tactical Talk

"BOBBIE, I KNOW YOUR TIME CONSTRAINTS, BUT IT'S IMPORTANT FOR OUR UNIT THAT YOU AND YOUR EXPERIENCE BE AT THAT MEETING. WE'LL DISCUSS YOUR WORKLOAD LATER....IT'S ALSO IMPORTANT FOR YOU. YOU'VE HAD SOME GOOD RESULTS WITH PRESENTING OUR CASE, I'D LIKE FOR YOU TO GET MORE EXPOSURE..."

"WE AGREE YOU SHOULD HAVE A REASONABLE WORKLOAD. LET'S EXAMINE THE ALTER-

NATIVES AND SEE WHAT WE CAN DO IN-
STEAD..."

"BOBBIE, I KNOW YOU WANT TO MOVE UP AND
I WANT TO HELP YOU. SO I THINK YOU SHOULD
BE AWARE OF CERTAIN PERCEPTIONS OTHERS
HAVE ABOUT YOU..."

"I GET UPSET WHEN I REALIZE WE MAY LOSE
AN IMPORTANT CONTRACT IF WE DON'T HAVE
THE RIGHT PRESENTATION..."

Tip: When your subordinates are exploitative, help them
build their self-confidence. Also check yourself to make sure
they're not reacting to your manipulating them: (1) Do you
try to get them to do something by making them feel guilty?
(2) Do you expect too much? (3) Are you making deals ("I'll
do this for you if you'll do that for me.")?

12.2 SNITCHERS

Snitchers are squealers who tattle on their peers and spread
malicious stories about them.

Sometimes Snitchers tell tales because they're jealous or
vengeful. It's a childish way of trying to make themselves
appear better by making a coworker look bad. Subordinates
often resort to squealing and squawking because they feel
frustrated at being unable to advance from their present level.
They take on the role of informant, hoping to gain an advantage when some position does open up. If that's the case, you
have to tighten your managerial reins. Look at your existing
or nonexisting measurable objectives, how you are rating and
rewarding good performance, and the quality of your discussions with each of your workers.

When faced with malicious fault-finding, look beyond the
gossip to the forces that are producing it. Why are these workers feeding the grapevine or coming to you with their stories?
What power struggles are going on? Are the results inconsequential or are innocent people being harmed?

What You're Thinking

Andrew told me a couple of things about Jim that could possibly be important for me to know. According to the grapevine, Jim and his wife are having some problems. Maybe this wouldn't be a good time for Jim to take on a new and challenging assignment. On the other hand, maybe Andrew told me that so that I'd ask Andrew, instead of Jim, to do that highly visible job. Andrew also complained that Jim was late with the monthly figures. Jim is too good a worker to let this go by. I'd better have a talk with him to find out what is really going on here.

A Snitcher's Thoughts

I think I planted that tidbit about Jim pretty well, offering it as a possible explanation for Jim's work not being up to the usual high standard. If the boss goes by the water cooler, he'll hear the same thing. It doesn't take long to get wall-to-wall coverage on fresh gossip.

Strategy

Your goal is to sort the information you get from Snitchers. You have to separate harmful, spiteful gossip from useful intelligence data.

(1) *Teach tattletales to solve their own problems.* In considering jealous back-stabbing, ask yourself why they are trying to use you. Have you become the indirect means for dealing with problems they refuse to face directly? Force subordinates to take responsibility for themselves. Don't get caught in the in-fighting.

(2) *Determine if you have to change procedures that might be encouraging tattletales.* You don't have to reveal your source when following up on some report that was given you, such as a worker who's having a problem or a customer who was dissatisfied.

(3) *Be alert for clues to potential patterns, problems, and changes.* Go to lunch often with your colleagues. Listen when your subordinates talk to each other. Stay tuned.

You'll unearth what's really going on in your organization that you ought to be thinking about or planning for. When you're at an office party, keep your ears open and watch to see who is talking to whom. Chat with secretaries and mail clerks, anyone who's in touch with the many levels of your organization.

Tactical Talk

"ANDREW, IT SEEMS TO ME THE PROBLEM IS BETWEEN YOU AND JIM AND I DON'T WANT TO GET CAUGHT IN THE MIDDLE. BUT IT IS IMPORTANT THAT YOU WORK OUT SOMETHING BECAUSE WE CAN'T HAVE PETTY SQUABBLING INTERFERE..."

"JIM, ARE YOU FACING SOME DIFFICULTY? I NOTICED YOU WERE LATE WITH THE MONTHLY FIGURES. IT ISN'T LIKE YOU TO BE LATE WITH ANYTHING. IS THERE ANYTHING I CAN DO TO HELP?"

Tip: If there's a lot of snitching going on around your office, look at how you're motivating your subordinates. They may feel dead-ended and resort to being informants to carve a place for themselves when a new position does come to pass. Weigh what's being said against what the squealer has to gain by telling this to you.

12.3 RUMOR MONGERS

Rumor mongers are gossips who spread unverified facts of questionable origin.

Rumor Mongers, like Snitchers, also spread stories. However their focus is broader than personal mud-slinging. Their intent is to gain attention for themselves by aggrandizing untrue or partly true messages. They often embroider the story, filling in the blanks to make it appear more important or believable or how they think it "should" be. They may go the other way, forgetting details, remembering only vivid parts and distorting the facts by omitting vital information. Rumor Mongers interpret what happened or is about to happen based on their own interests. Their own experiences, expectations, and views color and limit how they report a situation.

The difficulty for you is deciding which story or how much of a story to believe.

What You're Thinking

Uh-oh, here comes Loose Lips Louie. I wonder what he's going to tell me today. I have to pay attention to what he's saying, even though he gets only a part of it right. Things may be happening in the company that might affect my department.

A Rumor Monger's Thoughts

That may be an important piece of information I heard from my friend in the Manager's office. Why would those bigwigs have had a secret meeting? I'd better tell the boss about it right away. Now, let me try to remember what I heard...

Strategy

You never know if a Rumor Monger is telling a story that is true, partly true, or entirely false. Your goal is to listen and sift information for parts that can be verified and, if necessary, acted upon.

(1) *Keep your door open.* Let the Rumor Monger come in and talk to you. You want to hear about problems that can affect your operation before everybody else does.

(2) *Cut short discussions that are obviously meaningless and spiteful gossip.* Respond in a disinterested, noncommittal manner.

(3) *Ask a lot of questions of the Rumor Monger.* Try to find out where the story originated and how reliable the information is. Determine if this is a first-hand or seventh-hand account.

(4) *Check the facts.* How much is true and how much has been distorted? What are the dangers of acting—or not acting—on this information immediately?

Tactical Talk

"THAT'S AN INTERESTING STORY, LOUIE. WHERE DID YOU HEAR IT?...WHO TOLD YOU THAT?...WHO TOLD THAT TO HER?..."

"DO WE HAVE ANY EVIDENCE THAT SUCH A MEETING TOOK PLACE? ARE THEY PREPARING ANY SORT OF REPORT?"

"KEN, I'M TRYING TO TRACK DOWN A RUMOR THAT COULD BE A BOMBSHELL. AND YOU'RE THE ONE WHO'D KNOW WHAT IS REALLY HAPPENING. I WAS TOLD THAT... CAN YOU CONFIRM THAT?...WELL, I'D LIKE TO SUGGEST THAT THE BOSS ISSUE A STATEMENT BEFORE THIS WILD RUMOR GOES ANY FURTHER."

Tip: You can listen to the Rumor Monger without condoning idle gossip. It's important to keep your ear to the ground and find out what is going on that might influence your part of the world. But as with any rumor, you have to trace it, verify it, and deal with the reality.

Staying on top of the latest information is an important part of your job. Some subordinates try to manipulate you by flattery. Others dangle bits and pieces of news you can use. Don't accept these messages on face value. Question the motivation. Dig for the source. Verify everything.

PART FIVE

DEALING WITH RUDE/ABRASIVE PEOPLE

When managers allow insensitive acts, or are themselves abrasive, some workers brood and finally quit. Other employees pick up the managerial tone and imitate the acts. People with legitimate complaints, who are made to feel they're interrupting the staff if not cheating the company, are, in turn, rude trying to get someone to listen to them.

Rudeness is a vicious cycle that starts at the top and eventually permeates every strata of the organizational structure. Businesses waste a fortune by tolerating rudeness in the workplace.

So there you are, surrounded by ill-mannered people. You're mad because they are inconsiderate, insolent, and insulting. Bosses scoff at your efforts. Peers and subordinates talk down to you. Coworkers interrupt and embarrass you. Your bosses or cohorts or workers are so wrapped up in themselves they don't know they rub everyone the wrong way. If you respond with rudeness, you are letting their bad behavior rub off on you. It's a little tricky to remain polite as you hold your own with the vexingly discourteous.

CHAPTER 13

WHEN YOUR BOSS IS DISCOURTEOUS

13.1 Clods
13.2 Ridiculers
13.3 Condescenders

Discourteous bosses don't even try to understand anything from your point of view. You and other workers become nonpeople, there solely to produce the company's product or service. They show no respect for your thinking or your feelings.

Of course, we all have bad days. Occasionally, the best bosses snap, scowl, and scream at the innocent. And if you can't ride with the tide, if you let your feelings of self-worth go up and down with the boss's good and bad moods, look within yourself for the cause of the problem. On the other hand, if you have a boss who is habitually abrasive and emotionally abusive, learn to restore some respect for yourself.

13.1 CLODS

Clods are insensitive, inconsiderate bosses who ride roughshod over your feelings.

You had set aside certain important items to discuss as you eagerly awaited your private weekly meetings with your boss (a ritual which was the boss's idea). You're trying to get some advice or make a point and the boss keeps interrupting you to take calls or see callers. The precious scheduled time has just evaporated.

Perhaps the boss has his head down, nodding as you speak, while he's reading some mail instead of looking at you and giving you his full attention. Are you boring him? Isn't he interested in what you're doing? Of course, he is. But by trying to do two things at once, he fails to recognize his rude insensitivity as well as his decreasing effectiveness as a manager.

At other times your boss makes changes that directly affect your work and neglects to tell you about it. You have to hear the news from someone else. It's embarrassing, as well as undercutting, not to know the latest decisions made about a unit you're supposed to be running.

What You're Thinking

I might as well be a piece of furniture for all the notice the boss pays to what I'm saying. He certainly is a thoughtless character. Look at this memo. He's lopped a considerable sum off my budget. Granted, he has every right to do that. But why couldn't he have warned me that this was coming? Why do I always have to read these things in a memo or hear it through the grapevine?

A Clod's Thoughts

Let's see. This morning I have three separate meetings with staff people which should be pretty much routine, a stack of mail to go though, some important calls should be coming in with information I need on the Clarion decision, and Ralph has to drop by to give me the go-ahead on the new deal.

Strategy

Your boss is so product/profit focused, he doesn't see his staff as individuals. Your goal is to get him to show you the respect you deserve. Remain calm and firm, and keep your remarks simple.

(1) *Don't compete with the rudeness.* When someone is being impolite (talking to someone else during "your" time, reading while you're speaking, and so on) excuse yourself and leave, or at least offer to come back.

(2) *Ask questions.* This lets you know if the other person is listening to you and also rekindles his interest by getting him to express himself. To maintain that interest, keep your comments as succinct as possible.

(3) *Explain the problem in terms of the trouble it creates for the boss.* You can't come right out and call your boss a cold-hearted, mindless nincompoop, but you can show how it is to his advantage to have better communication with his people.

Tactical Talk

"BOSS, YOU'RE OBVIOUSLY TOO BUSY FOR US TO CONTINUE. I'LL SCHEDULE WITH YOUR SECRETARY A TIME THAT'S MORE CONVENIENT FOR YOU."

"BOSS, I SMELL TROUBLE UP AHEAD. I NEED YOUR UNDIVIDED ATTENTION FOR JUST FIVE MINUTES SO THAT YOU CAN AVOID A CRISIS..."

"BOSS, THERE SEEMS TO BE A COMMUNICATIONS PROBLEM IN OUR DEPARTMENT I KNOW YOU'D WANT ME TO BRING TO YOUR ATTENTION SO THAT YOU COULD CORRECT IT..."

Tip: You won't get respect until you expect it. When a rude boss bruises your ego, forget your fantasies on how to get even. Concentrate on being treated politely, with attention to your thinking and your feelings. Don't sit still while your boss walks over you—get up and leave.

Don't be quiet if you're bypassed on essential information—ask for it. Start by respecting yourself.

13.2 RIDICULERS

Ridiculers belittle you with taunting wit that scarcely covers their true intent.

Some rude bosses use sarcasm to thinly veil their criticism. They mistakingly think this brand of humor makes it easier for you to accept a correction. But you don't sense any jokes coming across. You just feel sharp barbs. You try to laugh when you really want to hide and sulk.

Other bosses pretend to be teasing you in order to hide their impatience, saying things like "Only my addled 90-year-old grandfather would take so much time to get me this information."

Good-natured teasing you can take. Criticism about your work you can handle. But these bosses taunt and humiliate you with personal attacks, especially in front of other people. To you, the implication is clear—he's telling the immediate world that he thinks you're an imbecile.

What You're Thinking

Why does the boss have to use sarcasm to tell me I'm doing something wrong? Why doesn't he come right out and say that I should be doing something another way? I think he has to keep proving to himself that he's better and smarter than the rest of us. There I was, talking to my client and the boss steps in and takes over, making a joke about how long it takes me to do the paper work. The infuriating put-down made me appear incompetent to the client.

A Ridiculer's Thoughts

It's been a while, but I'm still the best when it comes to closing a deal. Brenda's good, but she'd be there till next Christmas if I didn't step in.

Strategy

You sense that the boss is sending you a message through his sarcasm. Your objective is to get the boss to become more straightforward in telling you what he wants done and how he wants it.

(1) *Schedule a private meeting with the boss.* Be up front in admitting that you felt a little disturbed and want to clear the air. Do not criticize the boss for ridiculing you. Be professionally matter-of-fact so that you don't sound like a crybaby.

(2) *Ask the boss to explain what he meant by the remarks.* Open the door to receive good, constructive comments. Don't make excuses for yourself. Just listen and promise to improve.

Tactical Talk

"BOSS, I KNOW HOW IMPORTANT IT IS TO YOU THAT WE CLOSE EVERY SALE. I UNDERSTAND YOUR APPREHENSION WHEN SOMEONE ELSE IS DOING A CLOSING THAT YOU CAN DO SO WELL YOURSELF. BUT WHEN YOU TAKE OVER IN THE MIDDLE OF MY CLOSING, THE CLIENT LOSES RESPECT FOR THE COMPANY, WHICH IS EMBARRASSING FOR BOTH OF US.

"SO CAN WE DISCUSS THE BEST WAY TO PROCEED? WOULD YOU PREFER THAT I TURN OVER MY CLIENT TO YOU AT THE POINT OF CLOSING? OR MAYBE YOU COULD SHOW ME A BETTER WAY TO HANDLE IT MYSELF?"

Tip: Often bosses who utilize humor to correct or criticize their workers see themselves as stand-up comics. Unless you indicate otherwise, they will keep thinking that their sarcasm is a well-received way to soften an attack.

13.3 CONDESCENDERS

Condescenders patronize and talk down to you, doing you a favor to be with them.

These bosses have an exaggerated opinion of themselves and a devaluated opinion of others. Haughty and snooty, they are intellectual snobs who tacitly permit you to join the discussion. Then the Condescenders ignore your ideas, zapping you with put downs as they downplay your suggestions.

They are quick to grasp the full implications of a problem and faster than you are at seeing solutions. They are also insulting when they allow you to do something on your own: "This is an easy job. Pam can handle it."

What You're Thinking

My boss is really very smart about the business, but he never learned to act with tact. Everybody puts up with his abrasive manner because he gets results. I guess I'm fortunate that his rude comments aren't directed solely at me. He shares his arrogance among all of us. I make a point and he adds another aspect to it. Fine, but why does he have to preface it with, "What Pam was trying to say is..."? I am perfectly capable of expressing myself, so why do I let him make me feel like an idiot?

A Condescender's Thoughts

That was sheer genius, the way I got the Board to go along with the proposal. Anticipating every reaction, I had all the facts and figures to allay their concerns. My staff is still panting, trying to keep up with me. About my staff, I wish the troops would stop offering me their ideas after they get themselves into a mess.

It's their distorted thinking that brings on the problems in the first place and they need my clear analysis to bail them out. I must remind them before the next crisis to bring me only the problem, not their misguided solutions.

Strategy

It's safe to assume all their lives these bosses were applauded for accomplishments and no one ever bothered to teach them humility. They believe they are excellent administrators. It's unlikely that anything you say will change them or soften and mellow their overbearing rudeness. What you can change is your reaction to their lack of tact. Also, you can guard against a possible unwarranted attack.

(1) *Choose to dwell on how good you really are.* The boss can't make you feel bad about your self-worth unless you let him. In time, you won't even hear his tactless comments. You'll be too busy thinking and planning along with the boss for your next success.

(2) *Gently remind the boss you play a part in what he's accomplishing.* You want him to appreciate your trying, even if you don't quite measure up to his exorbitant standards. Prepare your remarks in advance of your staff meetings. Use progress reports to deftly and delicately tell the boss how capable you are, *quantifying* the efforts you expended. Numbers make a greater impression than adjectives. Let everyone bask in the glory of the finished product or service.

(3) *Pay close attention to your office grapevine.* An arrogant boss is an unlikely candidate for sharing the blame with you when things go wrong. Keep on top of developments to avoid becoming the fall guy. Don't wait for your problem to mushroom into a crisis. Ask early for the boss's help, but wait until he asks before you suggest solutions.

Tactical Talk

Boss: "THE NEXT AGENDA ITEM IS THE ATTITUDE SURVEY. PAM, I DON'T SUPPOSE YOU WERE ABLE TO—"

Pam: "BOSS, AS YOU KNOW THIS SUBJECT IS STEEPED IN MYTHS. UNLESS WE PLAN A COUNTERACTION, WE WILL BE FACED WITH UNREALISTIC DEMANDS TO...ACCORDING TO OUR SURVEY, 64% SAID THAT...AND 87% EXPRESSED A WILLINGNESS TO..."

Boss: "PAM WAS SURPRISINGLY CLOSE TO WHAT WE NEED, BUT SHE NEEDS TO FACE THE REALITY OF..."

Pam: "IT'S YOUR CALL, BOSS. CONSIDER, HOWEVER, THAT THE COSTS WILL INCREASE BY ROUGHLY 22% IF WE WAIT UNTIL..."

Tip: The boss's condescending remarks will diminish in ratio to the amount of increased respect you are able to earn. He's clever and conceited; you can be clever and considerate. Be ready with facts that you've double- and triple-checked for accuracy. Acknowledge that he's the boss, but when you do get the go-ahead, move quickly and confidently. And keep him informed.

The most important point about dealing with rudeness is that you don't have to take it, even from your boss, even when you fear your job is on the line. No matter what the gender of the offender, the first step is believing that you deserve respect because you won't get it until you expect it. Then you can respectfully show a boss how he benefits by being polite. If you think your boss is using rude remarks to mask a complaint, he probably is. Find the trouble and correct it. You can dispel rudeness by being up front and minding your own manners.

CHAPTER 14

WHEN YOUR COLLEAGUES ARE DISCOURTEOUS

14.1 Interrupters
14.2 Left-Handed Complimenters
14.3 Snoops

With peers, as with bosses, you can't afford to feud with the rude. That only drains your time and energy, escalates the problem, and doesn't help you get what you want. Nor can you just accept the rudeness or you'll feel yourself getting increasingly agitated. You want to stop the discourtesies, but the thought of telling the people you work with every day that they are being rude embarrasses you. So you sit there wondering why they act like juvenile brats.

Sometimes coworkers are too immature to be polite or are brash because they feel insecure. Whether they interrupt your work, make snide remarks, or mind your business for you, recognize the common thread. These egocentric offenders are all so interested in themselves, they are not giving you or your feelings a second thought. You need two guidelines to point them in the right direction—honesty and courtesy.

14.1 INTERRUPTERS

Interrupters rudely break into your discussion, burst into your office uninvited, or pester you on the phone.

What irritates you most about Interrupters is that they nibble away at your peak productive hours. They plop down at your desk during the time you had set aside to plot a potentially big project. After they leave or you finish their calls, you can't recapture the thoughts that were interrupted. Almost as annoying is when they waste your time at meetings by getting the discussion off the track. They speak in stage whispers to fellow workers when you're trying to hear the boss's comments on the latest marketing report. They never let you finish the point you're making.

Usually, Interrupters don't know they are regarded as pests or long-winded bores. Their crime is being self-centered and inconsiderate. Their punishment, eventually, is being ignored. In the meantime your stress level is climbing to the breaking point.

What You're Thinking

Peter seems to have made me his father confessor. I'm glad to talk to him when I have the time, but he keeps interrupting my work by popping in and out of my office. I've got to find a way to put a stop to this without hurting his feelings.

An Interrupter's Thoughts

Ike is a swell guy. He's been a real help talking to me the past few months on this new job. Today the boss sent me a new production figure that somehow doesn't seem right. I'll call Ike and ask him what he thinks about it and how I should handle it. Better yet, I'll stop by his office right now.

Strategy

Your aim is to break your colleague's thoughtless behavior pattern. To do so you have to interrupt the Interrupter. But handle with care or your Interrupter will become antagonistic and this could lead to other problems.

(1) *Be polite when you do the interrupting.* Smile, start with the person's name, and couple your friendly tone with sensitive phrases. Be considerate even though your Interrupter is not.

(2) *Be straightforward in explaining why you can't be interrupted now.* People understand when you're under pressure. You don't need phony gimmicks, such as knocking on your desk in order to fib to the telephone caller that someone's waiting for you. Just explain you have a deadline, a report to prepare, or preconference materials to gather. If you don't have time to talk right then but want to continue, suggest a time that's mutually convenient.

(3) *Snatch back control when your conversation is intercepted.* Interrupt your Interrupter for a minute or two to finish making your point.

(4) *Stop the rambler with sharply focused comments and questions.* Bring the discussion back to the stated purpose. Politely break in to summarize an Interrupter's unending monologue.

(5) *Discourage Interrupters from coming in and staying in your office.* Reposition your desk so that passersby can't catch your eye. Limit the number of chairs and stack them with reports or phone books. Stand up when an Interrupter comes in and remain standing.

Tactical Talk

"PETER, HOLD ON A MINUTE. FROM WHAT YOU'RE SAYING, I THINK YOU NEED TO BE TALKING TO THE BOSS, NOT ME, ABOUT THIS."

"PETER, IS THIS REALLY IMPORTANT? I'M TRYING TO GET READY FOR A MEETING. IF YOU NEED MORE THAN A MINUTE, WE'LL HAVE TO TALK LATER." or "I'D LIKE TO TALK, BUT I CAN'T NOW. HOW ABOUT LUNCH?"

"I'M SO GLAD TO HEAR FROM YOU, BUT I'M ON MY WAY OUT. I'LL CALL BACK AS SOON AS I CAN."

"YES, THAT MAY BE SO, BUT PLEASE LET ME FINISH. WE HAVE TO FOLLOW THIS ROUTE BECAUSE..."

"WE SEEM TO HAVE SHIFTED THE TOPIC FROM THE PURPOSE OF THE MEETING. AS I UNDERSTAND IT, YOU'RE SAYING THAT...HAVE I STATED YOUR VIEW CORRECTLY?"

"I THINK THAT ABOUT COVERS IT, DON'T YOU?" or "JUST ONE MORE POINT BEFORE YOU GO." or "I'VE TAKEN UP TOO MUCH OF YOUR TIME."

Tip: Interrupters either are not aware or do not care that they are selfishly imposing their needs on others. You can refuse to accept this form of rudeness and yet be gracious yourself. So if you're being interrupted and can't think of what to say, remember George Bernard Shaw's observation: "Silence is the most perfect expression of scorn."

14.2 LEFT-HANDED COMPLIMENTERS

Left-Handed Complimenters start by praising you and end with a qualifying put down.

The first time this happens you're caught off-guard. You felt so good about the praises you didn't realize there might be a negative implication tied to it. A little later, you wonder if you just imagined the slap or if it was really intended.

The next time the Left-Handed Complimenter strikes, you know the affront was definitely not your imagination working overtime. The two-sided remark was meant as a barb. Trying not to show signs of being stung, you feel yourself smile and you hear yourself sputter thanks while knowing that's not the way you ought to respond. Then you kick yourself for having thanked somebody who just got away with putting you down.

What You're Thinking

I find myself trying to avoid Laurie. I don't know why she's zinging me, but she seems to delight in building me up and knocking me down at the same time. Maybe I'm getting paranoid—was there a hidden meaning when she said I'm looking so much better these days? What's wrong with the way I looked before? And that crack about my report being great—*this* time. I've got enough problems without worrying about her.

A Left-Handed Complimenter's Thoughts

Frances is acting so high and mighty these days. I've asked her to go to lunch with me a couple of times and she's always too busy. She's determined to get ahead of the rest of us. I resent the way she's causing everybody else to work up to her pace.

Strategy

Your goal is to maintain your composure as you seize control of the conversation. In some cases, you may need feedback from your alleged offender before you're sure you are really dealing with a culprit.

(1) *Keep your cool and question the intent of the remark.* When called to account for their inappropriate comments, Left-Handed Complimenters duck for cover. They try to blame you for misinterpreting. But they are also less likely to pick on you now that they see you're not as vulnerable as they had believed.

(2) *Dig a little deeper for an underlying cause.* What you interpreted as a left-handed compliment may actually be the surface of hidden resentment or anger toward you. A pleasant confrontation may clear the air.

(3) *Divide the remark into two parts, praise and put-down.* Accept with sincerity the compliment that pleased you. Correct or ignore the implied insult.

Tactical Talk

Laurie: "THAT WAS A GREAT REPORT, FRANCES. WHY CAN'T YOU DO THAT KIND OF WORK ALL THE TIME?"

Frances: "I'M GLAD YOU LIKED MY REPORT. I WORKED HARD ON IT, AS I DO ON ALL MY PROJECTS. THE BOSS TELLS ME HE'S VERY PLEASED WITH MY PERFORMANCE."

Laurie: "YOU'RE LOOKING SO MUCH BETTER THESE DAYS, FRANCES."

Frances: "THANK YOU, LAURIE. BUT I'M A LITTLE CONFUSED. IN WHAT WAY DO I APPEAR TO LOOK BETTER TO YOU?"

Laurie: "WHY ARE YOU ACTING SO TOUCHY?"

Frances: "WHAT MAKES YOU SAY I'M ACTING TOUCHY? LAURIE, I SENSE THAT YOU MAY BE UPSET WITH ME. IF I'VE DONE SOMETHING TO OFFEND YOU, PLEASE TELL ME SO THAT WE CAN STRAIGHTEN THINGS OUT."

Tip: If you try to swallow real or imagined insults, you'll choke on them. When you feel colleagues use disguised barbs to inflame your feelings, stop to verify your assumption. Once convinced, you free yourself to respond pleasantly to the complimentary part while ignoring or tossing back the negative aspect.

14.3 SNOOPS

Snoops are unduly inquisitive, prying when it's none of their business.

Snoops are yet another type of rude colleague. Overly inquisitive and nosy, they seldom realize how offensive their questions and actions actually can be. Curiosity is admirable when one is doing legitimate research, but these peers dig for data like they're preparing a feature story for the *National Tattler*. They act as though the information in your confidential files or about your private life ought to be public information and they, if not the entire public, have a right to know.

Their curiosity *has* to be satisfied. Not content with impertinent or presumptuous questions, you also find them waiting for you in your office—reading through your files. Don't worry so much about hurting their feelings because they're usually too insensitive to be hurt.

What You're Thinking

Every time Matt comes snooping around here, I end up telling him more than I want to. I didn't want the nature of my recent illness to be general knowledge. I know I'm physically up to taking on more important work, but if word gets around I may lose the chance. Why did I let Matt pry that out of me?

A Snoop's Thoughts

I wonder if Allan is going to apply for the new position that's opening up in a couple of months. He was pretty vague with that story about a bad virus that kept him home for a few weeks. What if it's some sort of condition that saps his stamina? I better find out what's really happening.

Strategy

You probably can't stop the Snoops from being so snoopy, but you can aim to stop them from prying inappropriate information out of you. What's more, you can do this without sounding rude or antagonistic.

(1) *Give them the benefit of the doubt.* Act as though the snoops don't know they are asking for information that is too personal or confidential to reveal.

(2) *Remember that just because someone asks, you don't have to answer.* Briefly explain why giving away such information would be inappropriate. If you can pull it off with a smile on your face, you could even ask them why they want to know.

Tactical Talk

Matt: "BOY, THAT WAS SOME KIND OF VIRUS THAT KEPT YOU OUT OF WORK SO LONG. WHAT EXACTLY WAS THE PROBLEM?"

Allan: "I'M SURE YOU'RE NOT AWARE, MATT, THAT YOU'RE ASKING ME A VERY PERSONAL QUESTION. WHY DO YOU WANT TO KNOW?"

Matt: "WELL FRANKLY, ALLAN, THERE'S THAT NEW SLOT OPENING SOON AND I WAS WONDERING IF YOU'RE UP TO HANDLING IT."

Allan: "THANKS, I APPRECIATE YOUR CONCERN. AND YES, I'M BACK TO FULL STRENGTH."

Tip: You are under no obligation to answer queries that are too personal. To soften a refusal you can say you can't answer because that would be violating a confidence.

You can politely stop the Snoop you find reading your mail as you return to your office. Smile as you ask, "Hi, Matt, what can I help you find?"

Rude colleagues wear many faces. The abrasiveness of their inconsiderate behavior becomes increasingly irritating. It's like wearing a tight shoe until the day a blister sidelines you. Don't wait to erupt before you take action. You don't have to continue taking it and you don't have to blow your stack. Just be straightforward and polite in standing your ground.

CHAPTER 15

WHEN YOUR SUBORDINATES ARE DISCOURTEOUS

15.1 Snippy Talkers
15.2 Defiers
15.3 Needlers

When bosses are disrespectful and deflating, workers say they're arrogant. When subordinates behave like that, supervisors call them impudent or presumptuous.

Surprisingly enough, this discourteous attitude is sometimes triggered by bosses who are too good to be true. Bosses who go out of their way to be nice and considerate. Bosses who are careful to let their subordinates solve their own problems. Workers who are looking for more direction from above and not getting it may constantly feel they're in a state of crisis. They may, for example, need a clear division of who's doing what steps in the operation by what dates. When their bosses are "so nice" that subordinates can't complain to them, their frustration may manifest itself by workers being snippy or defiant or needling.

If being too nice isn't your problem, your rude workers may be feeling pressure from some other source and simply not know how to cope. They take out their anxiety or anger on you or their fellow workers. Whatever the cause, you want to tone down the tension in the office.

15.1 SNIPPY TALKERS

Snippy Talkers make cutting, impertinent remarks.

These subordinates are miserable and unpleasant to be around. They seem to be aching for an argument. Almost every day something sets them off soon after they get to work. A late delivery, for instance, might trigger their spending the rest of the day snapping at anyone who walks by.

Since snippy people are concentrating so intently on themselves, they are devoid of common respect and courtesy toward others. They'll toss their sharp verbal darts at a boss as well as a cohort. Because people want to avoid their line of fire, they've been allowed to get away with their taunting remarks.

What You're Thinking

Ned's work is very good and he's certainly demonstrated time and again that he's loyal to me. But I think he's mainly responsible for much of the petty bickering that goes on in this office. He appears to be overprotective of his turf. He can be impatient and insulting and quick to answer me or anyone else with a snippy response no matter who else happens to be standing there.

A Snippy Talker's Thoughts

I thought I could count on the boss for support. You just can't trust anyone but yourself. How can I do my job if the boss goes over my head and instructs my people? He knows the importance of respecting the chain of command. I feel hurt and angry to be treated in this way. After all I've done for him, the least he could do is back me up.

Strategy

When people act snippy, they are probably reacting to something or somebody that made them feel hurt or that interfered with their plans. Your goal is to get them to express their anger so that you can dig out the real problem and get it resolved.

(1) *Reexamine your management style.* Why doesn't your subordinate feel free to talk to you about whatever is bugging him? Have you done something that discourages such discussion? What's he afraid of? What does he think is at risk if he levels with you?

(2) *Put the subordinate at ease.* Enable him to talk to you. When he starts talking, just nod with an "I see" to show you comprehend, but don't interrupt him.

(3) *Ask questions.* Together, as a team, probe deeper to get at the root of the problem or misunderstanding. If the focus shifts to something your subordinate hadn't considered, and he needs a little more time, suggest meeting soon again.

Tactical Talk

"NED, YOU APPEAR TO BE EDGY LATELY. LET'S TALK ABOUT THIS. WHAT SEEMS TO BE THE TROUBLE?"

"WELL, NED, I'M GLAD WE COULD CLEAR UP THE MISUNDERSTANDING ABOUT THE CHAIN OF COMMAND. BUT WHAT DO YOU THINK YOU CAN DO TO DEAL WITH YOUR ANGER INSTEAD OF RESORTING TO SNIPPY REMARKS? YOU WANT TO MOVE UP AND THAT KIND OF BEHAVIOR WILL HOLD YOU BACK."

Tip: Start by assuming snippy subordinates snap and yap because they're frustrated. They don't know how or are afraid to express their feelings. Once you can get them to talk, you're on your way to reducing their anxiety, curtailing their rude behavior, and lowering office tension.

15.2 DEFIERS

Defiers are insubordinate and disrespectfully oppose established policy.

You give an order to some subordinates and they won't do it, don't do it, or delay doing it. They meet each and every assignment by confronting, resisting, challenging, and daring you to do something about their defiance. Eventually the work gets done, but you're worn out from the battle.

What You're Thinking

Marie deliberately defied my directives. I guess, technically, she's guilty of insubordination, but I couldn't prove it even if I wanted to. Marie is bound and determined to handle the job her way even though that creates other problems for us. She keeps arguing with me that her method is better. I've got to put a stop to her undermining my decisions.

A Defier's Thoughts

The boss made me responsible for the project and I can't do my job if she's going to hamstring me at every turn. All those stupid regulations! She's got to set me free to develop this my way.

Strategy

Your objective is to get peak performances from all your workers. You want to be reasonable with each one while you keep your eye on the big picture. Your vantage point is not available to your subordinates unless you explain to them how it looks from where you sit.

(1) *Check your own attitude.* When workers are defiant, ask yourself if you're being open and playing fair. Do you request or command adherence? Are you explaining the importance of doing something a certain way? Do you turn mistakes into learning experiences for both of you? Do you resist dangling promises unless you're sure you can keep them?

(2) *Get right to the point of your meeting.* Don't beat around the bush or make small talk. Immediately put your subordinate at ease by expressing your desire to continue your working relationship.

(3) *Let the defiant worker get his gripe off his chest.* Listen carefully. Then bend where you can, but explain why certain procedures must be followed. In a calm, professional manner, ask him to explain why he deliberately disobeyed a directive. Get him to tell you the probable consequences of such actions. Ask him how he plans to deal with the situation.

Tactical Talk

(from demanding) "GET ALL THOSE NOTIFICATION CALLS DONE BY 10 AM."

(to requesting) "WHEN WILL YOU HAVE ALL THE NOTIFICATION CALLS COMPLETED?"

(putting the subordinate at ease) "I APPRECIATE THE MANY CONTRIBUTIONS YOU HAVE MADE TO THE COMPANY, AND I HOPE YOU'LL CONTINUE MAKING THEM, BUT FIRST WE HAVE TO SETTLE THIS MATTER OF FOLLOWING ORDERS..."

Tip: A subordinate working on one segment of the operation can't have the same global picture as his boss who's supervising the whole show. While workers' views are invaluable and need to be discussed in group meetings, and while workers have to be free to complain to you, it's still up to you to enforce company policy and important procedures. If you are tactful, both you and your defiant subordinate will feel you won something in the discussion.

15.3 NEEDLERS

Needlers use sharp-pointed humor to provoke and goad you and your team.

It's a delicate matter to criticize a boss even when you're on the friendliest of terms. Needler subordinates have discovered that masquerading smart, sharp, stinging remarks as humor is a way to complain without being labeled an attacker. They attempt to control a situation without being held accountable for the new direction. Needlers need an audience such as the rest of your staff or a client. If you protest their antics, Needlers claim it was supposed to be funny. Why aren't you laughing while your ego is being deflated?

What You're Thinking

Noel knows I really need him because he's one of our best workers. I tried to show him I was on his side by offering to talk over any problems he was having. When I told him that some people found his needling remarks to be offensive, he just got huffy and defensive. He claims no one in this group has a sense of humor. What am I going to do about this Needler and how can I get him to stop needling me?

A Needler's Thoughts

Can't they see what's wrong with this outfit? You work for years, giving it all you've got, and what do they do? Bring in somebody from outside instead of promoting from within. I should have that job my new boss has. If I criticize her, I'll get into trouble. But if I disguise my jabs in some needling, I can't be blamed and I'll be able to let everyone see how inexperienced the new boss really is.

Strategy

Your objective is to force the Needler to come out of hiding and be open with his criticism. Get right to the point and needle the Needler. To accomplish this, it's essential that you come across as pleasant and friendly.

(1) *Ask repeatedly for clarification.* Using a variety of phrases, request that the Needler make his criticism clear by being more specific.

(2) *Shift the Needler's direction.* Get him to move away from jabbing at you and other people and start jabbing at issues. The Needler may be on to something important. Maybe some changes are needed and the procedures have to be reexamined.

(3) *Talk privately to the Needler.* With a smile on your face, let him know his "jokes" didn't accomplish their purpose. Then reassure him that his thinking is invaluable and that you, he, and the rest of the team will be considering his suggestions in depth. Toss him a challenge, some additional problem he might start thinking about how to resolve.

Tactical Talk

(in front of the group) "NOEL, PLEASE EXPLAIN THAT TO US AGAIN...WHAT SPECIFICALLY IS BOTHERING YOU ABOUT THIS? ...WHAT EXACTLY ARE YOU OBJECTING TO?... ...SOME OF US DON'T QUITE UNDERSTAND THE POINT YOU ARE MAKING..."

(in private) "NOEL, AS YOU PROBABLY GUESSED, I DIDN'T THINK YOUR LITTLE JOKES AT THE MEETING WERE VERY FUNNY, BUT I DO WANT YOU TO KNOW THAT I APPRECIATE THE FINE WORK YOU'VE BEEN DOING... THE TREND SEEMS TO INDICATE SOME EXPANSION IN YOUR AREA. THERE ARE AT LEAST TWO PROBLEMS THIS COULD CREATE FOR US THAT I'D LIKE YOU TO BE THINKING ABOUT ALONG WITH HOW WE MIGHT STREAMLINE..."

Tip: In trying to disguise his criticism with humor, the Needler often misses the point. To win people over, the critic should include himself in the joke. Otherwise, he appears to be sneering or scolding and that's offensive. With that in mind, you can beat the Needler at his own game. Include yourself in discussing the problem. Also, don't let the Needler see that he gets under your skin. Once you start, in a playful, pleasant, and professional manner, the others will join you in needling the Needler.

It takes only a few rude and abrasive workers to make a whole office feel tense. Sometimes they openly attack with snide or rebellious remarks. Other times they try to disguise their criticism through joking, but malicious, insinuations. Since these troublesome subordinates are often good workers, simply subduing them can destroy whatever amount of team spirit is left. The anger just smolders. To come out with boss and worker both winning, deal with discourtesy right away without threats. In a professional and friendly manner, ask questions that get to the cause. Let them talk. Once you're paying attention to each other's needs, the tension dissolves and you can start influencing your workers to become more productive.

PART SIX

DEALING WITH EGOTISTICAL AND SELF-CENTERED PEOPLE

According to Disraeli, the nineteenth-century British prime minister, "If you talk to people about themselves, they'll listen for hours." Many of us are flattered by attention and all of us need to be noticed. But egotists go to extremes. A thing has value only according to how it relates to their interests. They think you should be as interested in them as they are in themselves.

Some even want you to keep reliving with them their past glories. These boring braggarts forget that to maintain acclaim, in the conference room as on the stage or on the football field, you're only as good as your last effort. Their grossly overdeveloped yearning to be admired often turns them into grandstanders. They butt in, they take over. Selfish people are doubly difficult because they can't be team players. They believe that if they help you, you score and they are denied the limelight they desperately seek.

In dealing with egotists, it's natural to want to expose their conceit and self-centeredness. Don't be diverted. Although these bosses, colleagues, and subordinates are troublesome, you can deal with them and still concentrate your energy on your own legitimate goals.

CHAPTER 16

WHEN YOUR BOSS IS SELF-SEEKING

16.1 Brush-Offs
16.2 Neglecters
16.3 Yakitty-Yakkers
16.4 Show Offs

Egotistical bosses are centered on themselves. They promote their own interests without concern about how their actions might affect their subordinates. They usurp decisions that should be yours to make. They won't let their managers manage because they believe they have more expertise.

When bosses talk endlessly and won't leave you alone to work, or snip the chain of command by going over your head and directly ordering your subordinates, the help isn't helpful. Egotistical bosses also can be irritating constant checkers who set no deadlines but call you every day. Some go to the other extreme. They can appear too engrossed in their own quests to bother with you or even be interested in what you're doing.

16.1 BRUSH-OFFS

Brush-off bosses curtly dismiss you. They are too busy to answer your questions or supply what you need.

Why are these bosses too busy for you? They may not admit it even to themselves, but that's the way they want it. They get bogged down in tasks that others should be doing. Not only aren't you getting the help you need, they also keep others from assisting you. Brush-off bosses have trouble delegating. For one thing, they believe they can do everything better than everybody else.

Another reason is the fear that if they build up their staffs and let go of some of the tasks, others will no longer regard them as vital to the operation. As a result, they stifle their own growth. They leave themselves no time to plan important future moves, and they leave you feeling frustrated.

What You're Thinking

I could see the boss resented my asking Holly for some advice while he was away on Thursday. He's given me responsibility without authority to act. It's always my fault if something goes wrong. I sure needed help. Now I really need those papers before I can proceed and he keeps dismissing me with "I'll handle it." I understand he's busy, but he doesn't have to be so abrupt and brusque. He shows more respect for the office equipment than he does to me.

A Brush-Off's Thoughts

These people can't conceive the enormous responsibility I have running a large department. You'd think they would show me some consideration and realize that I'm under great pressure. Paul, for example, keeps pestering me for those papers. Why can't he just go away and wait until I'm ready for him?

Strategy

Your objective is to complete the jobs you've been assigned. That includes extracting necessary data from a busy boss.

(1) *Punt—don't confront.* If you tell the boss he's wrong, he has to defend his ego with a counterattack. So don't even give the appearance of arguing with him. Often you

can turn the ball over to the boss just by asking him his opinion or to make a choice.

(2) *Focus on his needs, not yours.* You lose ground if you complain. Force yourself to totally ignore his curt manner and talk instead about the options he has for enhancing his reputation or achieving his objectives. He's more apt to help you if he views the action as helping himself. Your positive suggestions can light the way.

Tactical Talk

"BOSS, WITH THE PINOCCHIO PROJECT BEHIND SCHEDULE, DO YOU THINK IT WOULD BE BETTER TO VISIT STREETER OR WRITE HIM FIRST ENCLOSING A LIST OF POINTS WE NEED TO KNOW TO COMPLETE THE FORMS?"

"BOSS, I HAVE AN IDEA THAT CAN HELP YOU FREE UP SOME TIME. WHAT IF YOU USED A GRAPH LIKE THIS TO INDICATE THE STAGES OF ACCOMPLISHMENT?"

Tip: You look better when you help your boss look good. Egotistical bosses worry about the perception their supervisors and colleagues have about their professionalism. Give them ideas that they can claim as their own: "I thought about this yesterday when you were discussing cost-saving procedures..."

16.2 NEGLECTERS

Neglecters are indifferent to what is needed and uncaring about inconveniencing you.

Unlike Brush-off bosses who are too busy to help you, Neglecters are laissez-faire leaders too disinterested to do anything. They're happy to let you decide the way to go and glad to let you take the blame if you fail. Some won't give you advice or opinions because they refuse to take risks. Generally, Neglecters are so involved with their own personal pursuits, they don't care enough to see that their subordinates have what's needed to perform well.

What You're Thinking

I can't decide whether the boss won't give me any suggestions because he wants to play it safe or if he just doesn't care enough to make the effort. In the meantime, he's letting me drift and I feel like I'm going in circles. Should I go ahead and make the decisions myself? How far should I stick my neck out calling the shots that my boss ought to be calling?

A Neglecter's Thoughts

My workers are capable people. They really don't need me. Besides, they'll learn if they make mistakes. I've got a lot of other things to attend to.

Strategy

Your objective is to maneuver around your boss's apparent disinterest and, if possible, turn this situation to your advantage.

(1) *Determine first if the boss is simply forgetful.* He may mean well but can't seem to remember to do what he promised. If so, the boss will regard your asking him about whatever he was supposed to do as your way of expressing interest.

(2) *Try to extract a little direction.* Even if it's like pulling teeth, at least make the attempt.

(3) *Fill the leadership vacuum.* If your boss neglects to point you in the right direction, move slowly on your own. Decide on a few measurable objectives. Achieve these and set a few more. But always *keep your boss informed* about what you're doing. Show him your planning sheets before you set your design in motion. Put your reports in writing as proof that you did keep him informed.

Tactical Talk

"BOSS, WHATEVER HAPPENED WHEN YOU SPOKE TO BOB ABOUT APPOINTING ME TO SERVE ON THE OPERATIONS COMMITTEE?"

"I SENSE THAT YOU FEEL I'M VEERING OFF COURSE, BOSS. WHAT SPECIFICALLY SHOULD I ADJUST? AM I PUTTING EMPHASIS IN THE WRONG PLACE?"

"HERE I'VE SKETCHED OUT THE STAGES FOR ACHIEVING MY MAIN OBJECTIVES OVER THE NEXT SIX MONTHS. IF YOU HAVE NO OBJECTION, I PLAN TO PROCEED IN THIS WAY."

Tip: Establish your own self-protection practices. While Neglecters seem to ignore you, they can resent your doing well by ignoring them. Reduce to writing conversations when your boss refuses to commit himself or tells you to do deeds he should be doing (e.g., "Attached is a synopsis to be sure I understood you correctly"). Send copies of your progress reports to someone besides the boss who also would have a reasonable right to be kept informed.

16.3 YAKITTY-YAKKERS

Yakitty-Yakkers trouble you with their idle, excessive gabbing that interferes with your work.

When your peers interrupt you, you can tell them you have a deadline and politely escort them to your door. It's much harder to end the conversation when your boss is constantly interrupting.

Yakitty-Yakkers are chronic talkers. Too frequently gabbers recite idle prattle, meaningless war stories of little interest to you because you didn't know the participants. They very much want your admiration and assume you want to share all their interests and experiences. If they were relevant, you'd be happy to, but you find your ear-bender boss an egocentric, inconsiderate imposer.

What You're Thinking

Why can't the boss just tell me what she wants? Why do I have to hear a whole introductory chapter before she gets to the request? The background in some cases would be useful, but for these simple requests a clear-cut directive is all I need to know. However, I'm treading on shaky ground. She's the boss, and if I respond too abruptly, I'll hurt her feelings and pay the penalty.

A Yakitty-Yakker's Thoughts

I must remember to tell Victor why they enacted this rule. If he knows the history, he can appreciate how hard we had to work to get it passed. Let's see, that must have been nine years ago when we had our offices in the old building, that place where we never knew if the elevator was going to get stuck, and...

Strategy

Your goal is to stop the idle talk without offending the boss.

(1) *Ask for clarification.* Very politely, ask the boss to relate the unending chatter to what you're currently working on.

(2) *Recap the lengthy list of directives.* Put them into your own crisp, precise words.

(3) *Tactfully excuse yourself.* Arrange to continue the history lesson during a coffee break when you won't be so rushed.

Tactical Talk

"BOSS, I'M NOT SURE I UNDERSTAND THE CONNECTION BETWEEN THIS EXECUTIVE ORDER AND THE ALLIANCE THAT WAS FORMED FIVE YEARS AGO..."

"LET ME SEE IF I'VE GOT IT STRAIGHT. YOU FEEL IT'S BEST TO COMPUTE ALL THE POTENTIAL FROM THESE CONTACTS BEFORE WE ATTEMPT TO SCHEDULE..."

"BOSS, I'D LOVE TO KEEP TALKING, BUT AS YOU KNOW I HAVE THIS DEADLINE...LET'S FINISH THIS TOMORROW."

Tip: Stop being intimidated by the Yakitty-Yakker because he's your boss. If you can sift through the verbiage, you'll probably find some gems. When time is short, treat the boss as you treat other interrupters—honestly and politely and get on with your work.

16.4 SHOW OFFS

Show Offs are conceited and aloof bosses, ostentatious about their achievements.

Show Offs are similar to Yakitty-Yakkers in their desire to impress you. But instead of interrupting you, they snub you. These bosses are snooty and snobbishly superior. Being high achievers, they consider themselves in the exclusive realm of ruling potentates.

What You're Thinking

Okay, he's smart and maybe he has a right to be conceited. And yes, the boss does have responsibility for the tough decisions. But why does he have to make me feel so stupid? He tricks me into giving him inappropriate answers. I get the feeling that he's toying with all of us on his staff to satisfy his insatiable ego.

A Show Off's Thoughts

My staff people have great potential, of course, or I wouldn't have selected each and every one of them. They have to understand the opportunity for growth that I offer them by working with me. I don't want any surprises from them that could embarrass me. A little intimidation should prevent that. They're going to have to earn my trust. If they're as smart as I think they are, we will get some excellent work done here.

Strategy

Keep your eye on your goal. You want to succeed in the organization. You have the chance to learn from a master.

(1) *Keep still and observe.* Your confidence grows out of knowing what you do well and working on what you want to improve. You alone determine if you want to keep positive or negative thoughts in your head. No one can make you feel stupid except yourself. So don't get into a bragging contest with a braggart, especially one whose office is decorated in Early Show-Off, with acclamations adorning every inch of wall space.

(2) *Deserve your boss's confidence.* Prove yourself by your good performance. Learn the way the boss wants you to process assignments and report progress. Let him know if you anticipate trouble up ahead, but don't tell him how to resolve the problem unless he asks for your suggestions.

Tactical Talk

"FROM THE GOALS WE AGREED ON, I'VE PREPARED THIS PERT CHART, INDICATING THE OBJECTIVES FOR EACH GOAL, WHOM WE MUST CONTACT, BY WHAT DATE, AND THE VARIOUS APPROACHES WE'LL USE...HOW DOES THIS LOOK TO YOU?"

"BOSS, YOU MIGHT WANT TO TAKE A LOOK AT THESE FIGURES. IT'S POSSIBLE THAT A PATTERN MAY BE DEVELOPING THAT COULD PRESENT SOME DIFFICULTY WHEN WE TRY TO IMPLEMENT THE NEW METHOD..."

Tip: Make your motto "listen and learn" when you're working for a clever, conceited Show-Off boss. You needn't bow down in the presence of intellectual royalty, but do lend your ear to his lordship's pronouncements.

Whether or not they have earned the right to be exorbitantly proud of themselves, egotistical bosses provide you with opportunities. If, on the one hand, the boss is a pompous bubblehead, he'll probably be happy for you to leap in and lead the group—provided you are above board and tactful about it. If, on the other hand, your boss is bright, then swallow your pride and absorb whatever you can. This may prove to be one of your best learning experiences.

CHAPTER 17

WHEN YOUR COLLEAGUES ARE SELF-SEEKING

17.1 Inflators

17.2 One-Uppers

17.3 Know-It-Alls

17.4 Pulley Operators

Although you're on the same peer level as your egotistical colleagues, they act as though their jobs are more important than yours. Whatever you're doing, they know more about it than you do. Whether they are real experts or phony pretenders, you resent their acting as though they are the center of the universe.

More than that, you're upset that they allow their arrogance and conceit to mislead you and deceive you and even humiliate you in order to make themselves appear more important.

17.1 INFLATORS

Inflators exaggerate their own importance to win your admiration or attention.

Pompous, pretentious, misleading mavens can talk with such assurance you're absolutely convinced they speak the gospel. You learn the hard way that they are phony incompetents. Quite often they fool themselves as well as you into believing they are the experts they pretend to be.

They take the smattering of information they've absorbed and expand upon it. From reading a couple of articles or studies and hearing a couple of lectures, they patch together a position that sounds reasonable. They want you to admire them and offer this "knowledge" to win your respect, but they waste your time with their inflated claims. When the information backfires, they accept no responsibility for steering you wrong.

What You're Thinking

How could I be so stupid as to let myself be taken in again by Jan, the Instant Expert On Every Subject? From the articulate way she explained the new law, she made it all sound so clear and logical. But I've been stuck before because of Jan. Why does she tell these whoppers? She's not actually lying, though. She seems to have convinced herself she has all the answers. I think she believes what she's saying, at least while she's saying it.

An Inflator's Thoughts

From what was discussed at the conference, the new law would apply only in certain cases. This looks like one of those cases. Yes, it feels right to me. It must be so. I'll tell Bill and he'll be impressed with how much I know.

Strategy

Your objective is to stop the Inflators from misleading you. They are puffed up with their own importance. While you can stick pins in hot-air balloons and watch them quickly disintegrate, it's better to let them off the hook in a slower, kinder manner.

(1) *Gently press for details.* Ask them to interpret. Inflators generally are reduced to doubletalk gibberish when asked to elaborate or give examples.

(2) *Give them a way out.* Use questions, rather than authoritative statements, to point out a mistake. Suggest it's a common boner to shift certain points out of alignment.

Tactical Talk

"JAN, COULD YOU MAKE THE DISTINCTION A LITTLE SHARPER AS TO WHEN THIS IS APPLICABLE? A FEW EXAMPLES WOULD HELP US SEE THE DIFFERENCE."

"PERHAPS YOU MAY BE REFERRING TO A SIMILAR LAW WHICH ALSO CAME OUT LAST YEAR. EXCEPT FOR A FEW POINTS, THEY'RE SO MUCH ALIKE I SOMETIMES GET THE TWO CONFUSED MYSELF."

Tip: Resist the temptation to puncture pompous egos even though it takes gall for them to think they know it all. When you have to continue working together, better to discourage than disparage. Inflators pretend so much, they talk themselves into believing they know what they're talking about. Being brainy midgets, they fidget next to informed colleagues. Soon they move on to try to impress someone else.

17.2 ONE-UPPERS

One-Uppers have to top whatever you say and go you one better.

Braggart colleagues come in two brands—ept and inept. Both types have an extraordinary need for your admiration and choose an irritating way to get you to think they're important. They blatantly lay claim to a mastery of procedures, sharpened technical skills, friends in high places—anything to impress you with how much they know or who they know. And they don't mind exaggerating to make the point.

What You're Thinking

I am every bit as capable as Cindy. I resent her implication that she can do anything better than I can. Even the last time I was out sick, she bragged she was sicker! She talks with such confidence and overabundance of pride, I wonder if she realizes that she keeps putting me down. She says, "My reports are sharp and crisp" or "My staff always exceeds our production goals" in that super-confident tone that implies I don't measure up. She's friendly enough, but I'm sure that's a phony act. I can see right through it.

A One-Upper's Thoughts

I envy the way Nicolle speaks so effectively before the group. I wish she could see that I can do a lot of things well, too. In fact, I don't know how some of my teammates ever got to this level. They don't belong, but I'll smile and be friendly to them. That's the politically smart way to act.

Strategy

To relieve your own stress, you want to bring about a friendlier atmosphere. This will require *mutual* respect and acknowledgment. Stop playing the One-Upper's "I can do anything better than you can" game.

(1) *Tease one-uppers in a light, friendly tone.* Show sensitivity even though they don't by gently interrupting the self-aggrandizement act. If you find yourself tempted to brag back, smile, excuse yourself and take a seat on the other side of the room.

(2) *Give One-Uppers the recognition they've earned.* Find specific areas in which they actually do excel. You'll win their friendship and cooperation by bolstering them with sincere, genuine compliments.

Tactical Talk

(*smiling, without sarcasm*) "CINDY, HERE'S A GLASS OF WATER. YOUR THROAT MUST BE DRY. TAKE

A BREATHER. YOU'VE BEEN TALKING NONSTOP FOR THE PAST 10 MINUTES."

"LOOK, CINDY, NO ONE CAN HOLD A CANDLE TO YOU WHEN IT COMES TO ORGANIZING YOUR STAFF. YOU'VE GOT US ALL BEAT WITH YOUR ABILITY TO COORDINATE. BUT ON THIS ISSUE WE HAVE AN ADDITIONAL FACTOR THAT MUST BE CONSIDERED. WHAT DO YOU SUGGEST WE DO ABOUT THE TIME LIMITATION?"

Tip: Give One-Uppers the one thing they want most—your attention—and they won't be as desperate to point out their great achievements. They feel justified in assuming an arrogant air because they think you, in some way, have belittled their efforts. Consider their expressed conceit a cry for your compliments.

17.3 KNOW-IT-ALLS

Know-It-Alls are smart alecks, arrogantly claiming to know everything about everything.

Bursting with self-confidence, Know-It-Alls are obnoxious extroverts who cram their opinions down your throat. Masters at promoting themselves, these colleagues usually know a great deal, as opposed to Inflators who only pretend to be well informed.

Know-It-Alls flaunt their intelligence, with their vanity shining through every line. Because they are competent, efficient, and thorough planners who cover all the angles, they have little use for your input and they have no tolerance if you subject their opinionated statements to debate.

What You're Thinking

Richard appears harmless. He conducts himself with dignity, but I can feel his attitude of superiority. After talking the boss into having a meeting program, Richard lectured the rest of us about achieving company goals by improving our working techniques. I've carefully analyzed my notes and I've concluded a few of the techniques he advocated are potentially dangerous because they violate employee rights. I have this tremendous urge to expose the holes in his argument because of his condescending tone.

A Know-It-All's Thoughts

Although I'd never say anything, it's obvious to me that my colleagues can be pretty dense. If the boss doesn't shape them up, I think I should. My talk at the meeting should show them I know all the answers.

Strategy

Since Know-It-Alls are usually right, your goal is to extract and utilize the clever thoughts that make them crow without letting their words stick in your craw.

(1) *Listen carefully to formulate good questions.* Don't interrupt with counterarguments, but with strong, solid questions. Ask, for example, how this compares, what results have been reported, over what period of time, what resources are required.

(2) *Do your own homework.* Verify the information. If you think Know-It-Alls are wrong, matter of factly present contradictory data. Don't directly challenge their expertise, but suggest another way to view the situation.

Tactical Talk

"HOW WOULD THAT AFFECT THE RATE AND WHAT IS THE ESTIMATED COST FOR THE FIRST YEAR?"

"I KNOW THIS WON'T SOLVE OUR PROBLEM, BUT WHAT IF WE WERE TO START HERE INSTEAD. DO YOU THINK THAT MIGHT GIVE US THE IMPETUS WE NEED?"

Tip: Know-It-Alls are bright and usually right. On those occasions you're sure they're wrong, if you try a frontal attack or back them into a corner, Know-It-Alls will bombard you with a fusillade of irrelevant data to support their position. They consider any opposition a personal affront. The only way to quiet them is to offer them a gracious way to save face.

17.4 PULLEY OPERATORS

Pulley Operators believe by pushing you down they elevate themselves.

They deliberately humiliate you in order to become the center of attention. These cohorts feel threatened whenever you do well because they hold themselves up in comparison to you and feel compelled to attack. According to their screwed-up value system, if you perform well that automatically means that their performance is worse than yours. However, work must be judged on its own merit. The value is constant. It doesn't fluctuate by comparison. Your good job can't make others appear worse (or better) than it actually is. You're not good because someone else is bad. You and they are as good—or bad—as you always were, independent of each other.

Nevertheless, Pulley Operators, lacking faith in their own abilities, need to push you down so that they can feel that they've risen to or above your level.

What You're Thinking

Since the boss assigned Herb and me to switch jobs, Herb's been unable to let go. He makes statements to clients that he was better at my new job than I am. He says that I don't belong there, as he did, because I don't have his instincts for meeting client needs.

A Pulley Operator's Thoughts

What is Jason trying to do, show me up? Well, I'll show him. If I can get them to see how weak Jason appears, they'll appreciate how strong I really am.

Strategy

Your goal is to help Pulley Operators feel confident in their own abilities without using comparisons as a measuring stick.

(1) *Acknowledge their expertise.* Give or share credit with Pulley Operators for improving a poor situation. If you let them feel important, they'll feel less need to tear you down. Be extra sensitive about soothing wounded egos. Then if trouble erupts involving your unit, they are more likely to come to you first before running to report it to the boss and others.

(2) *Keep abreast of what's happening in other units.* Meet often or have weekly lunches with the Pulley Operators and your other peers. Establish and maintain good rapport. Discuss ways to cooperate and help each other.

(3) *Find little ways to involve your colleagues.* Whether it's taking them into your confidence, asking for advice, requesting a small favor or to do a small segment of your project in return for your doing something for them, attempt to make them a small part of what you're doing. Now they have a vested interest in your doing well.

Tactical Talk

"HERB, I MUST SAY YOU HANDLED THAT CRISIS VERY SMOOTHLY AND CALMLY. IF YOU HADN'T, WE COULD HAVE HAD A REAL EMERGENCY HERE."

"THE DIVISION DIRECTORS ARE GETTING TOGETHER INFORMALLY FOR LUNCH ON TUESDAY. I HOPE YOU CAN JOIN US, HERB, BECAUSE I THINK WE CAN HELP EACH OTHER SOLVE SOME MUTUAL PROBLEMS."

"LOOK, HERB, IN THE INTEREST OF TIME AND EFFICIENCY, WHAT WOULD YOU SAY TO JOINING FORCES, WITH MY DIVISION DOING THIS PART AND YOUR DIVISION DOING THAT?"

Tip: It's difficult to mold a team when some members are driven by compulsive self-interest. Being terribly impressed with themselves, they not only affect you but also can damage morale of all subordinates—yours and theirs—with such outbursts as "Don't you know who I am? I'll have your job!" When Pulley Operators step on you and stomp on your workers, save your sanity by building up their self confidence.

When the actions and habits of self-centered colleagues interfere with your work, decide it's time to make friends, not enemies. Arguing with the egotistical easily escalates to rancor. Look beyond the conceit and stay calm for your own interest. Note how Thomas Jefferson exercised self-control in this excerpt from his writings: "When I hear another express an opinion which is not mine, I say to myself, he has a right to his opinion as I to mine; why should I question it? His error does me no injury...It is his affair, not mine, if he prefers error."

CHAPTER 18

WHEN YOUR SUBORDINATES ARE SELF-SEEKING

18.1 Empire Builders

18.2 Prima Donnas

18.3 Slipshods

18.4 Magnifiers

Egotistical subordinates are preoccupied with their own welfare and advancement. They weigh how some thought or deed will affect their position before they take action. Some demand special consideration because they happen to have important contacts or possess an unusual skill that you desperately need.

If they can't see how it benefits their particular job or project, these self-indulgent workers are unconcerned with the big, broad picture. With no obvious personal gain or advantage, they can become careless in their performance or concentrate only on those parts of the job which will further their goals. When you're trying to supervise and motivate a team, they're a demoralizing influence.

18.1 EMPIRE BUILDERS

Empire Builders are climbers. Their interest in others is limited to how well they serve as stepping stones. With a one-track mind, egocentric subordinates go about their work as though they are the only ones who count. The view of most of the crew is that Empire Builders don't carry their share of the load. They aren't team players but grandstanders who love to hog the limelight and pitch in when they know they'll get attention. They're not motivated by what's good for the group but by the amount of personal glory an action can generate.

Empire Builders are astute in understanding the political implications of an issue. They've memorized the little boxes on the organizational chart. They know the flow of information and where decisions are made. Doing favors (and, in turn, being owed favors) is their way of amassing a combination of multi-level supporters. Their giant egos and insensitivity enable them to use people as stepping stones in building their little empires.

What You're Thinking

Bobbie is charming, animated, and persuasive when it serves her purpose. At our staff meetings, she's quick to volunteer and is full of helpful suggestions. I've heard grumbling, though, that when it's time to work on a team project—a joint effort—Bobbie either does a vanishing act or manages to seize control of the group. If she can't milk the activity for personal recognition, she disappears and talks someone else into doing her assignment. On the other hand, if the project has the potential for favorable publicity, she takes over offering a better way to implement the planning.

An Empire Builder's Thoughts

I think it's important to get the boss to assign me to our division's planning team. From what I read in the company newsletter, that project is in line with the major emphasis the CEO articulated in his talk to the Board. I think I see a way to expand our results beyond our own division, gradually including all the other divisions. That would allow me to work with several key people I might not otherwise have the chance to know and hopefully win favorable attention from the higher ups.

Strategy

Your goal is to walk a tightrope. Maintain the Empire Builders' enthusiasm and effectiveness while preventing them from dumping on fellow workers in order to promote themselves.

(1) *Applaud the Empire Builders' talent for exciting the crowd.* Empire Builders can help you establish teams either as part of the production or the problem-solving process or both. You can safely assume all your people want to improve the emotional climate in the office. One tested way is to allow each one to act as a member of a team. This enables each worker to acquire more identity and recognition than he would by working alone by himself.

(2) *Set a limit on the Empire Builders' behavior.* Decide on the point beyond which you won't tolerate. You can't change the Empire Builders' personality, but you can change the way you interact with them.

Tactical Talk

"BOBBIE, YOU HAVE SUCH A GREAT ORGANIZING SKILL, I'D LIKE YOU TO SET UP A CONTEST BY DEVISING FOUR PLANNING TEAMS FOR OUR DIVISION, EACH TO EXPLORE FRESH WAYS TO ACHIEVE THE OBJECTIVES..."

"BOBBIE, EXPLAIN TO ME WHY YOU FELT YOU HAD TO HAVE WAYNE TAKE OVER FOR YOU WHILE YOU ATTENDED THAT DEPARTMENTAL MEETING...WAYNE'S ALREADY CARRYING A HEAVY LOAD AND ANYTHING MORE IS A SERIOUS IMPOSITION. FROM NOW ON, IF YOU WANT TO CHANGE ASSIGNMENTS, SEE ME FIRST."

Tip: Empire Builder subordinates are both a help and a hindrance. Encourage them to lead but insist on their adherence to your rules.

18.2 PRIMA DONNAS

Prima Donnas are temperamental workers, demanding that you give them special treatment.

Often conceited and vain performers, Prima Donnas have a way of intimidating and manipulating you into believing the company will fold without them. We can speculate that they were spoiled as children and learned early how to get others to do their work for them. They aren't lazy, but shrewd. They use many tricks, such as issuing ultimatums, to get special attention. In return for certain demands, they dangle prizes you long for, such as promising to introduce you to decision makers who can close a deal. Generally, Prima Donnas are moody and have short fuses. The danger is that they wear down your resistance.

What You're Thinking

Most of my staff gladly cooperate when I make assignments, but I can count on Gregg to give me a hard time. There's always some special circumstance why he can't work late or on the weekend or head the project. He gets excited when he's faced with doing something he obviously doesn't want to do. Rather than start a scene, I've been giving in to his temperamental antics. Gregg is driving me crazy because he makes it so difficult for me to treat each subordinate impartially.

A Prima Donna's Thoughts

I've given this company plenty of my time and energy. I don't see any reason to take on any extra work. The others may fall for that line about all of us having to pitch in to reduce the caseload. Well, let the peasants perform. I'm going to get out of it because the boss is afraid to antagonize me.

Strategy

Your objective is to maintain control by guiding the Prima Donnas to act more responsibly.

(1) *Call their bluff.* Stop acting intimidated and allowing Prima Donnas to interfere with your operation. Whatever Prima Donnas have that you want, it's better to do without it than have them usurp your authority and destroy team spirit.

(2) *Help them become part of the team.* Be friendly, but very firm in insisting that your procedures be followed. If you want your whole group pulling together, you have to treat each one the same way. Also, you can enlist the support of the Prima Donnas' peers to apply pressure on them to join in.

Tactical Talk

"WELL, GREGG, I'M AFRAID YOU'RE GOING TO HAVE TO CHANGE THAT APPOINTMENT. I NEED YOU TO TAKE THESE CASES. THAT'S THE ONLY FAIR WAY TO DISTRIBUTE THEM. THANK YOU FOR UNDERSTANDING THE SITUATION."

"GREGG, THE MANAGEMENT TEAM HAS COME UP WITH A PLAN TO REDUCE THE CASELOAD. IT INVOLVES YOU, JODI, GEORGE, AND WALT BECAUSE WE CONSIDER YOU THE BEST WORKERS. YOU'LL FORM A TASK FORCE THAT WOULD TAKE ONLY THOSE CASES THAT..."

Tip: Recognize the games that Prima Donnas play. Like children who pout, stamp their feet and throw tantrums, they use a variety of irritating techniques to wear you down and get their own way. You have to reinforce your rules and stick to them.

18.3 SLIPSHODS

Slipshods are careless workers, unconcerned that their negligence affects others.

Lately, you seem to have some subordinates who are inattentive and negligent. They show little or no concern for the company's end product and even less regard for the needs and feelings of their fellow workers. These are employees who are capable of doing but, for some puzzling reason, don't want to perform.

There are many possibilities that could account for good workers becoming thoughtless, careless, reckless, and rash. Usually, explanations relate to the newly irresponsible workers feeling disillusioned.

What You're Thinking

Kurt skirts the rules and is just getting by with his work. He used to be one of my best workers. Now he's late with assignments, especially with producing those segments others on the team are depending on. Does he think he's invincible? Is he so enamored with himself that he thinks everybody loves him and will forgive him his trespasses? How can I get Kurt to perform up to his potential?

A Slipshod's Thoughts

Why try? You work longer and harder and for what? No one gives you any reward for knocking yourself out. No matter what I do, whether I perform poorly, well, or extraordinarily well, it's the same to the boss, the department, and the whole darn organization. They don't really care about me or what I think, and they certainly don't appreciate any extra effort I put into this job.

Strategy

Your goal is to motivate demoralized workers and restore their team spirit.

(1) *Demonstrate personal warmth and concern for them as individuals.* Express your belief that each one is important. Use private discussions to probe the problem and discover what's troubling them.

(2) *Review your incentive system.* Go over with each one the bonuses paid for money-saving suggestions, the all-expense paid educational leaves to attend workshops and

conferences, the pay raise and promotion policies. If you have a good plan, don't assume your subordinates are familiar with it. If you don't have one, work on it.

(3) *Design a system for exchanging ideas.* Not a haphazard inquiry, but regularly scheduled formal or informal get togethers for this specific purpose, with all participants notified in advance of the issues to be discussed. Follow up by letting them know which ideas will be implemented.

(4) *Keep your staff informed.* Let them know what's expected of them and how they're doing. Frequently pick up your phone to deliver quick compliments. Write short memos to report latest developments that will affect their jobs. Consider a regular column in your company newspaper to address employee concerns and give special recognition for effort.

Tactical Talk

"KURT, WE HAVE TO TALK ABOUT WHATEVER IT IS THAT'S BOTHERING YOU. I'M NOT ANGRY THAT YOUR WORK HASN'T BEEN UP TO PAR, BUT I AM DISAPPOINTED IN YOU. LET'S SEE IF WE CAN STRAIGHTEN OUT THE TROUBLE."

"KURT, I THINK YOU HAVE A GREAT DEAL OF UNTAPPED POTENTIAL, BUT YOU NEED TO SHARPEN YOUR SKILLS. YOU COULD BENEFIT FROM ATTENDING THE ALL-DAY WORKSHOP NEXT WEDNESDAY, AND THE COMPANY, IN TURN, WOULD BENEFIT FROM YOUR ACHIEVEMENTS. YOU MAY NOT BE FULLY AWARE OF OUR INCENTIVE SYSTEM..."

Tip: Workers who lose interest and turn inward have an even greater need to be noticed and recognized. What appears to be a self-centered subordinate may be a disenchanted one. The magic in motivating them is showing sensitivity and giving them a sense of belonging.

18.4 MAGNIFIERS

Magnifiers blow minor tasks out of proportion to make themselves appear more important.

Some wag once said an egotist is a braggart who puts his feat in his mouth. Magnifiers go further. They enlarge *whatever* they do, making even the insignificant a very big deal. They are immature in their desire to impress others with unimportant work although, admittedly, the busywork may be well executed.

Magnifiers often complain they haven't time for their important assignments. They're too busy attempting to get noticed by giving each little job all they've got whether or not it deserves the effort. These subordinates have to grow up emotionally.

What You're Thinking

Gilbert spends far too much time designing fancy charts that we really don't need. I guess I've been too subtle with him and I'm going to have to clamp down about priority items. Also, for someone so new to the job, Gilbert certainly presumed to have all the answers. He was determined to call attention to himself before gaining any experience in *this* position when he volunteered an article for the company journal. Imagine his telling everyone how our services could be improved only to learn a little later that many of his conclusions are unworkable at this company. His determination to make his job bigger than it is embarrasses me and the rest of my team.

A Magnifier's Thoughts

I want them all to see that this new kid on the block is going to make a big difference to the company. I've made some elaborate color-coded drawings tracing the routes of our various systems. I've also prepared a series of charts breaking down all the information. I know the boss will understand that I haven't had time to get to some of the things he asked me to do, but I'm sure he'll be pleasantly surprised to see what a grand job I've done in compiling this data.

Strategy

Your goal is to help Magnifiers distinguish between assignments that are top priority and those to be dispatched quickly with minimum effort.

(1) *Differentiate between important tasks and make-work.* Explain that one should feel justifiable pride for achieving high standards where it is warranted and no pride for wasting time on the unimportant. Until they learn the difference, avoid giving Magnifiers assignments that must be handled immediately.

(2) *Develop a rating code and deadlines.* You can, for example, use simple A, B, C categories to indicate the time and effort required for different tasks. Make it clear that their designated tasks must be completed by the deadline date before working on anything else.

Tactical Talk

"GILBERT, YOU ARE CAPABLE OF FINE WORK AND IN TIME YOU WILL BE RECOGNIZED FOR MEETING THE HIGH STANDARDS OF THIS DEPARTMENT. BUT FIRST YOU HAVE TO STOP ENLARGING MINOR TASKS TO MAKE THEM APPEAR GREATER THAN THEY REALLY ARE AND CONCENTRATE ON COMPLETING YOUR ASSIGNMENTS."

"I'M CONFIDENT YOU WILL DO WELL HERE ONCE YOU LEARN TO FOLLOW A FEW SIMPLE PROCEDURES..."

Tip: Magnifiers insist on overstating and overemphasizing every little task they perform to try to increase your perception of their importance. Such behavior indicates emotional immaturity and requires your firm hand.

As the manager, you're charged with building a strong and effective team. You can't allow any self-centered subordinates, regardless of the value of their contributions, to dictate to you what, how, when, and if they will do what you ask. You can show sensitive concern for individuals and sincere appreciation for effort, and still maintain necessary discipline with fair and impartial treatment for all.

PART SEVEN

DEALING WITH PROCRASTINATORS AND VACILLATORS

People who *irrationally* postpone what they have to do generally have a vulnerable self-esteem. Although others may praise and encourage them, these bosses, colleagues, and subordinates doubt themselves and keep putting off decisions and actions. Just one critical comment can result in another delay.

The delays affect the entire operation. Procrastinators and vacillators cause last-minute scurrying accompanied by tension and arguments. Decisions and output are not quite as good as they might have been if it all hadn't been so rush-rush.

Procrastinators frequently blame their habit of putting things off on not having enough time. Of course, they have the same number of hours as everyone else and may try to do too much at once or fritter away their time on the insignificant. The stalling, however, is not rooted in a time shortage but in fear or rebellion. Fear that what they do or say won't meet their own excessively high standards or fear they can't do the deed correctly. Rebel-stallers find that holding up the whole office gives them a measure of control over the bosses or colleagues they want to avenge.

CHAPTER 19

WHEN YOUR BOSS CAUSES DELAYS

19.1 Stallers
19.2 Over-Committers
19.3 Chameleons

The whole organization is thrown out of kilter when the procrastinating or vacillating attitude starts at the top and runs downhill. Some bosses stall until they get up their nerve to act. They lack a leader's confidence. Some bosses change their minds because they never wanted to make the move in the first place. They start out with a pleasant teasing of "We'll see," and eventually agree only to avoid an argument. Others seesaw between yes and no as easily as a chameleon changes its colors.

While problems facing procrastinating and vacillating bosses vary, your direction in dealing with them is clear. You have to move them—and yourself—out of the stuck position.

19.1 STALLERS

Stallers believe if they stall long enough, the problems will disappear.

The one thing you can depend on with Staller bosses is their indecision. They're afraid that they can't or won't make the right choice. A mistake isn't simply an error or even a terrible boner that you or I might pull. When they make a mistake, their sense of security disintegrates. It diminishes the value they place upon themselves. Maybe, they reason, if they can put off taking action for a while, the need for it will lessen or go away. So they don't fix what's broken and don't buy what's needed and don't give you their decision. That behavior leaves you pacing up and down, confused by mixed signals as you await the boss's action.

Besides shirking responsibility by avoiding decisions, Stallers also neglect certain tasks because they regard them as unpleasant. They avoid duties that appear meaningless to them, especially those that don't seem to further their future with the company.

What You're Thinking

The boss keeps stalling on the allocation of funds for the new copier. The way that machine's been acting up, I know its days are numbered. He keeps burying the problem, saying he'll look into it later, but it's going to erupt again very soon. This office moves on its paper work. If the copier goes, we are all immobilized. I have to get the boss to take some action right away.

A Staller's Thoughts

Trina keeps complaining about the copier and I know that eventually we will have to replace the one we have. But in the last few years they have come out with so many new models and features, I'll never be able to figure out the one that best meets our needs and the price range we should be considering. Maybe we have another year or two before we have to be concerned about purchasing a new copier.

Strategy

Your goal is to get the required action by tactfully pushing the boss from stall to start.

(1) *Supportively relate how problems affect the boss.* Investigate, research, do the leg work to provide information that makes it easier for the boss to reach a decision or take action. Suggest solutions that show your concern for your boss's standing in the company.

(2) *Assume power without waiting for it to be handed to you.* When the boss is indecisive or stalling, take over those tasks he doesn't like to do or neglects doing. Just be sure your actions are above board and you keep all the parties informed. Staller bosses are usually happy with one less item to worry about and your reputation as an important problem solver grows with each responsibility you add to your list.

Tactical Talk

"BOSS, THERE'S A GREAT DIFFERENTIAL IN THE COST OF NEW COPIERS. I MET WITH SALESMEN FROM SIX LEADING COMPANIES AND COMPILED THIS COMPARISON OF FEATURES AND PRICES."

"BOSS, I KNOW YOUR CONCERN WILL BE HOW TO SAVE THE DEPARTMENT EMBARRASSMENT WHEN OUR REPORTS ARE LATE BECAUSE THE COPIER DIED, NOT EXACTLY UNEXPECTEDLY. I'D LIKE TO SUGGEST TWO POSSIBLE WAYS WE MIGHT HANDLE THE EMERGENCY..."

Tip: Yes, it's presumptuous to take over a task the boss doesn't want to do without being invited to do it. However, if properly executed, this maneuver is usually received as welcome relief. Provide tactful reinforcement by rallying other staff support. Don't comment to your peers on the boss's inability to act (for instance saying, "It's making me nuts the way the boss can never make up his mind!") Should the boss somehow be offended by your takeover, simply apologize, say you were trying to help, and don't do it again. But usually, this strategy is well worth the risk.

19.2 OVER-COMMITTERS

Over-Committers are nice people who can't refuse anyone and then find they have no time to follow through.

Just as you can depend on Stallers to be indecisive, you can count on Over-Committers to love harmony. These bosses agree with whatever everyone asks of them because they hate to argue. A confrontation could hurt someone's feelings and therefore has to be avoided.

But by *pretending* to agree in order to prevent a fight or a fuss, they promise too much or promise to do something they don't really agree with. Overburdened and unable to handle it all, they put off action or decisions and break their promises. They don't mean any harm, but you certainly resent the way they've messed up your timetable and failed to come through with whatever you were depending on.

What You're Thinking

Promises, promises, my boss keeps breaking promises. I end up looking foolish because I had reassured my staff that the boss would have an answer for us today regarding the holiday schedule. She's always disappointing us. All that agreeableness is a phony facade and "we're all one big happy family" is just a line. I'm losing respect for her. What's worse, how can I ever trust what she says she's going to do?

An Over-Committer's Thoughts

I'd like to agree to the staff's request granting permission for them to leave a few hours early on Friday before the start of the holidays. But I'm concerned about getting out the quarterlies on time. Maybe we'll need those extra hours to finish up. I know I promised them an answer today, but I'm going to have to give this more thought. What can I do to keep the crew from getting upset?

Strategy

Your goal is to help your boss make decisions without feeling threatened by unpopularity.

(1) *Claim the problem as your own.* When you sense the boss is stuck on the horns of a dilemma ("Do I please the company or please my workers?"), remove one of the horns so that the boss no longer has to choose. Step forward and accept the problem as *your* responsibility.

(2) *Bring the priorities into focus.* Assist in finding ways for the boss to do the right thing. It's possible to carry out a manager's responsibility to the organization and, at the same time, lessen the anticipated negative impact upon subordinates. Study the situation and examine everyone's needs and then offer potential solutions. You can probably negotiate a win/win compromise.

Tactical Talk

"BOSS, I'VE BEEN THINKING THAT THE RE-QUEST WE MADE FOR EXTRA HOURS OFF ON FRIDAY MIGHT HAVE PUT YOU IN AN AWK-WARD POSITION. HOW ABOUT MY KICKING AROUND SOME IDEAS WITH MY STAFF ON HOW THIS COULD BE MANAGED AND STILL STICK TO OUR ORIGINAL SCHEDULE?"

"BOSS, MY STAFF SUGGESTS THAT THEY CAN FINISH THE QUARTERLIES BY WORKING LATE ON THURSDAY, SUBSTITUTING THOSE EXTRA HOURS FOR TIME OFF FRIDAY AFTERNOON. IS THAT OK WITH YOU?"

Tip: Over-Committer bosses create dilemmas for themselves when they take their eyes off their priorities and become overly concerned with pleasing the immediate world. You can best move them to action either by removing one side of the di-lemma or by offering additional options that allow the boss to escape through the dilemma's horns.

19.3 CHAMELEONS

Chameleons are changeable, indecisive, and keep wavering on their decisions.

While the Over-Committers break promises in the name of harmony, Chameleons go back on their word because of their insecurity. Sometimes Chameleon bosses are incompetent. They may have been promoted beyond their capabilities. Rather than admit they don't know what they're doing, they delay deciding what to do. They say one thing today and the opposite tomorrow, deliberately muddying the water.

Sometimes Chameleons are looking for the absolutely perfect decision. They think they've found it, then discover a flaw in the chosen option and change their minds again.

Wishy-washy and inconsistent, Chameleons sway back and forth. Organized types (who plan for every contingency except individual idiosyncrasies) find it particularly infuriating when they believe the boss has settled an issue only to find it really wasn't settled at all.

What You're Thinking

I'm supposed to be my boss's assistant, but I'm finding it very difficult to help him. It seems to me that he's unsure of himself. He doesn't know if he's doing the right thing so he waffles on his directives. The Fenton deal was typical. Last week he wanted to proceed with the contract full steam ahead. This week he tells me to cancel our meetings and stop the negotiations. It's impossible to get anything accomplished when bosses keep changing their minds.

A Chameleon's Thoughts

I thought when I took on this job it would be an easy transition. After all, everyone knows that managerial skills are transferable. The problem is, without knowing the history and politics of this division, I really have to be terribly careful not to make a horrendously costly error. Right now, I'm not sure which staff people I can trust.

Strategy

Your goal is to expedite definite decisions so that issues that have been left hanging can finally be resolved. This requires your making a special effort to earn the boss's confidence.

(1) *Refine the content of information.* Even if the boss isn't new to this job, fill him in on essential background data, but don't give your boss more information about a subject than he needs to know in order to decide. Analyze, then summarize. Offer the boss suggested solutions instead of just dumping problems.

(2) *Negotiate the level of information.* Does the boss really have to make *all* those decisions? Can you agree that, as an assistant, you can be delegated responsibility for signing off on specified types of actions? In your discussions, maintain a calm manner in order to be more persuasive.

(3) *Monitor the flow of information.* Keep a careful tickler file. Depend on a reminder calendar to flag your attention, well in advance of deadlines, about the status of your projects. If you don't wait until the last minute to check progress, you can usually avoid a gridlock.

Tactical Talk

(instead of "What should we do about...?") "BOSS, AS YOU KNOW, WE'RE LOOKING AT THREE ALTERNATIVES: (1)...(2)...(3)...IT WOULD SEEM THAT THE SECOND OPTION IS BEST FOR US AT THIS TIME BECAUSE...DOES IT STRIKE YOU THE SAME WAY?"

"BOSS, AS YOU KNOW, I'VE BEEN WORKING ON THIS FOR SEVERAL YEARS. WOULDN'T IT HELP EASE SOME OF YOUR BURDEN IF I OK'D THE FIRST TWO STEPS AND YOU GAVE FINAL APPROVAL ON THE LAST THREE?"

Tip: Bosses who vacillate often can be bolstered by receiving clear, concise, pertinent information. They're not supposed to be experts on everything. Recognize the areas where your boss needs additional support. Supply the vital information in a form that can be immediately utilized and you'll earn your boss's trust.

You're not your boss's keeper. How he chooses to act is his own responsibility, so don't complain about the delays the boss causes or make excuses for it. Your aim is to help facilitate the operational flow. Your boss may have been selected to head your project because he has certain talents that aren't obvious to you. When the boss causes delays, you can assume he's probably afraid of failing or feels threatened. You can help by supplying him with whatever data is needed to make good, solid, final decisions.

CHAPTER 20

WHEN YOUR COLLEAGUES CAUSE DELAYS

20.1 Socializers

20.2 Perfectionists

20.3 Dawdlers

Like their bosses, your colleagues' delaying tactics may also be rooted in fear of failure, but there's often another component. Generally, peer procrastinators are so wrapped up in pursuing their own objectives, interests, or pleasures that they don't realize how their actions are affecting the entire office.

Some are too busy being friendly, others are too concerned with their own image, and some are too careless about deadlines to meet their responsibilities.

20.1 SOCIALIZERS

Socializers put off work while they desk-hop and make personal phone calls.

They don't seem to take anything seriously, these socializing peers who are dedicated to having fun. In their pursuit of happiness, they overstep the line between friendliness and responsibility, accenting the former and ignoring the latter. Socializer colleagues are outgoing and truly want to count everyone as a friend. They stop by your desk for a long chat, they get the group together for lunch, they're always on the phone or taking a coffee break. They have time for everything except the finished product they promised you. Maybe the work is too difficult for them. Maybe they're afraid they'll get it wrong. Maybe they disapprove of the system. Whatever is making them procrastinate, one thing we do know—they certainly feel it's more pleasant to be doing something other than the assigned task.

Socializers are happy, friendly people and you enjoy their company. But they interrupt everyone else's routine and cause serious delays. You find yourself getting increasingly agitated by their antics.

What You're Thinking

Ernie is a great guy, big heart, and lots of fun. But he reminds me of the kid who won't stop playing long enough to do his homework. It's not my place to lecture him. I just wish I had a magic wand that could get him to settle down and do his work. I can't move on this project until Ernie gives me his estimates.

A Socializer's Thoughts

I really enjoy working here. This is such a pleasant office and I've made a lot of good friends. Which reminds me, I have to call the gang to see if we can meet for lunch today, and if we're going to get that softball team organized...

Strategy

Although you have no authority over them, your goal is to persuade the Socializers to cooperate and finish their assignments.

(1) *Spell out the importance of the task and the roles they play.* Let Socializers know the benefits to the company/department/workers if the assignment is done well and the consequences if it is not. Impress upon them that they control an essential segment in making it happen. Be sincere—no phony line.

(2) *Limit your request to your immediate concern.* Don't ask for anything except the exact piece of work you need from them at this moment. Keep the focus and the discussion on that one item. Build grace periods into your original planning (for example, setting deadlines for their work the week before you actually need it) to allow for their delaying tactics.

(3) *Push politely without revealing panic.* Control your temper and hide your annoyance. Be pleasant about asking for what you have to have, but don't apologize for interrupting them. Act friendly and self assured to win their confidence.

(4) *Ask them for their opinions.* Help them to feel more involved, that they are truly a part of what is going on. You may hear ideas for changes that could unblock a logjam or even improve results.

(5) *Tie together what you want with their particular longing or interest.* As you chat, you'll hear the Socializers express their desires ("I wish that I could...", "I wish that I had..."). Try to see a situation the way *they* see it and suggest how finishing the task will help them achieve that desire.

Tactical Talk

"FRANKLY, ERNIE, I KNOW YOU'RE A FAIR PERSON AND YOU WANT TO DO YOUR PART. THE FACT IS, WE'RE STUCK BECAUSE YOU ARE THE ONLY ONE WE HAVE WHO KNOWS HOW TO FIGURE THESE KINDS OF ESTIMATES, AND WHAT WE NEED RIGHT NOW IS JUST THAT ONE FIGURE."

"DO YOU HAVE ANY IDEAS ON WHY WE GET SO JAMMED UP? WHAT DO YOU THINK WE MIGHT TRY TO MOVE THINGS A LITTLE FASTER?"

"THIS WILL CALL FOR A CELEBRATION WHEN WE FINISH AND YOU'RE OUR RESIDENT EXPERT IN HOW TO HAVE FUN."

Tip: Socializers missed their calling. They'd be great recreation directors. To win their cooperation, first win their trust by leveling with them. Don't plead for yourself but press for them to do what is important for themselves and for the company. Then link that effort to whatever it is they hanker for.

20.2 PERFECTIONISTS

Perfectionists keep polishing their work which never meets their extravagant standards.

These colleagues expect too much from themselves. They think everything they attempt should meet their excessively high expectations. As smart as they usually are, Perfectionists are consummate worriers.

They're afraid the work won't come up to the ideal they have in their minds or they may not get it perfect on their first try. If their workload prohibits their spending extra time to hone, and hone, and hone some more, they feel frustrated. So they keep putting off finishing the assignment. The more they worry, the less they produce. If they don't turn the work in, nobody will know it hasn't reached this artificial idealized goal they've created in their minds.

What You're Thinking

Lloyd may be gumming up the works. As our visuals specialist, if he doesn't come through I'm going to be in real trouble. I have to make the presentation to our new client on Thursday. So far, all I've seen is his original outline for the video part of the presentation. He says it's almost finished but he needs to fine-tune it with a little more editing. I'm nervous because Lloyd is never satisfied with what he produces. What do I do if he doesn't have it ready on time? I can't keep running to the boss to make Lloyd speed up. I wish I could make Lloyd understand what's at stake here.

A Perfectionist's Thoughts

I really thought this video for the new client was going to be great. It could be if people would leave me alone and let me smooth all the rough edges. I can't hand it in now. I need more time. I wish everybody would stop bugging me to turn over my work before I'm ready. Maybe the rest of them are satisfied with a less than excellent performance, but I'm not. When my name is on something, it has to represent the very best of my ability. I would be humiliated with anything less than that.

Strategy

Your objective is to help Perfectionist colleagues focus on what's important to the company as well as to themselves and to dovetail their priorities with company goals.

(1) *Help perfectionists deal with reality.* Organizations are limited in the amount of funds allocated and the time and staff assigned to certain projects. This is a hard lesson for all good workers to swallow, but Perfectionists choke on the limitations. If the company can't afford a standard as high as one wants, this shouldn't diminish the worker's self-esteem.

(2) *Reassure them that not everything has to be perfect.* Some projects have to be done post haste or an opportunity will be lost forever. Then the priority shifts from doing an excellent job at a normal pace to doing a good job quickly. If workers don't produce gems with every try it doesn't mean they're failures. Therefore, at times it's not only all right to turn in certain things that can't match your expectations, it's expected.

(3) *Help them with time management.* Suggest how work can be broken up into smaller steps or stages. Perfectionists need to enjoy a sense of accomplishment which they can get from checking more (and less complicated) completed tasks off their list. Explain that they'll have more time for important projects if they shorten time spent on the less significant ones.

Tactical Talk

"LLOYD, WOULD YOU LIKE TO TALK TO ME ABOUT THE VIDEO PART OF THURSDAY'S PRE-

SENTATION? IS THERE SOMETHING IN PARTIC-
ULAR THAT BOTHERS YOU ABOUT IT? MAYBE
IF WE WORKED TOGETHER WE'D GET THE BA-
SICS DONE FOR NOW AND IF THAT'S NOT UP
TO YOUR STANDARD, YOU COULD POLISH IT
MORE FOR FUTURE, MORE ELABORATE, PRE-
SENTATIONS."

"LLOYD, I KNOW HOW DIFFICULT IT IS TO TURN
IN WORK THAT'S LESS THAN YOUR BEST BE-
CAUSE YOU AREN'T GIVEN ENOUGH TIME. YOU
KNOW THE SAYING, 'THERE'S NEVER TIME TO
DO IT RIGHT, THERE'S ALWAYS TIME TO DO IT
OVER.' BUT THE FACT IS, SOME PROJECTS ARE
PEGGED AS GIVING LITTLE RETURN FOR EFFORT
INVESTED, SO THE MANAGER SCALES BACK THE
RESOURCES GOING INTO THEM. WE HAVE TO
DISTINGUISH BETWEEN THESE AND THE PRO-
JECTS THAT ALLOW US TO SHINE. IF IT'S ANY
CONSOLATION, EVEN PEOPLE IN BUSINESS FOR
THEMSELVES SOMETIMES HAVE TO BE SATISFIED
WITH LESS THAN THE IDEAL."

Tip: Don't confuse delaying Perfectionists with closet Perfectionists who, in a highly competitive climate, sneak their work
home to enjoy the polishing process on their own time. Without the right encouragement from superiors, they may suffer
from stress, but are no problem to you because they produce
on time. Delaying Perfectionists, on the other hand, throw the
rest of you off schedule. To move them more in sync with
you and your peers, they need to feel they're part of the team.
So talk team effort and team competition and plan some team
reward or celebration upon project completion.

20.3 DAWDLERS

Dawdlers waste time while you wait for their work in
order to complete your own.

Dawdlers are late for work, late for meetings, and late for
appointments. They may feel insecure about their abilities and

try to forestall the results by being late. Their problem becomes your problem when they put off getting you the information you need, signing the orders you request, completing their reports, and letting you cool your heels awaiting their late arrival.

Wasting time over trifling matters, they loiter and linger. Dawdlers often sit on the fence because they can't reach decisions. It's better, they tell themselves, to gather *all* the facts and hear from everyone before starting. Or they may move from one task to another, never completing anything.

What You're Thinking

This is the third time in a month that Rona has held us up because she didn't process the requisitions that have been sitting on her desk! I don't think she's lazy, but she seems to get distracted easily. Also, it seems to me that she goes through an unusual amount of checking before she okays an order. I suspect she's either not well organized, or she's unsure of herself, or both. Still, if I cover for her again, *I'm* the one who will appear incompetent.

A Dawdler's Thoughts

I know I was late processing Marge's requisitions and she's annoyed with me. But with the last warning I got from the boss, I just can't afford to make another mistake. Actually, the crux of the problem is old equipment. With a new computer, I could stay on top of all those orders with a quick update of current price lists. However, it's clear that nobody wants my opinion. They just want to yell at me for being unreliable.

Strategy

Your goal is to free yourself from your colleagues' apparently irresponsible behavior, but if you can direct Dawdlers toward improvement, that's a bonus for all of you.

(1) *Ask for a clarification of responsibilities.* Request that your boss review deadlines and work flow patterns with the whole staff. The responsibility for handling nonper-

formance by fellow workers is with the boss, the appointing authority. If you keep covering up for Dawdlers, the real core of the problem can never be uprooted.

(2) *Help Dawdlers get organized without criticizing them.* On assignments in which you are jointly involved, agree in advance on a reasonable amount of time needed. Discuss potential obstacles and how they can be met or skirted. Together produce your task/deadline plans.

(3) *Teach Dawdlers to be punctual.* Start without them rather than hold up a group meeting for the chronically tardy. Plan appointments with them in *your* office. Their being late won't bother you so much if you can continue working until they show up. Also tell them an earlier time than you actually expect to start. Don't throw your other appointments off because of Dawdlers. If their being late means you can't finish with them, stop at the allotted time and reschedule.

Tactical Talk

"RONA, I CAN'T KEEP COVERING FOR YOU. FROM NOW ON, IF YOU CAN'T GET YOUR WORK DONE ON TIME, YOU'LL HAVE TO HANDLE THE PROBLEM YOURSELF. THERE'S SOMETHING WRONG HERE THAT YOU'LL HAVE TO SETTLE WITH THE BOSS."

"BOSS, I THINK IT WOULD HELP US ALL IF WE COULD DO A QUICK FLOW CHART SETTING FORTH OUR DEADLINES AND SHOWING HOW OUR INDIVIDUAL ROLES IN THIS PROJECT MELD."

"ANDY, PLEASE TELL RONA I COULDN'T WAIT ANY LONGER. I HAVE TO LEAVE NOW OR I'LL BE LATE FOR ANOTHER APPOINTMENT."

"BOSS, RONA AND I AGREED ON DEADLINES TO AVOID FUTURE HOLDUPS WITH ITEMS I ORDERED. OUR PLAN IS NOT WORKING OUT. I NEED YOUR HELP."

Tip: First distinguish between the two basic classes of colleague Dawdlers—those who are late because of some fault within the system and those habitually late with everything. The former need your help in suggesting procedural revisions. The latter's irresponsible actions should be dealt with by their supervisors. In either case, you're not helping your peers by covering up their bad habit or the organization's bad system.

Procrastinating and vacillating colleagues cause their co-workers unnecessary stress and strain. Quite often, some quirk in their personality prevents them from following through with their responsibilities. They pursue their own objectives, failing to see the connection between helping the company and helping themselves. Since you have no authority over your peers, if your attempts at personal persuasion don't work, you have to let the boss handle their nonperformance. Sometimes, however, the reason for the delay is a fault within the system and procrastinators aren't really offenders but victims. In that case, suggesting revisions could prove most useful.

CHAPTER 21

WHEN YOUR SUBORDINATES CAUSE DELAYS

21.1 Clockwatchers

21.2 Duds

21.3 Rebels

Subordinates who seem bored, scared, or resentful and who dilly dally instead of doing what they know has to be done create conflict among other workers. Untreated, the tension can grow into a serious loss in productivity. But before looking at three common types who cause delays—those who won't do, those who can't do, and those seeking revenge—you should carefully examine the atmosphere in your office. If the air engulfing procrastinating subordinates is too stressful, rigid, or frigid, some part of the problem is not with the people but with the system.

CHECKLIST FOR MANAGERS DEALING WITH PROCRASTINATORS

Do You Create Good Rapport?

( ) Do you establish a good emotional climate in which workers are free to learn, produce, and try innovative approaches?

( ) Do you put procrastinators at ease so that they're comfortable talking to you, sensing that you identify with their needs?

( ) Is it pleasant and sometimes fun to work in your office?

( ) Do you avoid humiliating workers publicly with shouts and threats, or clobbering them privately after each mistake, or bribing them to do more?

( ) Do you reinforce the procrastinators' identity with their group through informal office get-togethers, events, and friendly competition?

Do You Eliminate Contributory Factors?

( ) Do you check that disturbing noises, poor lighting and ventilation, wrong tools, malfunctioning equipment, and insufficient training don't contribute to delays?

( ) Do you have enough staff, not expecting one person to supervise too many workers?

( ) Are you certain your rules don't overlap or require endless steps to get permission to carry out tasks?

( ) Do you make the objectives, directions, and time frames absolutely clear?

( ) Do you firmly enforce the deadlines you've set and make clear the consequences of nonperformance?

Do You Take the Time to Motivate?

( ) Do you explain to subordinates how their jobs contribute to the total effort?

( ) Do you reassure them of your confidence that they can perform well and deliver honest praise when they do?

( ) Do you discover your workers' ego needs and help them feel important?

( ) Do you link what you want done with the personal goals they've set for themselves?

Have You Instituted Helpful Mechanisms and Systems?

( ) Do you have a plan in place that allows subordinates' ideas to bubble up to the top?

( ) Do you show workers how to break up their jobs into logical parts?

( ) Have you designed a system to reward completion of major stages?

( ) Do you use display charts to graphically show status, improvement, and comparison of results among units?

( ) Have you a system for rewarding workers with recognition events, additional training, raises, and promotions?

21.1 CLOCKWATCHERS

Clockwatchers try to get away without working and have a "it's not my job" indifference.

These subordinates look lazy and unconcerned. They resemble dead wood, shirking work and playing hookey from meetings and projects. Clockwatchers are capable, but refuse to put forth a drop more effort than they have to.

Frequently their indifference stems from a lack of pride in the company's product/service or in their particular part in producing it. Nobody ever told them what they do is important or appreciated. Sometimes, when you scratch below their apathetic surface, you find subordinates who are frustrated by red tape or a specialty rut. If they're bored, unchallenged and underutilized, they may deliberately delay turning in their work just to get a little excitement going. They may use procrastination to create problems so that they can be recognized for solving them.

What You're Thinking

I don't know what happened to Cheryl. When she first came here, she was so full of promise and excited about working in this company. Now I can't seem to penetrate her what's-the-use attitude. The more I talk, the slower she works. Because we have to process so much data on a daily basis, when Cheryl doesn't finish, I have to give the remainder of her work to the faster workers who, of course, resent the overload. They feel they're being punished for working faster. All this has given me one big morale problem.

A Clockwatcher's Thoughts

When I first came to this office, the boss said they were looking for people able to implement the projects that would move us ahead. I wish I had taped that conversation to play back to him! I am so bored that it's torture to turn out my assigned work. My talent is untapped. I have no chance to contribute even though I'm sure many times I know a better method than the one they're using. The only way to get any notice around here is to be late with an assignment.

Strategy

Your goal is to get Clockwatchers to assume responsibility for performing their assignments on time, enabling you to treat all your workers fairly with an equitable workload.

(1) *Look first at your instructions.* What's crystal clear to you can be blurred confusion to your subordinates. Be sure you've spelled out specific objectives and deadlines.

(2) *Ask what's wrong instead of accusing.* Give Clockwatchers the chance to talk. Ask their opinions and suggestions and say you'll consider them—which doesn't mean you'll use their ideas, but will *think* about using them.

(3) *Begin a pride in the company/department/job program.* Implement a comprehensive approach including individual involvement such as discussion groups or quality circles, team competition, recognition system, and better channeling of internal and external communications. Seek subordinates' ideas and allow subordinates to make some of the decisions affecting the outcome of their tasks.

(4) *Create challenge, excitement, fun.* To make room for the spontaneous, eliminate extraneous regulations that tie workers down. Utilize their untapped potential. Not using their potential wastes a valuable resource and can be a root cause of worker dissatisfaction. Let subordinates learn something new by attending workshops, seminars, conferences, and training programs.

Tactical Talk

"FRANKLY, CHERYL, I WAS ANNOYED THAT YOU DIDN'T FINISH THIS ON TIME UNTIL IT OCCURRED TO ME THAT I MAY NOT HAVE MADE CLEAR TO YOU THE IMPORTANCE OF THIS DEADLINE..."

"WHY DO YOU THINK YOU'RE HAVING TROUBLE COMPLETING YOUR ASSIGNMENTS? ARE THERE SOME OBSTACLES YOU WANT TO TALK ABOUT? WHAT WOULD YOU SAY WILL HAPPEN IF YOU CONTINUE...? CAN YOU SUGGEST SOMETHING WE CAN DO TO GET YOU BACK ON TRACK?"

"I SENSE THAT SOME OF YOU ARE GETTING A LITTLE BORED, SO I'D LIKE ALL OF YOU TO DISCUSS AND RECOMMEND NEW WAYS TO MAKE YOUR EFFORTS MORE SATISFYING. AN EXAMPLE: ROTATING JOBS SO THAT EACH OF YOU COULD LEARN THE MAJOR ASPECTS OF THE OPERATION."

Tip: Don't nag. Learn why Procrastinators drag behind. Many Clockwatchers aspire to go higher. They're competent enough, but are frustrated because they are hog-tied or unchallenged. They feel stuck in a job that doesn't fit their ambitions and needs. If you're considering a development program for them, be sure other workers don't perceive this as a reward (as in "I work fast and get loaded down with his unfinished work. He works slowly and gets more training!"). Plan learning opportunities and job rotation as part of the broad picture, colored by input from the entire staff.

21.2 DUDS

Duds put off asking for the help they need and delay everyone else.

Clockwatchers know how to proceed. Duds don't. Although they are paralyzed by the fear of making mistakes,

Duds are ashamed to admit they don't understand some concept or don't know how to accomplish an assignment. Complex procedures perplex them, but they don't want their bosses or their peers to judge them as incompetent.

Easily frustrated, fearing failure and plagued with anxiety, they procrastinate rather than risk doing something wrong or poorly. It's the only way they can see to cope with the potential blow to their self-worth.

What You're Thinking

George keeps promising me that survey I asked for, but he doesn't deliver. This isn't the first time that I've depended on him and he didn't follow through. I need that survey for the planning session with the staff next week. I wonder why he's stalling. I never thought of George as lazy, but maybe I've been wrong. Could I have overburdened him with other assignments? I have to do something about this situation immediately.

A Dud's Thoughts

I keep telling the boss I need a little more time to finish the survey. I didn't want to upset him by saying I couldn't get it done on time for the planning meeting, but I had to have the extra time to plow through the books in order to check my work. I'm still not sure I've done it right. I wish I could hide until this problem goes away. It's not going to go away and I'm going to be fired!

Strategy

Your goal is to strengthen procrastinators you suspect are fear-ridden so that they are able to finish their work on time.

(1) *Free them to seek help when needed.* Let them know you expect to be asked when something isn't clear or if they need more information or other resources in order to proceed. Don't spoon-feed them, but nourish and support them to increase their self-confidence.

(2) *Get them to agree their procrastination is a problem.* Don't assume that they know the trouble their behavior is creating. Be clear about your priorities. Get them to identify the root cause of the delays and the probable consequences if they continue acting that way. Be calm, non-threatening and a good listener.

(3) *Decide together how the problem will be solved.* Consider if they've been mismatched in their jobs or overloaded and if you have to do some shifting of responsibilities. Agree to interim, smaller, measurable objectives and reasonable deadlines. Plan with them, not for them. Schedule times for future meetings.

(4) *Follow up with feedback and recognition.* Reward them with honest praise when they finish each stage to help them feel a sense of accomplishment. If the work isn't done on time, express your disappointment and encourage them to do better. Reinforce good completed work with other incentives.

Tactical Talk

"GEORGE, I WANT YOU TO KNOW THAT I'M AVAILABLE EVERY AFTERNOON AT 3 IF YOU HAVE ANY PROBLEMS. YOU'RE GETTING A LITTLE BEHIND SCHEDULE, WHY DON'T YOU COME IN AND WE'LL SEE WHAT WE CAN DO ABOUT IT?"

"DO YOU UNDERSTAND WHAT HAPPENS IN THE REST OF THE OFFICE WHEN YOU ARE LATE WITH YOUR PART OF THE WORK? I NEED PEOPLE I CAN DEPEND ON TO SUPPLY DATA FROM WHICH WE CAN MAKE GOOD DECISIONS. I WANT TO BE ABLE TO DEPEND ON YOU. WHY DO YOU THINK YOU'VE DELAYED TURNING IN YOUR SURVEY? THINK ABOUT THAT AND WE'LL TALK AGAIN TOMORROW, SAME TIME."

"I WISH YOU HAD COME TO ME SOONER WITH THIS, GEORGE. HERE ARE SIMILAR TYPES OF SURVEYS THAT YOU CAN USE AS A GUIDE TO

> CHECK YOURSELF. IF YOU NEED MORE HELP,
> GO SEE HARV. WE ALL NEED A HAND AT TIMES.
> IT'S NO SIN TO ASK FOR ASSISTANCE. THE SIN
> IS IN NOT ASKING FOR IT. FROM NOW ON I
> KNOW YOU'LL SPEAK UP."

Tip: Make sure your procrastinating subordinates feel comfortable about asking for help just as soon as they get stuck. Impress upon them why your priorities must be met.

Coach the Duds, reassuring them that you know they're trying. After you've done your best to relieve their fear and anxiety, and given them any additional training that's called for, a few may continue to procrastinate. Try to find a better match of worker and job or help them transfer to more suitable work.

21.3 REBELS

Rebels use delaying tactics to get even with you. Because they're afraid to tell you why they're angry, these spiteful Rebels want to get back at you without taking any risks. The tactic they choose is procrastination, using neglect, carelessness, or deliberate misbehavior to result in late and bungled projects.

Their actions may have been triggered by the way you said something or a company policy or procedure they regard as offensive. Whatever it was, it bruised their ego or made them feel inadequate, and they think the safest way to get even is to cause a slow-down in office operations. Interfering with whatever you want done gives them the satisfaction of gaining a measure of control over you.

What You're Thinking

Theo does a pretty good job of hiding his hostility, but I still sense it. I suspect that it was he who intentionally messed up the quarterly report so that it would have to be redone. Also, Theo gave me some lame excuse when he held off placing those important orders. Whenever I want to talk to him he's taking an extended lunch or out on sick leave. He must know that his delaying tactics are wrong. He's got a good job, good pay, good benefits. Why is he being a troublemaker? I have to straighten him out.

A Rebel's Thoughts

I was told during my interview that this job would give me a chance to make a difference. Instead, I find they settle for substandard results. My boss doesn't seem to care because she has her favorites to take care of. Why do we have to adhere to her stupid time schedules when there are so many other factors to be considered? There's no room here for imaginative and creative thinkers who can see more potential for the organization. We're so entrenched in procedures, we don't even know why we're working. The last time I made a suggestion, I got slapped down. I won't risk any more rejection. I'm not a part of what's going on. Well, they can just wait for this darn report while I take my time and do it over the right way. I'll show her I won't settle for her criteria.

Strategy

Your goal is to regain control by getting the Rebels to stop hiding their hostility. Until you can get them to speak to you honestly about what's troubling them, instead of resorting to procrastination as tactical revenge, you can't get them back on track.

(1) *Blame the system for the problem.* Shifting the blame away from them lets Rebels save face and gives them an opening to express themselves. Explain the situation as it appeared to you and why you consider it a problem. Listen to the response without interrupting.

(2) *Ask questions.* Put aside threats and attacks. Successful probing requires a light, friendly tone. Clear the air by making it easy for them to be open and candid with you in a private discussion. In effect, give them permission to unleash their hostility toward you.

(3) *Express agreement whenever possible.* Without getting defensive, you can be firm in that you won't allow the

operation to be jeopardized. Help them understand why they procrastinate. Together, identify potential ways to handle the situation.

Tactical Talk

"THEO, THE QUARTERLY REPORT IS QUITE LATE. THAT PRESENTS A PROBLEM FOR OUR DEPARTMENT. HOW DO YOU SUGGEST I EXPLAIN THE DELAY TO THE BIG BOSS?"

"WHY DO YOU THINK WE HAD THIS TROUBLE? THEO, PLEASE FEEL FREE TO BE FRANK. REALLY, IT WON'T BOTHER ME AND I WON'T HOLD IT AGAINST YOU IF YOU CRITICIZE SOMETHING I'VE DONE."

"YOU MAKE A GOOD POINT, THEO. BUT AS YOU KNOW WE HAVE TO TURN IN THOSE REPORTS ON TIME. WHAT WOULD YOU RECOMMEND TO CORRECT THIS SITUATION?"

Tip: Don't assume that workers who don't criticize openly, aren't critical. However if you give Rebels a chance to clear the air and let them have a say in decisions affecting their responsibilities, most of them will be glad to get back to work.

When your subordinates are procrastinating, don't just sit there and smolder until it's time for their annual evaluation. First determine why they are causing delays. If they're bored, often the ennui will flee if they're given a challenge and a voice in suggesting solutions. If they're paralyzed by fear of failure, make it easier and more acceptable for them to ask for help immediately. If they're stalling to seek revenge, get them to articulate the hostility they've been hiding. To maintain your control, you may have to (a) enable your subordinates to feel more freedom on the job and (b) explain how they benefit from your goals.

PART EIGHT

DEALING WITH RIGID/OBSTINATE PEOPLE

Rigidity kills creativity. The two are diametrically opposed. Those who demand that you do things their way because "it's the only way" wipe out any desire you have to be innovative. Rigid people have trouble adjusting to changing circumstances. Their tenacity and persistence, while admirable in pursuing goals, become detrimental as they hold fast to outmoded concepts and antiquated rules.

Unfortunately, almost every office has stubborn bosses, colleagues, and subordinates who just won't bend or budge. They're as stiff as the policies and procedures they claim are carved in stone. Some are severely strict despite the tension it produces.

Such obstinacy may be a cover-up, a way to mask fear, anger, embarrassment. Most likely, they've backed themselves into a corner and can't get out without losing face. To reach them, you first need to win their trust.

CHAPTER 22

WHEN YOUR BOSS IS UNBENDING

22.1 Comma Counters
22.2 Inflexibles
22.3 Pig Heads

At times your boss is like a race horse wearing blinders to hide his peripheral vision. Other times he's just plain stubborn as a mule.

Some bosses are so rigid about enforcing the fine print, they can't see the handwriting on the wall. Others are obstinate about making modifications even when current conditions cause hardship. Some won't change their minds because pride doesn't permit them to admit their position spells t-r-o-u-b-l-e.

In any event, you'll never reach the winner's circle telling bosses they're wrong. They'll just get defensive and become even more intractable. Especially if you embarrass them in front of others "with the facts that prove" your case. Even if they agree, they'll get back at you, consciously or subconsciously, at a later time.

Instead, start cultivating a polite, sincere, and relaxed manner. Bosses are more apt to listen when you try to show them how to get what they want while you get what you want.

22.1 COMMA COUNTERS

Comma Counters are stubbornly pedantic, demanding perfection on the insignificant.

These bosses have a petty outlook. They see the microscopic parts without also backing up to get a telescopic look at the larger picture. With overemphasis on minor details, they deify preciseness and undeviating conformity.

The problem for you is that they won't risk trying for a better way. Frequently, they not only lack imagination, but also have no *practical* understanding of what's involved in getting your job done.

What You're Thinking

My boss has tunnel vision. He's uncompromising when it comes to adhering to our procedures, clinging rigidly to our scheduling practices. Recent reports of data from other organizations show they are getting more mileage out of their facilities by slightly extending the hours and doubling the shifts. He won't listen. He just stresses the importance of keeping records and filling out forms.

A Comma Counter's Thoughts

Al is rocking the boat, but I am sticking with something I know I can depend on. The scheduling plan we've been following for years works perfectly fine. I'd better not catch him bending my rules or not completing every last one of the forms on time.

Strategy

Your goal is to help your boss get a broader view, a more comprehensive understanding of what's involved. Be straightforward. In a confident, calm yet enthusiastic tone, convey your sincerity.

(1) *Learn the history.* Maybe your boss has been burned before on that issue and, if so, let him know that *you* know he's had some experience with this. Express em-

pathy for his needs and concern for how your boss, personally, would be affected if the current practice is continued.

(2) *Present authoritative evidence whenever possible.* This is especially important if the boss believes you're asking him to put his reputation on the line. Stress the benefits that will be important to him and your organization, showing why the risk is minimal and how the changes also benefit the boss emotionally.

(3) *Scale down your request.* Keep the changes and costs to a minimum. Talk about taking smaller steps over shorter periods of time.

Tactical Talk

> "BOSS, MY CONCERN IS THAT OUR CURRENT SETUP IS NO LONGER A SAFE WAY TO GO. THE DRAIN ON OUR RESOURCES IS CAUSING..."

> "HERE'S A RECENT STUDY THAT SHOWS HOW WELL THIS APPROACH WORKED IN SEVERAL RESPECTED ORGANIZATIONS."

> "WHAT IF WE THINK ABOUT A TRIAL RUN LIMITED TO THREE MONTHS? IF THERE'S NO MARKED IMPROVEMENT OR NEW PROBLEMS ERUPT, WE CAN ALWAYS GO BACK..."

Tip: When bosses ignore larger trends, while stubbornly enforcing minor details, contrast the danger of being swept aside with the benefit of going with the flow. Reassure those who bury their heads in the sand, afraid to take risks. Talk about trial testing instead of permanent changes.

22.2 INFLEXIBLES

Inflexibles are iron-willed bosses who won't listen and stick tenaciously to their ideas.

They are in charge and don't you dare forget it. Their way is the only way because they say so. They rigorously and intolerantly impose unreasonable strictness.

Don't complain to these bosses if this causes you any difficulty. They don't want to hear why it would help you if, just this once, they'd make an exception. Their rigidity is unshakable, their resolve seemingly can't be curved, bent, or diverted. Your problems won't influence them to modify their views. They suddenly can't hear what you're saying, no matter how pointed your comment. They're too busy worrying about keeping control.

What You're Thinking

I want the boss to see that I'm smart and I can come up with good ideas. But I'm getting cold feet about making more suggestions. It's so hard to get her even to consider doing something another way or trying something new. She just wants to indoctrinate us with her ways, to follow exactly in her footsteps. The old ideas are so well insulated, new ideas can't penetrate the stone wall she's built up.

An Inflexible's Thoughts

I've got to watch Patricia a little more closely. I think she's questioning my authority. I can't have any upstart trying to diminish my power by coming up with plans for more participatory management. I'd be a fool to go along with that and lose my control over my workers.

Strategy

Your goal is to get your obstinate boss to let a friendly, fresh but critical air flow over your policies and precedents. To achieve more open discussions, try these tactics:

(1) *Understand where the boss is coming from.* In presenting your ideas, focus on management's concerns. Explain how your proposal meets the objectives the boss is always talking about. Point up probable consequences if the idea is not accepted.

(2) *Explain the mutual benefits.* Explain the benefits not only for the boss and the company, but also to you. Let the boss see how eager you are for this plan to work. Show your willingness to knock yourself out to make it succeed.

(3) *Acknowledge costs and obstacles.* If applicable, prepare a budget and list staffing suggestions. Explain how you'd overcome anticipated roadblocks.

(4) *Go in the back door by creating the market.* Begin by documenting demand, asking opinions from those who'd be using your product or service. When users become caught up with your idea, suggest how they can help you persuade your boss to bring it about.

Tactical Talk

"BOSS, I'VE HEARD YOU SAY HOW IMPORTANT IT IS FOR THE COMPANY TO INCREASE OUR NET... I SUPPOSE YOU'VE CONSIDERED CONSOLIDATING, BUT HOW WOULD IT BE IF WE WERE TO COMBINE ...?"

"I KNOW IT WOULD TAKE QUITE A BIT OF TIME TO FIGURE OUT THE LOGISTICS, BUT I'D BE HAPPY TO DO THIS ALONG WITH MY REGULAR ASSIGNMENTS..."

"I'M GLAD YOU LIKE THE IDEA. I WONDER, WOULD YOU BE WILLING TO HELP GET IT OFF THE GROUND? WOULD YOU FILL IN THIS BRIEF QUESTIONNAIRE SO I COULD TAKE YOUR THOUGHTS BACK TO MY BOSS?"

Tip: If your boss won't bend, reshape your request and repeat it. People refuse for one reason and agree for another. When bosses are determined to maintain the status quo by practicing thought control, help change their minds by pulling with them instead of against them. Tap into the potential of product/service users by getting them to change the boss's mind for you. Although you've violated no rule, should your boss accuse you of being aggressive, apologize. It's easier to say you're sorry afterwards than to get permission from an iron-willed autocrat beforehand.

22.3 PIG HEADS

Pig Heads hold to a course of action blindly, stupidly, and stubbornly. They are obstinate, poorly informed, balky bosses who stupidly and persistently adhere to some course of action. They won't listen to your arguments. You can't persuade, plead or reason with them because to get them to change their course, they'd have to admit they made a mistake. Pig Heads are prejudiced by some preconceived, unreasonable judgment they made before they had the facts and now, although the facts contradict their initial opinion, they won't budge. You feel trapped because your boss's bull-headed directives don't mesh with the tasks you're supposed to perform.

What You're Thinking

The boss doesn't know what he's talking about. He's too stubborn to listen and learn what's going on here. I'm going to be held responsible for his stupid idea that I know is going to fail. If I follow though, I get the blame. If I don't do it, the boss will dump all the lousy assignments on me.

A Pig Head's Thoughts

I may not have had actual experience in contacting new clients, but I studied the subject and I resent Sharon's arguing with me over the procedure to use. I've told all my people that I insist on everyone doing this according to my plan. If I let Sharon change the orders I gave her, that would be admitting her way is better than mine. I can't do that. It would be too embarrassing.

Strategy

Your goal is to refuse a direct order without causing resentment or being insubordinate. You want restrictions eased so that you can do your job with minimum interference and, hopefully, gain the boss's approval.

(1) *Present a substitute to the boss's plan.* Get new ideas from mentors, networks, seminars, or libraries, then ask the boss again. If you don't have time to prepare a full counterplan, you can still better the odds for success. Slip some sound suggestions into the obnoxious order.

(2) *Attempt to solve the boss's problems.* Before you present your idea, ask yourself how it would help cope with cutting costs, increasing sales, minimizing mistakes, or whatever other organizational matter is making the boss apoplectic.

(3) *Add an emotional appeal.* Link your idea to a personal longing. Do you think your boss wants to feel more secure, get more recognition, have more free time, find a stage to show off some skill?

(4) *Act as though you expect acceptance.* Your boss is more apt to agree if you anticipate agreement rather than hostility. Positive expectations encourage positive responses. Attribute to the boss traits he'd like others to think he has.

(5) *If the boss won't budge, obey the order precisely.* Don't criticize, but do get the order in writing to protect yourself. Document all your actions to show you were following the boss's orders. If you're lucky, your bull-headed boss could eventually get kicked out or transferred. If not, you've continued to do good work, armed against unfair accusations.

Tactical Talk

"FOLLOWING YOUR LINE OF THINKING, IT SEEMS THAT YOU'RE SAYING..." (*Insert your improvement. It's worth a try.*)

"I KNOW YOU AREN'T AWARE OF THE SITUATION BECAUSE IF YOU WERE YOU WOULDN'T ALLOW THIS DECLINE TO PERSIST. WHAT DO

YOU SUGGEST WE DO? WHAT WOULD YOU
THINK ABOUT...?"

"BOSS, I KNOW YOU'RE A REASONABLE PERSON
AND THE OTHER DIRECTORS OUGHT TO REC-
OGNIZE YOUR EFFORTS TO MAKE THE COM-
PANY MORE..."

"I'VE SUMMARIZED OUR DISCUSSION IN THIS
MEMO TO MAKE SURE WE PROCEED THE WAY
YOU WANT."

(You slipped in some changes and the boss balks.) "OK,
I'LL PREPARE ANOTHER MEMO FOR YOUR SIG-
NATURE CORRECTING THE ITEMS YOU
POINTED OUT." *(Once he signs, the boss—not you—
will be held responsible.)*

Tip: Do all you can to let your boss save face. Bolster him
instead of saying he's wrong. Ask if doing something else
might help. When a pig-headed boss refuses to budge and
your experience and instincts tell you that you're in jeopardy,
survival requires you protect yourself. Written records and
signed instructions become a bullet-proof vest. Arm yourself.

Concentrate on the wants of rigid and obstinate bosses.
If you hit the right button, they themselves will find justifi-
cation for doing what you suggest. If your boss believes that
you are really sincere in wanting to help him, that you've
somehow tied your future with the boss's, then he'll begin to
trust you. The stubborn walls will start tumbling down.

CHAPTER 23

WHEN YOUR COLLEAGUES ARE UNBENDING

23.1 Killjoys
23.2 Chapter and Versers
23.3 Stiff Necks

Rigid teammates bury their emotions. That allows them to treat other people as things to be placed or pigeonholed. That lets them appear uncaring about your strengths and weaknesses and inconsiderate of your feelings. Their tunnel vision is centered only on the concept or issue or regulation they want you to accept or follow.

To get stubborn cohorts to see another track besides the one they're on, stop looking for "either your way or my way" solutions. Hopefully, together, you can resolve the matter to your *mutual* satisfaction. Rather than one winning and the other losing, practice negotiating so that both of you get what you're after.

23.1 KILLJOYS

Killjoys give you moral or official reasons why it's wrong to enjoy the work.

Killjoys are so stiff that rigor mortis has already set in. They are doggedly determined to sap the pleasure out of anything you're working on. Their remarks take away every last drop of fun you used to get from working in the office.

Because Killjoys are angry, resentful, or bitter, they make it seem a sin to lighten up. They stringently limit their subordinates and try to carry over their rigidity to you, their peers. They won't let anyone enjoy a relaxed and pleasant working environment.

What You're Thinking

Telling Sandy to stop being so restrictive is like telling him to stop breathing. For some reason, he's feeling terribly unhappy and he's taking it out on everybody around him. Is that how he copes with unhappiness? Okay, so he's got some problem that's overwhelmingly complicated. Does that mean he can't allow other people to enjoy themselves while he's miserable?

A Killjoy's Thoughts

We're being paid to produce, not to have fun. What's the matter with these people? I try to tell them the right thing to do and they give me the silent treatment or they walk away. It's embarrassing to be left alone standing there. I feel so isolated in this office. Nobody ever includes me when they go out to lunch or asks me to join them for coffee. Well, at least now I've got them paying attention to me.

Strategy

Your goal is to improve the office climate by reducing the tension and bringing the Killjoys back into the fold.

(1) *Be a friend.* Their rigid behavior makes you want to isolate them. Your isolating them makes them more rigid. Break the cycle. Be willing to be the good listener, a sponge that sops up the anger or hurt that spills out.

(2) *Help them find answers.* Ask questions that get them to identify their viable alternatives for resolving their difficulty. Help the Killjoys get back on course.

(3) *Use laughter and gentle teasing.* Laugh, not in derision but in amusement, at their solemnity and rigidity. Play back their words. It's easier for them to say you misunderstood them than to admit they're wrong.

Tactical Talk

"SANDY, YOU SEEM SAD. IS THERE ANYTHING I CAN DO TO HELP YOU?"

"WELL, HOW DO YOU THINK THAT COULD BE COUNTERACTED? SANDY, WHAT WOULD IT TAKE?"

"IT'S POSSIBLE I DIDN'T HEAR YOU RIGHT, BUT, SANDY, DO YOU KNOW WHAT YOU JUST SAID? YOU SAID THAT...DID YOU MEAN TO SOUND LIKE AN OLD-FASHIONED SCHOOLMASTER WITH A HICKORY STICK?"

Tip: You don't have to suffer the Killjoys. If you didn't have a choice, you'd be stuck with accepting their dogmatism. But you do have alternatives than can lessen the tension you mention.

To expand your options, look at your need to reduce the stress and restore a pleasant climate. While it's a normal reaction to get back at Killjoys, it has the opposite effect and increases the strain. Try another tack and *help* the Killjoys to remove their dark clouds.

23.2 CHAPTER AND VERSERS

Chapter and Versers know and quote you every company rule and regulation.

Each policy and procedure is committed to memory. Touch on any topic and these colleagues will spout another executive order. Their knowledge is so detailed, itemized, and precise that they can recite the exact wording of every directive or taboo ever committed to the papers they shuffle.

Chapter and Versers are rigidly unfeeling. They seem to be numb to any personal needs and firmly unyielding when it comes to obeying the letter of the law.

What You're Thinking

We don't need a manual when Stuart is around. He's a self-proclaimed guardian of our procedures. Who appointed him the cop to keep law and order? Every time the discussion deviates from our directives he's ready to pull us back. Maybe we'd come up with good recommendations, but his one-track mind discourages us from even trying.

A Chapter and Verser's Thoughts

There's a right way and a wrong way to go about this. I can't understand why they don't follow the rules that have been set forth. Why are they being so stubborn? Yes, here it is, the order I told them about. Maybe if I show it to them in writing they'll see...

Strategy

Your goal is to work in a more relaxed manner by getting the Chapter and Versers to loosen their grip on all those rules.

(1) *Get them to go beyond what is to what might be.* Only when you do this will their droning stop and your mutual resentment dissipate.

(2) *Appeal to Chapter and Versers' self-image.* Talk about the way they see themselves, as the organized, efficient group's memory.

Tactical Talk

"STUART, WE KNOW YOU'RE TRYING TO HELP, BUT I THINK WE ALL NEED TO UNDERSTAND THE REASON FOR RULES. THEY EXIST TO FIT THE NEEDS OF OUR ORGANIZATION AND ITS PEOPLE. NOT VICE VERSA; WE DON'T EXIST TO FIT THE RULES."

"YOU HAVE SO MUCH KNOWLEDGE THAT COULD BENEFIT US AND I'M SURE YOU WANT TO. NOW AFTER WE ALL EXPLORE THE POSSIBILITY OF REALIGNING, WHY DON'T YOU HELP US ORGANIZE THE RESULTS OF OUR BRAINSTORMING? YOUR EFFICIENCY CAN TURN ALL THOSE LOOSE IDEAS INTO NEAT COMPARTMENTED PLATTERS WE CAN SERVE THE BOSS."

Tip: Don't let Chapter and Versers lace your creative efforts into a strait jacket. Win them over by promising to enlist their computer brains *after* you look for better ways.

23.3 STIFF NECKS

Stiff Necks are inflexible, arrogant co-workers who say they always did it this way and they always will.

These dogmatic colleagues don't need proof to preach that their opinions are correct. They are totally unbending in their beliefs and self-righteous (almost snobbish) in articulating them.

Stiff Necks refuse to change. They want to preserve the status quo, whatever the cost.

What You're Thinking

Melissa thinks if you don't agree with her you're wrong. You become the enemy. She doesn't see the subtle changes that are taking place in the market. There are trends and patterns emerging which Melissa refuses to acknowledge. We can't let her horse-and-buggy ideas influence our decisions and hold us back.

A Stiff Neck's Thoughts

If they knew a little more about the background of the organization, they wouldn't be so quick to want to change our policies. We struggled hard to get where we are. We went through the testing stages from which good, appropriate decisions evolved. I know we're on solid ground now. What they're suggesting is too risky.

Strategy

Your goal is to move in the direction that's best for your organization. This will take open-minded discussions and a willingness to examine all facets and viewpoints.

(1) *Stick to the issues.* Raise the level of discussion when it sinks to personal attacks. Soothe the wounded feelings of Stiff Necks who take the disagreement as an insult to themselves.

(2) *Let the Stiff Necks salvage their pride.* Let them save face so that they *can* change their minds. Give them a gracious way out.

Tactical Talk

"MELISSA, FROM WHAT YOU'VE TOLD US ABOUT YOUR EXPERIENCES, I CAN SEE WHY YOU FEEL AS YOU DO. PLEASE EXPLAIN TO US THE IMPORTANCE OF MAINTAINING..."

"WE UNDERSTAND YOU REGARD MARTY'S PRO-POSAL AS TOO PROGRESSIVE. SPECIFICALLY, HOW WOULD YOU COMPARE YOUR POSITION TO MARTY'S?"

"IT SEEMS TO ME THAT THE TWO POSITIONS AREN'T REALLY THAT FAR APART. WE ALL AGREE THAT (1)..., (2)..., (3)..., AND WE DISAGREE ON (1)... (2)... LET'S EXAMINE THOSE LAST TWO POINTS AGAIN AND MAYBE, BY PUTTING OUR HEADS TOGETHER, WE CAN COME UP WITH A BETTER POSSIBILITY."

Tip: Sometimes it's necessary to gently massage the Stiff Necks to get them to act cooperatively. They cling to the status quo because it makes them feel secure. Let them feel you respect their opinions and that *they have a part* in moving the group from the old position.

When rigid, obstinate colleagues bring about tense situations it's tempting to walk out or move to another part of the room, or better yet, to tell them off and embarrass them. But such responses only make matters worse. For your own sake, to help make your office a more comfortable place to be, disagree in a pleasant and friendly fashion. Bring them in instead of shutting them out.

CHAPTER 24

WHEN YOUR SUBORDINATES ARE UNBENDING

24.1 Silent Screwups

24.2 Unyielders

24.3 Clingers

Rigid and obstinate subordinates, like Mary, Mary, are quite contrary. They are growing a garden of goofs because they persist in some error or stubbornly stick to a procedure even though you've shown them a better way. If they oppose a rule, they ignore your orders for as long as they can get away with it.

These subordinates aren't anxious to hear any advice you have to give them. If you can't leave them alone, they want you to feel sorry for them or compliment them, anything but tell them how to do their jobs. Their dogged and often unreasonable resistance makes them hard to handle.

24.1 SILENT SCREWUPS

Silent Screwups need help, but are too proud and stubborn to ask.

They have false pride. They are usually ashamed to ask for help. They're afraid that their receiving assistance will somehow jeopardize their job.

As a result, they chronically botch up their assignments. They persist in doing something that may be wrong because they won't ask first for more information or some support. They can't understand that it's smart to get help, and their poor judgment in stubbornly insisting that they go it alone results in unnecessarily inept performance.

What You're Thinking

It's so hard to get through to Fred. He acts as if everyone were expected to know everything about every phase of our operation. By the time I finally realized that he was having trouble with his assignment, we lost a lot of valuable time. Why was he so stubborn about coming to me earlier?

A Silent Screwup's Thoughts

The boss is nice to me and I hate to disappoint him. But sometimes I can't figure out what the devil he expects me to do, especially on jobs I haven't handled before. Sometimes I fake it and it turns out okay; other times it's a mess. But if I ask the boss for more explanation or somebody to help me, he'll know I'm not as good as he thought I was. He'll send me back to my old unit.

Strategy

Your goal is to bolster the self-concept of Silent Screwups so that they feel secure enough to ask for help just as soon as they need it. Afraid or ashamed, they won't open up until they feel less vulnerable.

(1) *Be clear about your expectations.* Demonstrate your patience and reasonableness in anticipating their growth, along with being ready, willing, and able to help. Assign tasks that can develop their weak skills or increase their learning experience. Role play situations they find difficult to handle. Suggest outside self-improvement resources. Increase the frequency of your feedback.

(2) *Be sure your instructions are crystal clear.* Supplement your verbal orders with written instructions. Include

deadlines for every step, exceptions to the rules, who or where to turn to for help, what equipment or data to use, how to report the progress.

(3) *Help the Screwups accept responsibility.* Encourage their coming in early for help, but when they do, stretch their minds. Instead of telling them what to do, ask for their ideas on how to solve the problem.

Tactical Talk

"FRED, I REALLY BELIEVE YOU HAVE THE PO-TENTIAL TO GO AS FAR AS YOU WANT IN THIS ORGANIZATION. I WANT TO HELP YOU BE-CAUSE I THINK YOU'RE WORTH THE TIME AND EFFORT. HOWEVER, IF I'M GOING TO SUCCEED IN THAT WE'RE BOTH GOING TO HAVE TO MAKE SOME CHANGES."

"HERE'S A FOLDER WITH ALL THE INFORMA-TION YOU NEED FOR YOUR NEXT ASSIGNMENT. LET'S REVIEW IT FIRST LINE BY LINE AND DIS-CUSS HOW YOU THINK YOU SHOULD PRO-CEED."

"WHAT DO YOU THINK YOU MIGHT NEED TO FINISH IT?...HAVE YOU THOUGHT ABOUT DOING ...? DO YOU THINK IT WOULD HELP IF...?"

Tip: Silent Screwups need your reassurance that it's a sign of wisdom to know what you don't know, admit it, and get help. They aren't goof offs and they don't want to mess up. They just stubbornly refuse to open up until you assist them in overcoming their fear or embarrassment.

24.2 UNYIELDERS

Unyielders won't give an inch, can't relax, and create a tense atmosphere.

Unyielders are martinets, rigid soldiers who are sticklers for detail and overly precise. They can't comprehend exceptions to the rule or mitigating circumstances.

These subordinates won't move from the position they've taken no matter how you pressure or beg them to ease up and do something another way. They are taut and tense and make everyone else nervous.

What You're Thinking

Michael takes every directive so literally, he's not using his common sense. Nobody punches time clocks in this office, but he won't leave until he's put in exactly eight hours. He'd rather sit there twiddling his thumbs than go home early when he's through ahead of time. And when it would help us, he won't stay late when he's not finished. The other workers resent his unbending attitude. He makes his cohorts feel uncomfortable.

An Unyielder's Thoughts

The boss seems to have forgotten how he yelled at me for not following his orders. Well, I promised myself never again would I give him a reason to embarrass me like that. Now I dot every i and cross every t. I don't care what the others think about this, I'm playing it safe and following every regulation to the letter of the law.

Strategy

Your goal is to get the Unyielders to relax so that you can restore some calm in your office.

(1) *Determine why unyielders are being difficult.* They often act in an obstinate manner because they are annoyed or angry. Get their criticism to surface. If you don't have the power to correct the problem, take their complaint up to your boss.

(2) *Re-examine your procedures.* Look for an excess of red tape or superstructure, inequitable policies, infrequent or vague feedback.

(3) *Rubdown with humor.* As the boss, you set the mood for the office. It's okay to poke fun at the overdone preciseness but not at the overly precise workers.

Tactical Talk

"MICHAEL, YOU APPEAR TO BE SOMEWHAT ON EDGE LATELY. IS ANYTHING THE MATTER? CAN WE TALK ABOUT IT?"

"WELL, YES, MICHAEL, NOW THAT YOU BRING IT UP, I THINK THAT TYPE OF DECISION COULD HAVE BEEN MADE AT YOUR LEVEL. MAYBE I CAN TAKE SOME STEPS TO MODIFY OUR PROCESS."

Tip: Workers who are unbending aren't talking about why they act that way. When neither gentle coaxing nor forceful commands get Unyielders to relax, try instituting a system for listening to and gathering ideas. For example, invite a few of your workers at a time, on a rotating basis, to your inner circle management meetings.

24.3 CLINGERS

Clingers commit themselves to inadequately thought-out ideas and won't let go.

They hold on tenaciously to some opinion or proposal. Their stubborn firmness ignores logic. They hold fast because they've become emotionally attached to an idea or procedure. Stubborn and intractable, Clingers are particularly difficult to supervise because they go off half-cocked. They hastily and prematurely decide on a course of action without adequate preparation and then feel they have to stay glued to that decision.

What You're Thinking

I wish Ruth would analyze the issues more thoroughly and methodically before jumping to conclusions. She gets overly enthusiastic about an idea without fully comprehending what's involved. Sometimes with a little bit of luck, it works out okay. On other occasions, by the time she realizes that she moved too quickly, she's in too deep. To get out would be embarrassing, so she stubbornly holds on and tries to make it work. At times she can maneuver all of us enough to help save the day. Other times the combination of unrealistic optimism and stubborn pride is a disaster.

A Clinger's Thoughts

I know the boss thinks I get too carried away with some of my ideas, but if I sit around and wait for more studies to be done, I'd never get anywhere. If it feels right, you have to move on your instincts and take the risks. If it doesn't work out, I can usually salvage something without having to admit I made a mistake.

Strategy

Your goal is to help Clingers balance their optimism by giving their proposals more careful consideration before they act.

(1) *Be consistent in what you expect.* If some subordinates tend to oversimplify the problems and get themselves in a position where they can't back out, you may need to get firm. Demand that they first clearly define the problem and ask enough questions to spell out the many facets of the issues. If they learn to look before they leap, there will be less clinging to hastily and poorly conceived ideas.

(2) *Discuss consequences in advance.* They can't learn to be responsible if you assume their obligations and bail them out of difficulties. Talk about worst-case scenarios and ask the Clingers what they would do "if." Get them to include in their planning ways to avoid trouble spots or overcome obstacles. This will free them from stubbornly holding on to a bad call out of pride or embarrassment.

(3) *Shift the focus.* Move from harping on what they're doing wrong to what is needed to improve themselves. Convey an understanding and trusting tone.

Tactical Talk

"RUTH, YOU MAY HAVE SOMETHING VERY GOOD HERE, BUT IT'S IMPORTANT THAT YOU GET A BETTER HANDLE ON THE SITUATION. DO A LITTLE MORE RESEARCH, AND BE PREPARED TO ANSWER THE WHO / WHAT / WHEN /WHERE /WHY /HOW QUESTIONS BEFORE YOU GO ANY FURTHER."

"THIS LOOKS GOOD, BUT WE OUGHT TO BE PREPARED FOR POTENTIAL SNAGS. WHAT WOULD YOU DO IF SUPPLIES AREN'T HERE ON THE PROMISED DATE AND THE..."

"RUTH, YOUR IDEAS ARE EXCITING, AND I WANT YOU TO KEEP COMING UP WITH THEM. ONCE YOU PUT THEM ON A MORE SOLID FOUNDATION, YOU'LL HAVE REAL WINNERS."

Tip: Help Clingers maintain their enthusiasm without jumping the gun. When optimists get out of hand they need the careful inspection of pessimists for balance and to achieve a realistic plan. Once they've given advanced thought to what could go wrong, they can plan for it or change course without having to cling stubbornly to a losing proposition.

Fear, false pride, annoyance, and anger are largely responsible for subordinates acting rigid and obstinate. You can best cope with these attitudes and improve the climate in your office by helping your workers feel more secure. Put greater stress on clearly communicating your instructions and expectations, offering genuine support and improved feedback, listening for signs of hostility, and giving them a way out when they feel their pride is tied to their stubborn stance.

PART NINE

DEALING WITH TIGHT-LIPPED/TACITURN PEOPLE

It takes two to tango, tangle, and talk to each other. How exasperating it is to try to get a discussion going when the other person cuts you off with a clipped "yes" or "no" or becomes totally mute. You can't communicate unless both of you listen *and respond* to what you heard or think you heard.

Some uncommunicative bosses, colleagues, and subordinates are simply contemplative types who need more time to come to a conclusion. They may be the quiet type who keep thoughts to themselves, not commenting if what you're saying doesn't interest them. They easily become responsive, however, when you pose relevant, direct, open-ended questions.

More difficult are the taciturn types who are afraid to open up. Maybe you've hurt their feelings, but they depend on you for their security. Maybe their keeping your good opinion of them looms so large that they can't get a word out. Some are silent and stone-faced for fear if they reveal their emotions, you'll think they're out of control. Tight-lipped people clam up, sulk, stare, or grin to hide what they're thinking. Getting any of them to express their thoughts is a tough challenge.

CHAPTER 25

WHEN YOUR BOSS IS UNCOMMUNICATIVE

25.1 Icebergs
25.2 Clams
25.3 Evaders

You don't know where you stand because the boss isn't telling you. The word feedback is not in his vocabulary. Furthermore, you don't know if he's silent because he's displeased with your work but just doesn't want a hassle. Or he could be angry at you and expects you to read his mind. Maybe his silence has nothing to do with you; perhaps he's just the secretive type who keeps his thoughts tightly wrapped because he doesn't want to have to defend his decisions.

Whether bosses are unsociable, unresponsive, or evasive, their silence makes you feel, at the least, uneasy. Some of you allow their attitude to gnaw at your nerves until you are literally worried sick.

25.1 ICEBERGS

Iceberg bosses are unsociable, aloof, and disinterested in exchanging thoughts.

They are so cold you feel the shivers go up and down your spine as they approach. It's true some bosses *deliberately* try to intimidate you, using stony silence the way bullies use loud threats. But Icebergs are not out to scare or subdue you. They're not even thinking about you. They are merely reserved, undemonstrative, secretive people who've decided to button their lips.

You are often dealing with a loner, at least as far as decision making is concerned. Icebergs don't want your input. They don't care to share their plans or justify them to you. They're not interested in your arguments because they've already made up their minds.

What You're Thinking

If you can count the daily "Good Morning" grunt, the boss hardly says two words to me. I don't think he's angry at me. It's more like I hardly exist. No matter how hard I try, I'm just not very important to him. There's no way to bore through that polar block of ice that buffers him from his staff people.

An Iceberg's Thoughts

The operations seem to be progressing very well. I hope none of the staff people wants to see me this morning because I have some important decisions to make and I don't want to be disturbed.

Strategy

Your goal is to get the boss's attention and be reassured that you're on the right track. To get the boss to open up, find some way to help your boss and thereby help yourself. You don't have to become best friends, you just want the boss to feel friendly toward you. What do most bosses need? More time, less work, and good news.

(1) *Look for time savers.* In your own little niche, go over every step that involves the boss. Can you make your reports more succinct? Can you quantify and qualify data so that it's faster for the boss to utilize the information?

(2) *Look for work savers.* Is there some task you could offer to take over because it really doesn't require the boss's

high-level decision making? Are there items that can be combined for an easier and sharper review by the boss?

(3) *Look for morale boosters—yours and the boss's.* Accept your boss the way he is without taking his aloofness as a personal affront. Keep your finger on the office pulse. If you're not getting the latest news from your boss, get it from the grapevine. Recount to your boss positive reactions you've observed. Study your professional or trade journals to extract and report encouraging signs or trends.

Tactical Talk

"BOSS, I THINK WE COULD SHAVE QUITE A BIT OF TIME OFF OUR STAFF MEETINGS BY DISTRIBUTING BACKGROUND DATA ON AGENDA ITEMS IN ADVANCE..."

"BOSS, IF IT MEETS YOUR APPROVAL, I'D BE HAPPY TO PREPARE THE EXECUTIVE SUMMARY FOR YOUR REVIEW AND SIGNATURE..."

"GLORIA, I'M GLAD YOU COULD MEET ME FOR LUNCH. I WANTED TO ASK IF YOU'RE HAVING ANY LUCK GETTING THROUGH TO THE BOSS...COULD YOU FILL ME IN ON WHAT'S HAPPENING WITH..."

Tip: You have to pay the price to melt the ice. Exert more effort to meet whatever it is the boss needs. When Iceberg bosses play their cards close to their chest and refuse to deal you in on their plans, your move is to earn their trust and make them your friends. Unless you win their confidence, the Icebergs' frigidity will keep you at a distance.

25.2 CLAMS

Clams are unresponsive and refuse to tell you why they're silent. Like their namesake mollusks, these bosses retreat into their hard shells and clam up. They won't divulge what you want to hear. Their silence is intimidating because you don't know what it means. Your self-confidence erodes. You sweat and fret from lack of feedback.

Unlike Icebergs, Clams may use silence manipulatively. The absence of sound makes you feel uncomfortable and you start to blabber. You rush to stop the hush, spilling out information that you might otherwise not reveal. Perhaps being uncommunicative is the Clams' means of avoiding commitment. But there's no point in guessing their motives when what you need is data on how you're doing.

What You're Thinking

I worked hard on that proposal and I thought it was a darn good idea. Now I'm beginning to lose faith in my own judgment. Perhaps the boss needs more information before reaching a conclusion. On the other hand, maybe the boss doesn't like the idea or resents my coming up with ideas. Was it a bad suggestion or bad timing? Does his silence say my work is acceptable or that I'm incompetent? Is he still considering it? I don't have a clue because the boss isn't talking. How can I crack the shell?

A Clam's Thoughts

Terry's proposal on combined purchasing for the units has some merit even though he hasn't had as much experience as I have in dealing with that issue. But it's too early to commit myself. I don't want to say anything one way or another until I give this a lot more study.

Strategy

Your goal is to restore your confidence by getting some good, useful feedback.

(1) *Use questions to pry open the Clam.* Avoid queries that can be answered with a yes or no nod. Ask open-ended questions. Go after detailed, specific information.

(2) *Don't move a muscle until the Clam responds.* Ask your question, then wait, smiling—without uttering another

word—until you get a reply. Turn the tables and use the silence to your advantage. Don't rush your Clam, who may be deep in thought, weighing your words before reaching a decision.

Tactical Talk

"BOSS, SINCE YOU HAVEN'T SAID ANYTHING YET ABOUT MY PROPOSAL, I ASSUME YOU NEED MORE TIME TO ASSESS IT. ON WHICH TOPICS WOULD YOU WANT ADDITIONAL INFORMA-TION?"

"BOSS, LAST WEEK YOU LISTED SEVERAL OB-JECTIVES. I BELIEVE I COULD MAKE BETTER USE OF MY TIME IF I KNEW WHICH ONES ARE TAGGED AS YOUR TOP PRIORITY?"

Tip: Forget about psychoanalyzing bosses who clam up. If you don't get the feedback you need, generate some useful responses. Stop acting intimidated. If you'll carefully think through your questions before you ask, you'll be able to stay calm and composed. The underlying message that you send should be: We're on the same team, so what can I do to help you?

25.3 EVADERS

Evaders won't discuss issues because they dislike and avoid confrontations.

These bosses are nice people, but can be namby-pamby leaders. They don't like arguments and, consequently, won't discuss, debate, or dispute. They keep still because if they don't say what they're thinking, no one can think they're wrong.

Some became Evaders after they overcommitted themselves instead of saying no. In trying to avoid hard feelings or a fight, they ended up breaking their promise and causing the friction they were trying to avert. Evaders refrain from criticizing even when they're angry that something isn't done the way they want. To have a confrontation might look as though they were out of control. To them, it's safer to be silent.

What You're Thinking

I asked the boss what she thought about the new method of figuring depreciation. All I got was generalities. Nothing specific that I could work with. What should I do when I'm not getting the guidance I need? Should I go over her head? Should I stick my neck out and make my own decision?

An Evader's Thoughts

I didn't give Charlie a direct answer when he asked my opinion of the new method. I could see he was spoiling for a fight and he can just take his aggression out on someone else. Besides it will help develop his character to do more research and think something through for himself.

Strategy

Your goal is to force the Evader to come out in the open. If there's hostility, you both have to deal with it and get it resolved.

(1) *Make an appointment with your boss.* Don't go into any detail. Just schedule ten minutes of the boss's time. You can't keep avoiding each other or dismissing the fact that you're not communicating.

(2) *Get directly to the point of the meeting.* After expressing your desire to attain your mutual objectives, state what you are sensing. Be frank but friendly, and very careful not to show any signs of annoyance.

Tactical Talk

"BOSS, I KNOW WE BOTH WANT OUR OPERA-
TION TO BE AS COST-CONSCIOUS AND EFFI-
CIENT AS POSSIBLE, SO I THINK WE REALLY

HAVE TO TALK ABOUT THE BEST WAYS TO
ACHIEVE OUR MUTUAL GOALS."

"I THINK I MAY HAVE INADVERTENTLY UPSET
YOU, AND IF I HAVE, BOSS, I APOLOGIZE. HOW-
EVER, I DON'T KNOW WHAT I'VE DONE WRONG
OR WHAT YOU MAY WANT ME TO DO TO COR-
RECT IT."

Tip: When dealing with Evaders, you have to force their hand
because they'll go to any length to avoid an argument. If you
sense hostility, be particularly tactful and composed in order
to get the matter discussed. If you feel your boss is afraid of
taking risks, supply more concrete or dependable information.
If you're still not getting an answer, write a memo to the boss
stating what you plan to do and, upon hearing no objection,
do it.

Tight-lipped and taciturn bosses are particularly frustrating because they may or may not be reacting to something
you did or didn't do. But it's not good for you to continue
working under the stress of uncertainty. You must get your
boss to open up. The best way is to take the initiative and
politely, professionally, ask open-ended questions that can
give you the direction you're seeking.

CHAPTER 26

WHEN YOUR COLLEAGUES ARE UNCOMMUNICATIVE

26.1 Skeptics

26.2 Withholders

26.3 Glarer-Starers

You work side by side with colleagues who won't talk to you. You try, but you can't get through. Sometimes you get the feeling that they mistrust you although you believe you've acted honorably. Some coworkers are uncooperatively silent when you can't remember doing anything that might have offended them. Others you know are angry because they send you fierce and fiery looks, but they won't disclose why. They won't utter a word.

You've concluded that these colleagues are nursing hurt feelings. Apparently, they're annoyed or angry at something you said or did. However, their messages aren't clear and it's difficult to concentrate on your work once their negative vibrations have become transparent.

26.1 SKEPTICS

Skeptics are suspicious. They look for some proof before opening up to you.

Skeptics are not hostile or cold, yet they are barely luke-warm. They don't know if they can trust you. That makes them hesitate before they'll commit or confide.

They question your intentions, doubt your sincerity, and wonder if you're hatching some plot. As far as they're concerned, the jury is still out on your case. In the meantime, the climate in your office is getting a little sticky and damp.

What You're Thinking

I wonder why Roger reacts so slowly and begrudgingly when I make a suggestion or comment. I get the feeling that he's questioning my motives. But I'm not sure because he so seldom speaks to me and, when he does, it's usually a one-word response. I think it would help us both if we could talk.

A Skeptic's Thoughts

I'm still not sure about Jim. I don't know what he's up to or if I can depend on him. He suggested I join him in preparing that report. If I do, will I get left holding the bag? I'd better play it safe and remain noncommittal with Jim. The less I say to him, the better, at least for now.

Strategy

Your goal is to convince Skeptics that you truly aim to help your group/department/company. Show that your suggestions are not meant as self-serving.

(1) *Supply evidence of your good faith.* Let your good idea become "ours" rather than "mine." Report to Skeptics useful news they may not have heard. When you finish early, offer to help them.

(2) *Be up front.* Explain more carefully the mutual benefits, but don't hide the obstacles. Make a promise and keep it. Inspire confidence by your reassuring attitude.

(3) *Nudge, don't push.* Be willing to move slowly and gently instead of aggressively. Be sincere and honest in expressing compliments and appreciation.

Tactical Talk

> "ROGER, I'M THROUGH WITH MY DAILY STACK. CAN I GIVE YOU A HAND? DID YOU HEAR THE LATEST RULING THAT JUST CAME DOWN FROM PERSONNEL?"

> "I KNOW YOU CAN SEE WHY IT WOULD BE TIME-SAVING, BUT I SHOULD POINT OUT A COUPLE OF POTENTIAL PROBLEMS. MAYBE YOU CAN SUGGEST HOW WE CAN GO AROUND THE ROADBLOCKS."

> "TAKE YOUR TIME. THERE'S NO RUSH. BUT I REALLY WOULD APPRECIATE HEARING YOUR OPINION."

Tip: Trust isn't earned overnight. It's a slow, protracted process to persuade Skeptics that you're for real. If you've been pushing too hard, show more patience by first laying a good foundation for the trust you want them to bank on.

26.2 WITHHOLDERS

Withholders hold back telling you the information you need.

Withholding is sulking wearing a disguise. Withholders usually know more than you do about a given subject and are hurt that you haven't acknowledged their expertise. Consequently, in order to make you come to them, they tell you none or only part of what you have to know. They won't cooperate until you verbalize your recognition and appreciation of their knowledge. Their buttoning up is a frustrating tactic, but it sure gets your attention.

What You're Thinking

Gretchen has finished making the latest projections, but she's not parting with that information. She says it's too soon to be sure she's right, but that's just an excuse not to give us what we need so that we can proceed with our planning. Could it be that she's acting childish and just wants to be begged?

A Withholder's Thoughts

If they want my information, they can show me a little more respect. I stay late and go over my figures very carefully to be sure they're correct. Then they come by demanding my data without taking the time to recognize my efforts. They are completely uninformed in this area. They need me. You think they'd show some appreciation.

Strategy

Your goal is to get Withholders to give you the required information.

(1) *Give the devil his due.* Soothe their wounded egos. Couch your request more tactfully. Be more generous with warranted praise and appreciation.

(2) *Come in the side door.* When Withholders won't answer your direct request, ask them to confirm your conclusions or the limited facts you were able to gather. Admit your ignorance and ask them to fill you in. Inquire how they would go about tackling your problem.

Tactical Talk

"GRETCHEN, I DON'T KNOW WHAT THIS DIVISION WOULD DO WITHOUT YOUR TALENT. YOU'RE THE ONE WHO'S KEPT US POINTED IN THE RIGHT DIRECTION. I'M GOING TO NOMINATE YOU FOR EMPLOYEE OF THE MONTH."

"I REALIZE YOU'RE NOT READY TO SHARE YOUR PROJECTIONS WITH US, BUT I WONDER IF YOU'D LOOK AT THIS. THIS IS WHAT WE THINK WE'RE FACING. ADMITTEDLY, WE'RE ALL NOT SHARP ON THIS SUBJECT. MAYBE YOU COULD FILL IN A FEW GAPS."

Tip: Give Withholders the credit they deserve. Withholders are sulkers. You've hurt their feelings and they're getting back at you. Remedy the wrong, and the information you need will start pouring right out.

26.3 GLARER-STARERS

Glarer-Starers silently express their anger through fixed, hostile looks.

These colleagues bottle up their anger because they're afraid of a fight. Their body language, however, broadcasts their ire or indignation. They act as though you ought to be able to read their minds. That makes no sense because they give you no clues.

Sometimes, Glarer-Starers are so deeply hurt that they are unable to talk about the cause. You try to reach them and you're rebuffed.

What You're Thinking

I asked Larry what was wrong when he started with those contemptuous stares. All day he's been looking right through me as though I'm something less than human. He said nothing was wrong, with a childish pout, as if I'm supposed to know what ticked him off.

A Glarer-Starer's Thoughts

I'm furious at the way Bill is taking advantage and dumping his extra cases on me. Did I give him any indication that I was looking for more work? I don't think I helped bring about this situation, but I can't confront Bill about it. I'm so angry, I'm afraid I'll get emotional and start yelling and losing control. That would be unprofessional and I'll lose everyone's respect.

Strategy

Your goal is to get the Glarer-Starers to discuss the problem. If their actions seem childish, then it's up to you to remain in control.

(1) *Offer an olive branch.* Show you want peace by trying to get the problem out in the open where it can be resolved. Suggest a neutral setting, maybe meeting for lunch.

(2) *Be quietly persistent.* If your friendship offer is refused, try again. Keep trying, until eventually the Glarer-Starers reveal what's bothering them.

(3) *Prepare for the next controversy.* Discuss how you both want to handle disagreements.

Tactical Talk

"LOOK, LARRY, WOULDN'T YOU AGREE THAT UP TO NOW WE'VE HAD A PRETTY GOOD AND HONEST RELATIONSHIP? I WANT TO PRESERVE THAT."

"YOU SAY NOTHING IS WRONG AND THAT'S GOOD. BUT I FEEL THERE IS SOMETHING YOU WANT TO GET OFF YOUR CHEST. IF SOMETHING *IS* WRONG, I'M SURE YOU'D WANT US TO REMEDY THE PROBLEM."

"IN THE FUTURE WHEN EITHER OF US GETS MAD, WE'RE GOING TO HAVE TO BE MORE FRANK AND STRAIGHTFORWARD AND WILLING TO DISCUSS THE SITUATION, DON'T YOU AGREE?"

Tip: While silence and penetrating stares appear to be a juvenile approach, sometimes Glarer-Starers are not ready to discuss the problem. They may be deeply hurt with emotions still too close to the surface. Nevertheless, they usually do want to talk to you, so keep plugging away at being a friend.

Colleagues who figuratively or literally stop talking to you may distrust your motives or feel disappointed, hurt, or angry at something you've done. Since they refuse to tell you what that is, first concentrate on winning back their confidence before you continue playing detective.

CHAPTER 27

WHEN YOUR SUBORDINATES ARE UNCOMMUNICATIVE

27.1 Grinners

27.2 Worriers

27.3 Tongue-Tieds

You think you're a good, kind boss, and it surprises you to learn that some of your workers don't feel comfortable with you. They try to hide it, but they're scared. Whatever they ask you, however they respond to your questions, no matter what they do, they are afraid you'll think they're ignorant or foolish or incapable.

The desire to make and maintain a good impression can be so stressful when they think a job is shaky that it inhibits them from talking effectively to you. Fearful of botching their message, they say as little to you as they can get away with. Some won't speak out at meetings because of this fear.

To reach uncommunicative subordinates, it's important to pick up on and respond to their perceptions, wants, and interests before you try to get anything else across to them.

27.1 GRINNERS

Grinners won't voice objections and hide behind a grin when provoked.

They may be hurt or angry, but are afraid to speak out because they believe their job depends on pleasing you. They may be hiding their hostility from themselves as well as from you. Little nervous telltale gestures, such as staring at their shoes or out the window, signal that what they are feeling doesn't match the cheerful smile and pleasant words.

Grinners put on a happy face no matter what you ask of them. They are obedient, uncomplaining, and remain passive although they believe they've been pushed too far. You sense something is wrong. You can't quite nail down the incongruity but you know that eventually you will have to deal with it.

What You're Thinking

I had asked Dorothy to prepare a compilation before Wednesday. On Tuesday morning she turned in a list with one segment missing. I asked her why it wasn't finished. She said nothing and just stood there grinning. So I kept going with, "Well, do you need more time?" "Yes," she replied and left. I can't figure out what's happening. Dorothy didn't say that she was upset or stymied. Did I say something in anger that may have offended her? If so, why the grin and why isn't she talking to me?

A Grinner's Thoughts

The boss asked me to prepare that compilation knowing full well I would have to get a segment of the information from my old nemesis Bill. I completed everything except that segment, but I can't tell the boss why. He'd jump down my throat again. I don't feel secure enough to level with the boss. Until I know it's safe to open up, I'll shut my mouth and keep a lid on my real feelings.

Strategy

Your goal is to unlock the agony, annoyance, or anger that brought about the silent grin-and-bear-it routine.

(1) *Enable the Grinners to come to you.* When a problem comes up, show you are listening and more concerned with how the work is affected than in verbally thrashing

the workers for having the problem. Cool off first if you're angry. Then you can deal tactfully and directly with the issue.

(2) *Ask open-ended questions.* Queries that can be answered with a "yes" or "no" stop or discourage discussion. Instead choose questions that delve into what the Grinners are thinking and feeling to get a better understanding of their unresponsiveness.

(3) *Be still and wait for the reply.* Don't fill the void. Don't keep talking to stop the silence. Wait patiently, showing no irritation, until you get a response.

Tactical Talk

"WHAT DO YOU THINK CAUSED THAT AND HOW CAN WE CORRECT IT?"

"HOW LONG DO YOU ESTIMATE IT MIGHT TAKE? WHAT OTHER PROBLEMS MIGHT WE ENCOUNTER?"

"WHAT'S YOUR OPINION ABOUT...?"

"HOW DO YOU FEEL ABOUT...?"

"DO YOU BELIEVE IT'S AN UNREASONABLY SHORT TIME TO COMPLETE ...?"

Tip: Listen to what isn't said. If the Grinners aren't talking to you, for some reason they feel anxious or threatened. It could be that if they wait long enough to reply—and just stand there, grinning—you'll answer your own questions for them.

27.2 WORRIERS

Worriers are afraid to speak up and unable to talk out their problems.

One main difference between Worriers and Grinners is that Worriers aren't smiling. They may avoid seeing you, but they're not hiding their feelings behind a grin.

Their worrying often stems from a lack of feedback from you. After a while they begin to fret. Before long, they've built up a head of steam. You've been so busy with your managerial duties you didn't realize what was happening.

What You're Thinking

What's gotten into Alex lately? He ducks when he sees me coming or gives me quick, short answers when I try to talk to him. It's out of character for him to act shy or withdrawn. It's as though he's afraid or defensive. I don't know why. His work is good. In fact, I gave him an excellent rating on his last evaluation. Up until now, I was happy I had one less person to be concerned about.

A Worrier's Thoughts

At first I reasoned if the boss didn't say anything, I had his tacit approval. But too much time has elasped without any comment. That must mean he doesn't like my work. Look at this cryptic message he just sent out, announcing a major shift of staff with no explanation. I think my decision-making responsibility may have been cut. This memo is a signal my job isn't as secure as I thought it was. I guess I've blown it this time. I can't talk to the boss. He may be angry at me and if I say the wrong thing I'll get fired. I'll stay out of his way. The less I say to him, the better.

Strategy

Your goal is to reassure the Worriers and get them back on an even keel.

(1) *Examine your information system.* Perhaps you're being too formal, allowing stiff and stuffy memos to carry messages that require a personal and informal back-and-forth conversation. Memos go one way. Communication means both parties are participating.

(2) *Fill in future plans and anticipated consequences.* Worriers wouldn't become so nervous if you let them in on what you are setting in motion, why, and how they personally will be affected. Sometimes Worriers are afraid to ask you too many questions lest they be branded as troublemakers.

(3) *Assume withdrawal indicates unexpressed hurt.* Find out the reason without pressing them for an answer. Gently lead the way with open-ended queries.

Tactical Talk

"ALEX, I'VE BEEN MEANING TO TALK TO YOU AS A FOLLOW UP TO MY MEMO ON SHIFTING STAFF. DID YOU UNDERSTAND THAT YOUR TITLE AND SALARY REMAIN IN TACT?"

"YOU PROBABLY HAVE SOME QUESTIONS AND I'LL BE GLAD TO ANSWER THEM."

(if the Worrier doesn't respond after a few minutes of silence) "CAN YOU TELL ME WHY YOU HAVEN'T ANSWERED MY QUESTION?... ARE YOU AFRAID OF WHAT I'LL SAY? WHAT DO YOU THINK I MIGHT SAY?"

Tip: Don't take your good workers for granted assuming that if they give you no problems, they know you are pleased with their work. They don't know this for a fact. They need reassurance and feedback just like everyone else or they may turn into Worriers and stop talking to you.

27.3 TONGUE-TIEDS

Tongue-Tieds are inarticulate or shy. They can't seem to verbalize their thoughts.

They are so overly concerned that you think well of them that they get too embarrassed to speak. While their ideas may be worth considering, they're afraid they will sound foolish.

You ask for suggestions and they're too timid to answer the impersonal queries.

Some are afraid they might sound boring or dull or unclear. They may feel their opinions are neither necessary nor wanted. They suffer stoically rather than verifying their perceptions.

Other Tongue-Tieds are afraid they'll be judged as weak if they ask you for help. They won't ask a question that might make them appear ignorant, especially if they believe everybody else understands what's going on.

What You're Thinking

I know Luke is capable of intelligent, even spirited conversation. I've overheard him talking to his own workers. But he gets tongue-tied around me. And he's terribly ill at ease when he has to give a prepared talk, even a short report. That's a shame. If he could get over his reluctance to speak up and speak out, Luke has the potential to go far in this organization.

A Tongue-Tied's Thoughts

I'd like to comment when the boss asks us for ideas, but I'm so scared I'll make a fool of myself. Maybe the others will contradict me; maybe they'll show me up to be wrong. Maybe I won't choose the precise words and I'll seem ridiculous. I'd look like a moron if I asked a question and everybody but me knew the answer.

Strategy

Your goal is to help the Tongue-Tieds feel comfortable talking to you and talking before their peers and other groups.

(1) *Encourage their questions.* In private talks, you can help relieve their shyness by reassuring them that we all make mistakes because we're human and need more information. Suggest that for now it might be easier for them to participate at staff meetings if they were to write out their questions, and when they get used to that, to add a brief comment before the question.

(2) *Ask them direct questions.* At your meetings, turn to the Tongue-Tieds when you reach areas where you know they have experience or expertise.

(3) *Help them improve their meeting reports.* Mention practicing at home with a tape recorder to hear for themselves how they sound. Discuss the conversation-instead-of-a-speech technique.

(4) *Assign them to small committees.* The give and take discussions in smaller groups are so informal that they serve as good practice sessions. Here the Tongue-Tieds can gain confidence in expressing themselves.

(5) *Suggest public speaking courses.* Perhaps your company has a training programs in which the Tongue-Tieds can get assistance. If not, point out available community resources.

Tactical Talk

"LUKE, I KNOW YOU'RE GOOD AT PUTTING YOUR FINGER ON THE REAL PROBLEM. AT THE STAFF MEETINGS, WHEN YOU ASK A QUESTION THAT PINPOINTS THE REAL ISSUE, YOU PLAY A MOST IMPORTANT ROLE IN PROBLEM SOLVING."

(at a meeting) "LUKE, YOU WORKED ON THAT LAST YEAR. WHAT DO YOU THINK ABOUT THE IDEA OF REPEATING IT AGAIN?"

"WHEN YOU KNOW YOU HAVE TO GIVE A REPORT, DON'T TRY TO WING IT OR READ IT. WRITE OUT AND MEMORIZE ONLY BRIEF OPENING AND CLOSING STATEMENTS, THEN PRACTICE AT HOME FROM A KEY POINTS OUTLINE. WHEN YOU KNOW YOUR SUBJECT AS WELL AS YOU DO, YOU CAN DO MOST OF YOUR REPORT BY ANSWERING QUESTIONS FROM THE GROUP. THAT ALMOST ELIMINATES YOUR GIVING A SPEECH."

Tip: Some Tongue-Tieds need more than reassurance, especially if they're having difficulty with a prepared talk. Explain how this personal problem can hold them back and offer to help. If you can't coach them yourself, suggest places where they can get assistance.

Uncommunicative subordinates are usually afraid to speak. They are too angry, worried, or embarrassed to try. So it's up to you to encourage them to talk to you without dreading the outcome. Ask questions that will unearth the causes of their concern and then you can respond to what they're saying. You may need to relax your rigidity, provide better feedback, offer more reassurance, or in some cases, coach the poor public speaker.

PART TEN

DEALING WITH COMPLAINING/CRITICAL PEOPLE

We expect others to be thick-skinned while our own egos are as fragile as eggshells. If I give you my unsolicited opinion, it's to help you improve. If you give me your unasked-for advice, you're criticizing me. Giving and receiving top-notch criticism is an exceedingly delicate art.

Basically, your critic is saying: "You and I ought to have the same values, but you're not acting according to my standards." That's OK as long as you respect the other's right to an opinion and stick to dissecting the issues. Difficult bosses, colleagues, and subordinates never heard of those rules.

With them, you're automatically wrong. They make mincemeat of your dignity. They even singe themselves when making things hot for you. Some skillfully manipulate you with self-incrimination. Others are confirmed complainers who have no intention of fixing what's wrong. They shed their responsibility by telling you about it; now it's your problem.

Nevertheless, since the critics' behavior is predictable, you can plan ahead how to deal with them. You can also learn to be choosy—not every issue is worth doing battle about.

249

CHAPTER 28

WHEN YOUR BOSS IS A FAULT-FINDER

Some bosses are quick to make you their scapegoat. Others rip you apart when you *are* to blame. Only when it's your blunder does it really matter who's at fault. Then you have to own up to your mistake immediately, apologize, and suggest remedial action.

Pointing your finger at another culprit (boss, cohort, or subordinate) only makes you look weak to your boss. Whether or not it's deserved, criticism usually stings, and bosses get especially upset when you can prove they were at fault. That forces them to defend themselves and repair their egos. So forget that legitimate excuse; when fault-finding supervisors are manipulative, tyrannical, petty, or wimpy, you can use other tactics to deal with their complaints without coming unglued.

28.1 GUILT LADLERS

Guilt Ladlers manage to make *you* feel guilty, no matter the real reason.

Guilt Ladler bosses choose a roundabout route to criticize and complain. They use being hurt as a manipulative club over your head. They try to control you by making you feel guilty for their wounded feelings. As a result, you reproach yourself if you don't do what was asked of you, while getting angry at the boss for asking. But being angry makes you feel more guilty, so you comply. You've just been snared by the guilt trap.

Having convinced themselves that they're blameless, Guilt Ladlers deny responsibility. They've already shunted the problem to you. Although denial increases their guilt, they're unable to apologize. To get relief, they blame others and broadly hint they deserve to suffer. Wallowing in self-pity, they refuse your help as they lash out at you for not helping.

What You're Thinking

The boss tells me, "Look at what you've done to us. I really expected you to show more diligence. Everyone in our department has always scored highest in that program. What do you think the other managers are going to say now about me and my department? Don't be surprised if I go into cardiac arrest." I feel so drained from having another one of those conversations with the boss. I don't know how he can twist everything around. But he manages to make all of us lose sight of the real issues.

A Guilt Ladler's Thoughts

Verne told me it would be tough for him to carry his regular load and participate in the program, too, but he agreed to do it. He promised me he'd work hard. He ought to know how much it means to me to have the respect and admiration of all the managers. Why did he do this to me? I guess it's my fault for being so trusting.

Strategy

Your goal is to get out of the trap that the master manipulator has set for you.

(1) *State your feelings clearly.* Be honest about being hurt or disturbed by what the boss has said. You're not criticizing the boss if you are simply stating how you feel along with your desire to restore your damaged relationship.

(2) *Toss back the guilt.* Politely and calmly refuse to accept it. Point out in a straightforward manner the role that the boss has played.

(3) *Sever the boss's problem from yours.* The boss is showing signs of insecurity, so be careful to protect the boss's feelings as you do this.

Tactical Talk

"BOSS, I WAS DISTURBED WHEN YOU SAID I HADN'T BEEN DILIGENT ABOUT THE PROGRAM. I'VE ALWAYS CONSIDERED YOU A FAIR PERSON AND I BELIEVE WE'VE HAD A PRETTY GOOD RELATIONSHIP UP TO NOW, SO I'D LIKE TO CLEAR THE AIR."

"PERHAPS YOU'VE FORGOTTEN OUR TALK IN WHICH WE AGREED (1)..., (2)..., (3)..."

"NOW IF YOU FEEL YOU WANT GREATER PARTICIPATION FROM OUR DEPARTMENT ON THAT PROGRAM, MAY I SUGGEST THAT WE ADJUST..."

Tip: Don't wilt from the guilt. Guilt Ladlers try to shift the blame for their poor judgment or insecurity onto you. They criticize your actions as the cause of their hurt feelings so that you, in turn, feel guilty and they have more control. Refuse to buy the boss's ludicrous look at the world. Politely state the real facts and get on with resolving the problem.

28.2 NIT PICKERS

Nit Pickers are petty bickerers who find fault with inconsequential matters.

Nit Picker bosses insist on perfection for tasks that are not important. Understandably, they want painstaking, even finicky, accuracy when you prepare something consequential. But these bosses get their kicks from picking apart every detail on every effort as well as every past mistake for which you've long since paid your penance.

Usually Nit Pickers feel threatened and blame everyone else for problems that arise. They often work very hard themselves because they have trouble delegating. It's hard for them to trust others when they demand perfection where perfection isn't called for. Consequently, they try to do your work for you, continuously butting in when you should be allowed to proceed on your own.

What You're Thinking

The boss can't keep his cotton-picking hands off my assignments. What is he so afraid of that he has to constantly check up on me? He finds tiny flaws in my preliminary drafts when he knows darn well that I'll correct them after we make the major adjustments. If I didn't need this job so badly, I'd tell him off.

A Nit Picker's Thoughts

As hard as I try, I don't seem to be able to impress the top management. I keep a very careful eye on everything my staff does. I truly believe their work is as good as anyone could expect. Why, then, am I being passed over for the new post that's opening up? Maybe I have to keep an even more careful watch over my workers.

Strategy

Your goal is to get your smothering boss to back off and let you breathe. The relationship is choking you.

(1) *Adjust your focus to get a better perspective.* The situation is irksome, not critical. Stop reciting prolonged excuses to your boss. Instead of getting defensive, enroll your regained sense of humor. Try a little teasing. Or, if you caused a slight mistake, make a joke at your own expense.

(2) *Redirect your anger*. Relax and reflect. Compose yourself, then channel your energy into thinking up a plan you can feed to your boss in easy doses.

(3) *Divert the boss's attention to more meaningful tasks*. Encourage the boss to work on whatever the organization needs or toward any personal goal the boss has hinted at. Suggest ways the boss can find the time (by substituting this positive action for the checking-up habit).

(4) *Double check your work*. Make sure you're doing what you promised and getting your work in on time. Pay closer attention to your instincts when something doesn't feel right. Or, go back to the boss, ask if you understood correctly, saying why you're concerned. If there *is* an error, this enables the boss to correct it without embarrassing anyone.

Tactical Talk

"BOSS, I'M GLAD YOU FOUND THAT OVERSIGHT. NOW LET'S SEE, IF WE MOVE THE TOTALS INTO THE NEXT COLUMN, THAT SHOULD BE A BETTER ALIGNMENT."

"BOSS, I KNOW YOU'VE BEEN WANTING TO ATTEND THE CHAMBER OF COMMERCE LUNCHEONS TO DRUM UP NEW BUSINESS. I CAN HOLD DOWN THE FORT HERE WHILE YOU MAKE NEW CONTACTS FOR THE FIRM."

"PLEASE LET ME PROVE TO YOU THAT YOU CAN TRUST ME. HERE'S HOW YOU CAN MAKE SURE THAT EVERYTHING IS RUNNING SMOOTHLY..."

Tip: You need two prongs to deal with Nit Picker bosses—reassurance and temptation. Being worried and anxious, they give you assignments and then can't let go. They need to know they can trust you before they'll loosen their grip on the wheel. They also need incentive to busy themselves with something more important. Watch for clues so that you can dangle their desire in front of them.

28.3 HANGING JUDGES

Hanging Judges blame you before gathering or hearing the facts.

Take your pick of whodonits. The culprit is your boss, your cohort, or maybe it was an act of God disaster. In any event, you are not guilty. But you haven't yet pleaded your case and you're being convicted.

Blaming others for troubles they themselves may have created, Hanging Judges look for scapegoats. If they're at fault for a failing project, they can't admit it. Instead, they seek easily intimidated, vulnerable victims. You are picked as the sacrificial lamb because you're not likely to retaliate.

Hanging Judges aren't interested in finding answers. Of utmost importance to them is that they maintain control. To do this, they feel they must rid themselves of the failure tag. So, "Tag, you're *it*."

What You're Thinking

Wow, is the boss hopping mad! All those accusations and the name calling. If he's trying to intimidate me, he's doing a great job. But it was he who really caused the catastrophe. If I show him up, he'll resent it. If I don't, I get blamed unjustly. I'm really stuck.

A Hanging Judge's Thoughts

I told Judy to make certain that the team included a multi-ethnic mix. I also told her to hold off a week before adding any new people. But now what am I going to do? Somebody must have complained to the big boss about not being represented. I'll send Judy a reprimand telling her to straighten out the mess immediately with a copy to the big boss. That will let him know I'm right on top of the situation.

Strategy

Your goal is to stop being made the boss's scapegoat. You have to stand up for yourself while showing the boss you're more useful as his ally than his victim.

(1) *Let go of your hurt feelings.* Keep still until your anger subsides. To get a little objectivity, back away, pretending it's someone else's problem. In all probability, you're not the only one the boss treats this way.

(2) *Deal with the boss's hostility.* Politely show that you're not the weak and vulnerable victim the boss thought you were. To voice your objections use questions rather than accusations.

(3) *Criticize without doubting authority.* If the boss thinks you're questioning his actions, he'll become defensive and immovable. Don't blame *anyone.* Keep your disagreement on a professionally high plane to avoid a confrontation. Be cooperative, respectful, and stick to the issues.

(4) *Provide a gracious way out.* After the boss calms down and is rational, discuss objectives and suggest options. Find some points on which you can sincerely compliment and agree with the boss. Help him increase his own self-esteem.

Tactical Talk

"BOSS, I DON'T BLAME YOU FOR BEING UPSET. WHICH ORDER DID YOU WANT ME TO FOLLOW?" (rather than, "It was your order I followed to the letter.")

"IT SEEMS TO ME LIKE WE ALL GOT OUR SIGNALS CROSSED ON THIS ONE. MAYBE WE COULD AVOID THIS IN THE FUTURE IF WE WERE TO..."

"YOU'RE RIGHT ABOUT THAT, BOSS. FAIR REPRESENTATION IS CRUCIAL. NOW THAT I UNDERSTAND HOW YOU WANT TO PROCEED, I'M SURE YOU'LL FIND ME A GOOD TEAM PLAYER..."

Tip: When you're being blamed for something that's not your fault, don't yell "foul." Keep playing, even though the boss is changing the rules in the middle of the game. But come back strong, in a polite and straightforward manner. It's unlikely you'll get picked on again once the boss realizes you're more valuable as a supporter than a scapegoat.

28.4 MEAT GRINDERS

Meat Grinders are overly candid. Their cutting criticism rips you to shreds.

This time it *was* your fault. There's no way to hide this blunder that may blow your career chances. Panic takes over. Meanwhile the boss, always a stern Dutch uncle, is furious and unrelenting with his sharp accusations. But this time he has every right to be angry.

Don't answer the charges. Freeze in your tracks. Say, "I'll be right back" and leave the room or hang up the phone. Now take a few deep breaths and remember that everybody makes a mistake. It's how you face up to it that influences your future. Also keep in mind that bosses have the right to criticize your work, but that doesn't include the right to inflict cruel and unusual knock-out blows to your ego.

What You're Thinking

I know the boss told me to take care of the Lasser order before I did more work on anything else. I thought it could wait because I had so many other things I had to do that I considered more important. I was wrong. Lasser called screaming at the boss and the boss pelted me with his reprimands. He's not just mad; I think he's completely lost confidence in me. This is a mess I brought on myself. If this doesn't cost me my job, I'll be paying for it for years to come.

A Meat Grinder's Thoughts

Warren really blew it this time. If he lost us that Lasser account, it's going to be the last account he loses. He thinks he's so smart, that he knows more than I do. I just can't depend on him. I don't want to hear his excuses. What a day this has been. First the fight at home, then that idiot in the parking lot, and now this. Why couldn't Warren follow my orders? Now that it's too late, it might dawn on him that I was right.

Strategy

Your goal is to immediately remedy your mistake and get back in the boss's good graces.

(1) *Admit your error quickly and emphatically.* As soon as you realize that you, or someone under you, goofed, claim the blame. In the boss's mind, this computes as, "Aha, he sees I was right to criticize him, so I suppose he's not so dumb after all. Let's see what else he has to say." Denying your mistake only makes you appear spineless; delaying causes you unnecessary hardship.

(2) *Give no alibi or excuse.* If your subordinate was the one who pulled the boner, you still have to accept the responsibility. Get to the point without cushioning the misdeed. You were wrong. You are sorry. An alibi would only make the boss madder because it implies the boss accused you unjustly.

(3) *Offer a way to make it better.* Suggest your plan to correct the error. Restate your boss's criticism, transforming each negative into a positive objective. If, after having time to calm down, the boss continues hurling insults at you, hold on to your dignity by proclaiming that you accept the criticism as sound, but his being unnecessarily rough is delaying progress in working things out.

(4) *Seek agreement on the plan.* Whatever you two come up with, be sure you're in accord before you leave. If the boss has to bring someone else in to clean up your dirty work, this won't improve your relationship.

Tactical Talk

"BOSS, I USED VERY POOR JUDGMENT IN NOT TAKING CARE OF THE LASSER ORDER AS YOU HAD DIRECTED ME TO DO. IT WAS A STUPID MISTAKE. I WAS WRONG AND I'M SORRY." (after the boss yells, "You never follow orders!")

"BOSS, FROM NOW ON YOUR ORDERS WILL BE PROCESSED (1)..., (2)..., (3)..."

"BOSS, I THINK WE CAN STILL HOLD ON TO LASSER IF WE TELL HIM THAT WE OVERSOLD OUR NEW PRODUCT AND ... OK, THEN WE AGREE. I'LL GO OUT THERE THIS AFTERNOON AND STRAIGHTEN IT OUT."

Tip: Stop predicting doomsday because you made a mistake. Everybody does. The real danger is in compounding the error by not saying you're sorry or not apologizing soon enough.

It's a no-win situation to place blame on someone else. In a confrontation with the boss, if you win now you lose later. Don't blame anyone unless you're apologizing for yourself. Either way, move quickly to remedy the situation.

Prevention is the best defense against bosses' criticism—valid or otherwise. Keep them informed because bosses don't like surprises. Try to involve them in your assignment, especially at the planning stage. Avoid hurting their feelings. They instinctively strike back if you seem to be questioning their authority or goring their sacred cow. Keep your antenna out to pick up on ways to assist them in achieving their personal goals. Bosses you help are less apt to criticize you.

CHAPTER 29

WHEN YOUR COLLEAGUES ARE FAULT-FINDERS

29.1 Squawkers
29.2 Super-Sensitives
29.3 Wise Crackers
29.4 Wet Blankets

Critical colleagues are treasured gems when they help you develop better insight and discover new possibilities. But many of your peers don't listen supportively or bother to cushion their comments. They may have nothing against you personally, but they complain in general. Others react resentfully if they think you're criticizing them.

Usually, fault-finding peers want you to admit that you made a bad judgment call. You may not agree and, without sugar-coating that's a difficult pill to swallow. As a result feelings are hurt on both sides, team spirit is seriously injured, and productivity is side-tracked. For your own protection stand up for yourself but try to make friends with your critics before they attempt to damage your other relationships, such as with your boss, for instance.

29.1 SQUAWKERS

Squawkers are chronic gripers who grumble about everything—publicly and secretly.

It's their cruel and harsh manner of correcting you that sets your teeth on edge. For a minor infraction they'll ridicule you before the entire staff. Besides grumbling about you, their firing away at other colleagues leaves you wondering how to respond.

Even more destructive is the way they wrap complaints in "confidential" information and then tie you up by swearing you to secrecy. Instead of knocking out the problem with a frank talk right to the heart of the matter, you're left boxing at shadows.

What You're Thinking

According to Ellie, Paul is about to stick a knife in my back because he thinks his personnel unit and not my planning unit should be handling every aspect of orientation. Her information source swore her to secrecy, so Ellie says if I say anything to Paul she'll deny telling me and his staff will be in hot water. Ellie claims she told me this so that I could defend myself. How can I ward off an attack when I don't have all the information and I can't talk to the alleged perpetrator?

A Squawker's Thoughts

Eve and Paul cut me out of the orientation altogether. They completely overlooked my training experience and the good suggestions I could offer them. Well, I don't think they'll be trusting each other so much anymore. And the irony is that Eve will now feel she owes me one for tipping her off! Once the two of them start squabbling, I can let the boss know I'm available to handle the project.

Strategy

When being attacked, your first goal is to minimize damage and, secondly, try to convert your enemy into a friend.

(1) *Do a quick review.* Race over the facts leading up to this point. Did you inadvertently trigger the trouble? Have you assumed colleague support without bothering to check?

(2) *Don't play their I've-got-a-secret game.* Refuse to promise to keep confidential your peer's gossip or rumor. Get the issue on the table so that you can deal with it.

(3) *Dissolve the tension by talking.* You can't let cutting remarks fester. Politely confront your accuser. Then examine the system that allowed the problem to arise. Discuss options. If a colleague unfairly criticized you at a staff meeting, meet later in private to hash it out.

(4) *Touch base regularly with potential troublemakers.* Keep your peers informed about your projects. Involve them by coordinating appropriate segments. Before they squawk to the boss about you, listen to, understand, and be cooperative about their complaints. Suggest joint presentations with the modifications you agree on. And give them the starring roles.

(5) *Insist on respect for yourself and your peers.* Simply refuse to continue a conversation unless everyone is civil. If a peer complains about another colleague to you, you can't escape by keeping still. To a Squawker, *remaining silent means you agree.* If you think the third party is indeed causing a problem, decide how you are going to deal with it. If you disagree, speak up and say why you feel as you do.

Tactical Talk

"I'M SORRY, ELLIE, BUT IF I KEEP YOUR SECRET I CAN'T SOLVE THE PROBLEM. I AM GOING TO TALK TO PAUL WITHOUT MENTIONING ANY NAMES. I KNOW YOU DON'T REALIZE IT, ELLIE, BUT SOMEBODY IS USING YOU TO STIR UP TROUBLE. YOU DON'T WANT TO BE INVOLVED IN THAT, DO YOU?"

"PAUL, I HEARD YOU WERE CONCERNED THAT THE PERSONNEL UNIT IS NOT HANDLING THE ENTIRE ORIENTATION. WE'VE ALWAYS WORKED WELL TOGETHER. I'M SURE YOU HAVE SOME GOOD IDEAS FOR STRAIGHTENING THIS OUT."

"I CAN UNDERSTAND WHY YOU WERE UPSET, PAUL. WHY DON'T WE FIGURE OUT THE BEST APPROACH AND GO TOGETHER TO THE BOSS. YOU TELL HIM WHAT WE AGREE ON, AND I'LL BACK YOU UP."

"I REALLY DON'T WANT TO ARGUE ABOUT THIS. I'LL COME BACK WHEN WE CAN TALK CALMLY."

"WHAT YOU SAY ABOUT ARTHUR MAY BE TRUE, BUT MY EXPERIENCE WITH HIM HAS BEEN JUST THE OPPOSITE. I'VE FOUND HIM TO BE TO-TALLY DEPENDABLE. FOR EXAMPLE, WHEN I WAS HANDLING THE SPRING CONFERENCE..."

"HOLD ON A MINUTE, ELLIE. YOU HAVEN'T STOPPED GRIPING FOR THE PAST 15 MINUTES. WHY DON'T WE GIVE IT A REST AND TALK ONLY ABOUT PLEASANT THINGS FOR THE REMAIN-DER OF OUR LUNCH HOUR, OK?"

Tip: The trouble with Squawkers is that they do too much squawking and you don't do enough talking. When you're attacked, confront your accuser and resolve the matter. Early consulting and coordinating with them on a regular basis usually takes the sting out of their bite.

29.2 SUPER-SENSITIVES

Super-Sensitives are extremely touchy and take every comment as a personal affront.

What your colleagues do in their own bailiwicks is their business until it affects you. Then you have to talk about your mutual concern. But the Super-Sensitives get tense, touchy, and uptight. Without your criticizing them, they act defensive. No matter what you say, it's suddenly you against them.

Why the irrational reaction to imagined criticism? Super-Sensitives lack confidence in themselves or feel inferior to you, and they are hurt much too easily. You and your colleagues, having lost patience with immature behavior, avoid them like the plague and they don't know why.

But now you have to talk.

What You're Thinking

All I said to Barbara was that I wanted to talk to her about the delay in routing top priority items. She instantly jumped down my throat for my claiming the delay was her fault. She began reciting her virtues—she's the first one to show up for work, she puts in more hours than I do, she's not lazy like some other managers, and on and on. We never did discuss the routing problem.

A Super-Sensitive's Thoughts

When Eric came by to talk about the delay, I could see what he was up to. He was about to criticize the way I run my division and imply that I'm not as efficient as he is. Well, I resent his superior attitude and I guess I put him down a peg or two.

Strategy

Your goal is to overcome, or at least tone down, the Super-Sensitives' resentment. You want to resolve a difficulty or deliver negative feedback without getting into an extended hassle. When you're having trouble talking to the Super-Sensitives, the tactics in this checklist will help.

CHECKLIST FOR DEALING WITH SUPER-SENSITIVES

( ) *Do I Help Build Their Self-Confidence?* Ask them to review *your* work and suggest changes. Your gratitude will raise their self respect level.

( ) *Do I Help Them Balance Their Feelings?* Do I get them to express their hurt directly and honestly. If you contributed to their hurt feelings, apologize. If their feelings appear irrational, ask them to look again at the facts.

( ) *Do I Protect Their Pride?* They feel humiliated if you discuss a problem before others. Keep it private.

( ) *Have I Acknowledged Their Needs?* Recognize their requirements without assuming blame or guilt. Simply add what you, too, need and why.

( ) *Do I Soften the Sting?* Wedge a criticism between two compliments. Talk as teammates working together: "We did,"rather than, "You did."

( ) *Do I Let the Boss Handle Their Poor Performance?* If they don't do their job right, that's the boss's responsibility, not yours. When you poke your nose into somebody else's turf they have a right to resent it.

( ) *Do I Skip Lengthy Prologues?* Get right to the point. Otherwise they sense something is coming. Your stalling makes them anxious and exaggerates the importance of the discussion.

( ) *Do I State Issues Factually?* Be prepared with specific names, numbers, places, dates, frequency. Use questions to expose underlying problems.

( ) *Do I Keep the Discussion Substantive?* After you acknowledge their feelings, stick to facts, objectives, obstacles, and tactics. Skip the talk about attitudes, motives or who's to blame.

( ) *Have We Agreed on a Plan?* Develop specific stages or tasks to get from here to there. If the steps are complicated, remain upbeat as you both develop an outline.

Tactical Talk

"BARBARA, WOULD YOU MIND TAKING A LOOK AT THIS CHART I'VE DRAWN? DO YOU SEE ANY STEPS I MIGHT BE ABLE TO ELIMINATE?"

"PLEASE TELL ME FRANKLY WHAT IT WAS I DID OR SAID THAT SEEMS TO HAVE HURT YOUR FEELINGS?"

"I UNDERSTAND THAT YOU NEED...BUT I HAVE A TIGHT SCHEDULE THAT REQUIRES...REALLY, I'M NOT TRYING TO PUT YOU DOWN, I JUST WANT TO DO MY JOB A LITTLE BETTER."

"WE RUN INTO THIS SNAG ABOUT THREE TIMES A WEEK. HOW CAN WE REALISTICALLY CIR-CUMVENT THE ROADBLOCK?...THEN WHY DON'T WE WORK UP A NEW SCHEDULE?"

Tip: Reduce the resentment of Super-Sensitives by helping them deal honestly with their feelings. Usually, they've been isolated because of their foolish behavior. They need to regain their self respect and know they're capable of contributing. They have to distinguish between imagined slurs and real facts. You can make a big difference by becoming friends with these critics.

29.3 WISE CRACKERS

Wise Crackers toss flip, witty and sarcastic jokes about your flaws.

With Super-Sensitives, it's obvious they're upset. With Wise Crackers, you're left guessing. These colleagues are quick with quips and put downs that disguise their antagonism. They know your shortcomings and may suspect you created error, but they don't come right out and say so. Their non-assertiveness leaves you confused.

Wise Crackers enjoy subtle and indirect jabs, especially with an audience to appreciate their wit and protect them. You may be facing a very difficult situation, yet they feel free to criticize because they carry no responsibility for the out-come. In fact, they feel no responsibility toward you or your feelings. The buried, unresolved conflict leaves your alliance on shaky ground.

What You're Thinking

When Stan made that crack about my putting all those business lunches on the tab, he wasn't just joking. He meant to land a blow. How can I laugh at his remarks and keep overlooking the fact that he's holding me up to ridicule? Even if I did goof, there's no way I could have responded without losing face. I've got to find a way to stop him from repeatedly embarrassing me in front of the gang.

A Wise Cracker's Thoughts

Why should Hank get away with those long, expensive lunches? I resent the boss always asking him to talk to the prospective clients when I can certainly represent the company as well or better than Hank. My little jokes will let Hank know I've got my eye on him.

Strategy

Your goal is to minimize the effect of the Wise Crackers' remarks and, if possible, to curb their resentment or hostility.

(1) *Own up to a mistake.* If your error is exposed to a group, admit, apologize, and *briefly* explain. Assume your explanation will be accepted. If you expound, point by point, it looks like you expect them to find you guilty and they most likely will.

(2) *Make light of a public "attack."* Without getting defensive, move the subject away from yourself and talk policy or procedure. If the disguised jokes continue, seek peer support by asking if the others agree. Start teasing the Wise Crackers yourself. Their other victims in the group will probably be happy to join you.

(3) *Practice at home to take the offensive.* Hearing how you sound on your tape recorder will help you develop a confident and conversational tone. By role playing with a friend, you can practice direct eye contact as well as a sincere and relaxed manner.

(4) *In private, bring hostility to the surface.* Wise Crackers will claim they were only teasing but they persist in digging. Unemotionally, tell how you felt. Ask the Wise Crackers to be up front with you, then deal with the real problem.

(5) *Disarm your attackers.* Keep your colleagues informed. Give them a chance to buy into your project or proposal. Get them to express to you their thinking, suggestions

and disagreements in the early stages, rather than your springing the finished product on the group and inviting the wisecracks.

Tactical Talk

"STAN, SOMETHING YOU SAID YESTERDAY REALLY BOTHERED ME AND I'D LIKE TO SETTLE IT."

"MAYBE TO YOU IT WAS JUST TEASING. BUT TO ME, IT FELT LIKE I WAS RUN OVER BY A 16-WHEELER THAT HIT ME AND LEFT ME FOR DEAD."

"STAN, IT WOULD REALLY HELP US BOTH IF YOU'D LEVEL WITH ME AND TELL ME WHAT'S REALLY EATING YOU, SO WE COULD CLEAR IT UP."

Tip: Wise Crackers go far beyond friendly teasing during their public performances. Malicious intent lurks behind their brand of humor. Instead of getting defensive, change the channel and talk about what's wrong with the system. Then take the offensive and start teasing the teaser. Later, in private, deal openly with their hostility.

29.4 WET BLANKETS

Wet Blankets are very negative, throwing cold water on every idea.

When you're looking for sound thinking you need to hear from pessimists as well as optimists. Is the idea practical? Realistically, can it work? Colleagues who pull apart your idea by expressing legitimate concerns are not criticizing you. They help you avoid blunders or plan ways to overcome obstacles when they ask if the resources, experience, and timing are on target.

Wet Blankets, on the other hand, are convinced before they explore the possibility that it won't work. They don't want to carefully weigh the pros and cons. They sabotage discussion with premature pronouncements that you don't have enough time, power, money or study. They say, "There's nothing we can do. It just can't be done." Their defeatist attitude drenches your idea in a downpour. It's pretty hard to find your own enthusiasm after that kind of attack.

What You're Thinking

I still think it's a great idea. Without entailing too much expense and inconvenience, we'd get more office space, reduce noise interference and work faster. How much could it cost to add one inside wall and move the electrical over 12 feet? We never even got a chance to discuss it before Donald showered us with 66 reasons why it wouldn't work, and then stated flatly the boss would never approve it. We have to do something about getting more room, but every time somebody comes up with a plan Donald puts a damper on it.

A Wet Blanket's Thoughts

Don't they realize by now that the boss will never go for that? He never wants to approve spending for any budget item that's meant solely to benefit the staff. And they don't realize how expensive even minor renovations can be. Why let everybody get all excited over the prospects when they are only going to be turned down again?

Strategy

Your goal is to reach a realistic conclusion. You have to determine how much, if any, of the Wet Blankets' objections are valid.

(1) *Do your homework.* Before proposing your idea, get the facts and the figures, time frames and resources, along with the potential trouble spots.

(2) *Search for support.* Whenever possible, find cases where the idea has worked, or examples or studies that back you up. Find testimonials about products or people who'd be involved.

(3) *Present the situation and the options first.* Move from there to your proposed solution. If Wet Blankets inter-

rupt, don't surrender the floor until you finish the few points you wish to make.

(4) *Keep the mood optimistic.* Ask Wet Blankets for specific criticism, elements you may have overlooked, a worst-case scenario, and then respond to the objections without being argumentative. Be sincere in really wanting to hear what they have to say. If you sound reasonable and enthusiastic, you can keep their pessimism from permeating the air.

(5) *Be willing to modify your idea.* If the discussion points up changes that could be beneficial, go for pride of joint product instead of pride of sole authorship.

Tactical Talk

"I WAS TALKING TO LANNY IN PURCHASING AND HE SAID HIS DEPARTMENT DID SOMETHING LIKE THIS FOUR YEARS AGO. SO THERE IS PRECEDENT FOR OUR REQUEST..."

"DONALD, IT WOULD HELP US IF YOUR OBJECTIONS WERE A LITTLE MORE SPECIFIC. WHAT DO YOU THINK WOULD HAPPEN IF WE WENT TO THE BOSS WITH THIS PROPOSAL AND..."

"IF DONALD IS CORRECT ABOUT THAT, DON'T YOU THINK IT'S STILL WORTH A TRY? WE HAVE SO LITTLE TO LOSE."

Tip: Don't let the Wet Blankets drown your spirits. They are being negative in general. They're only helpful when they're negative with specifics and those things you can discuss and resolve. When they still insist, "It can't be done," tell them they may be right, but since the worst that can happen is..., why not try it? That should rally the rest of the troop and restore a realistic approach.

When colleagues find fault, you can accept the fact that someone disagrees with you without accepting the criticism itself. If you agree that you *are* at fault, immediately apologize and suggest a remedy. But when you consider the remark to be unfair, you can say we all have a right to our opinion and present your point.

Don't let yourself be pulled under by rumor mongers who swear you to secrecy, or the overly sensitive who fight unnecessary battles, or joking colleagues who mask their barbs, or peers who spread doom and gloom. Admittedly, their acts aren't amicable, but it's in *your* best interest to remain friendly and foster good team spirit.

CHAPTER 30

WHEN YOUR SUBORDINATES ARE FAULT-FINDERS

30.1 Blame Shifters
30.2 Whiners
30.3 Self-Beraters
30.4 Martyrs

If your subordinates are *constantly* complaining, the feedback line is probably clogged. You especially need an ongoing, flowing communications system that connects the thinking between you and your workers when dealing with fault-finding subordinates who charge you with their errors, snitch on their colleagues, or blame themselves for every error.

It's easy to second-guess others, so don't assume sinister motives. The worker who appears to be goofing off might see himself conscientiously laboring even though he's ill. Your assistant who labeled you Simon Legree never once told you that she feels overburdened. You don't know what people are thinking unless they tell you, and the best way to find out is to ask. Such dialogue moves you toward the mutual goal of improved performance. Most people want to do better and, as their boss, you want them to also. So learn to capitalize on their criticism by using it as a springboard for discussion.

30.1 BLAME SHIFTERS

Blame Shifters blame you for their own bonehead blunders.

They are buck-passers. Once they report a serious problem to you, it's your migraine. They've washed their hands of any further responsibility. When the anticipated disaster occurs, they have already transferred the sin to you, their scapegoat. It's all your fault.

Blame Shifters have difficulty handling pressure. If they feel you're criticizing them they have to relieve their hurt or fear or worry. So they remove the blame from themselves and hand it to you. You don't help them develop by promising to think about a matter they bring to you, that just saddles you with more worries about assignments that should have remained delegated.

What You're Thinking

Tina should have had that all the data for the application together by now. She said she informed me a few weeks ago that she was having trouble finding the information. She claims I told her I'd get back to her about it. I probably did say that, but with so much on my mind, wouldn't you think she'd check back with me? Now we don't have enough time to do a thorough job. I'm angry that I couldn't depend on Tina, while she acts as though *I* am totally responsible for blowing this opportunity.

A Blame Shifter's Thoughts

I was worried about making the deadline so I told the boss I was having trouble finding the information for the application. He was supposed to give me some direction and I'm still waiting for him to "get back" to me. Now he's blaming me for not following through with my assignment. You can't win in this job. Bosses always have to have someone to blame for their mistakes and the criticism only flows in one direction—down.

Strategy

Your goal is to get the Blame Shifters to accept responsibility for their own behavior. Start by reducing the emotional overload.

(1) *Let them voice their anger or frustration.* Be empathetic, anxious to know what they think. Listen, without responding to the charges. Blame Shifters will try to make you their victims. Even if you contributed to a misunderstanding, that doesn't relieve them of their obligations.

(2) *Suggest you meet soon.* You both need a little time to compose yourselves. Should the Blame Shifters' complaints be legitimate, you'll want to correct your action. When the atmosphere is calm again, start resolving the difficulty.

(3) *Define the real problem.* Start by complimenting Blame Shifters on specific matters they handled well. Then point out the trouble spots. Keep the discussion impersonal.

(4) *Don't do your subordinates' work for them.* Make them responsible for working on the solution and following through. Explain the consequences they face if they don't produce. Ask them to specify the tasks that have to be done and to set reasonable reporting deadlines. Now let go! There's a plan and a date; forget about the matter until then.

Tactical Talk

"TINA, MAYBE I DIDN'T MAKE MYSELF CLEAR... BUT NOW WE HAVE A SERIOUS MATTER WE HAVE TO DEAL WITH. I THINK WE BOTH NEED A LITTLE WHILE TO SORT OUR THOUGHTS. PLEASE BE BACK HERE AT 3 PM."

"TINA, I APPRECIATE THE AMOUNT OF WORK YOU'VE BEEN HANDLING, BUT I'M NOT PLEASED WHEN I DEPEND ON STAFF TO COME THROUGH AND THEN LEARN IT'S NOT DONE.

WHAT DO YOU SUGGEST WE DO ABOUT
THIS?...NOW THAT WE HAVE SOME IDEAS FOR
CHANGING PROCEDURES, WHAT WOULD YOU
NEED TO SALVAGE THE APPLICATION?...WHAT
KIND OF HELP DO YOU NEED?"

"OK, IF I ASSIGN KATIE AND TIM TO HELP YOU,
YOU UNDERSTAND YOU HAVE FULL RESPON-
SIBILITY FOR GETTING IT DONE ON TIME AND
YOU ARE AWARE OF WHAT WILL HAPPEN IF
YOU MISS THE DEADLINE. COME IN ON FRIDAY
TO TELL ME HOW YOU'RE PROGRESSING."

Tip: Foil Blame Shifters who try to victimize you by handing
you their mistakes and responsibilities. Don't contribute to
their antics by promising to give them an answer later on.
Help them by discussing the problem and let them suggest
ways to handle it. Then stay on top of the matter through
clearly defined reporting procedures.

30.2 WHINERS

Whiners are crybabies who voice protracted protests over
the unimportant.

Driven by childish insecurity, Whiners complain when
everything's actually going well. They love to exaggerate unfair workloads, tardy reports, broken rules—whatever they
can blame on somebody else. Although their work is good,
they're interested only in the success of their own unit. They
cause dissention and destroy team spirit by tattling on their
colleagues.

Occasionally, they hit on a problem with roots in the system, and this has to be hashed over and remedied. But usually
Whiners don't sound off about legitimate problems. Yet they
can be so persuasive you end up defending yourself and feeling foolish later. When Whiners warn you of trouble ahead
their intent is to establish an excuse in advance of a feared
failure. If the complaint involves their peers, they want you
to referee and decide in their favor.

What You're Thinking

I can hardly believe it. With all the critical decisions that are weighing me down, Sharon parades in here complaining that Margo keeps messing with the thermostat and the cold air is blowing down her neck and making everyone else uncomfortable. When I told her that was between her and Margo, she said Margo insulted her and they got into a fight. Now she wants me to referee. How did I get into this? And more importantly, how do I get out?

A Whiner's Thoughts

I told Margo that lowering the themostat was a very selfish thing to do and that she only cares about herself and has no consideration for anybody else. I warned her that if she didn't stop acting like that, I would report her. I'm glad I did. It's bad enough that I don't get the recognition I deserve around here without having to suffer physical discomfort as well.

Strategy

Your goal is to improve team spirit by helping the Whiners act in a more mature and professional manner.

(1) *Reassure the whiners.* They may be using petty complaints to get you to say something nice to them. Try more frequent feedback to recognize their accomplishments, allay their fears or insecurities, and offer your support. Keep checking to learn if things are OK before they hatch minor matters into full-scale complaints.

(2) *Lead them toward more appropriate behavior.* Ask them how they feel after acting in certain (inappropriate) ways and what part their behavior had in bringing about the result. You can be empathetic and noncritical and still help Whiners realize that they were part of the cause and should be part of the solution.

(3) *Refuse to be the referee.* Don't take sides, either in petty bickering or if the squabble blows up and the whole office is abuzz. When it gets that bad, you have to step in, but get the facts before you do. Don't blame anyone or let

them rehash accusations. To restore teamwork, get them to recognize they both have individual needs and they both must focus on how these needs can be met.

(4) *Distinguish between a whiner's exaggerated cry and a common complaint.* If you're concerned that the criticism may be more widespread than you first realized, use your staff meetings to resolve the problem. Give the group an exercise in finding solutions.

Tactical Talk

"SHARON, I'D LIKE YOU TO SET ASIDE 9 TO 9:15 EVERY THURSDAY TO MEET WITH ME. I'M STARTING A SEPARATE 'HOW'S IT GOING?' TIME WITH EACH OF MY STAFF, SO BE PREPARED TO TALK ABOUT ANY PROBLEMS OR IDEAS YOU WANT TO BRING TO MY ATTENTION."

"SHARON, I UNDERSTAND YOU'RE UPSET. I, TOO, FIND IT DISTURBING THAT YOU COULDN'T WORK OUT THE PROBLEM WITH MARGO. WHAT RESULT WERE YOU HOPING FOR?...HOW DID YOU FEEL AFTER YOU TOLD MARGO TO STOP?...DO YOU THINK THE WAY YOU ASKED MAY HAVE BROUGHT ON HER REACTION?...WHAT OPTIONS ARE OPEN NOW TO GET WHAT YOU WANT?"

"I'VE CALLED YOU BOTH IN HERE BECAUSE THE PRESENT SITUATION CANNOT CONTINUE. IT'S AF-FECTING THE ENTIRE OFFICE. I WANT THE PROBLEM SOLVED, HOW ABOUT YOU?...WE ALL KNOW WHAT LED UP TO THIS POINT, SO LET'S NOT REVIEW IT. LET'S DEFINE WHAT WE WANT TO ACCOM-PLISH...WELL, WHAT ARE YOUR NEEDS?...HOW COULD THAT BE PREVENTED?...YOU'VE MADE A GOOD START. YOU DON'T NEED ME ANYMORE TO WORK OUT A TENTATIVE ANSWER. TELL ME ON FRI-DAY WHAT THE TWO OF YOU HAVE COME UP WITH."

Tip: The Whiners' bid for attention is juvenile, but their need to be noticed is real. To bolster their sense of security help them focus on objectives and learn how to get along instead of tattle-taling on their peers. Don't fall into their trap by playing referee, or as soon as one complaint is resolved, Whiners will be ready with another.

30.3 SELF-BERATERS

Self-Beraters nag themselves and believe whatever went wrong was their fault.

Like Whiners, they are looking for reassurance. But instead of picking on their peers, they peck at themselves. They are overly critical of their own work. They dramatize how bad they're doing so that you'll contradict them. They claim blame for whatever went amiss hoping you'll grant them absolution. Actually, they perform well, but they are so insecure they have to plead for compliments.

Having such low self-esteem, Self-Beraters are always anxious and practically invite people to take advantage of them. Their way to avoid being hurt by others is to inflict the hurt on themselves before anyone else can do it to them. You find it difficult to criticize them because they've already attacked themselves more severely than you ever would.

What You're Thinking

Just to stop the emotional blackmail, I find myself tempted to give in to Doug's begging for compliments. Sometimes I think it would be less nerve-racking to assure him, over and over and over, yes, you're doing a great job. It's as though he's bracing himself to be hurt or scolded. Instead, when I do compliment Doug, he can't accept it graciously. His demand for reassurance is insatiable.

A Self-Berater's Thoughts

That report I gave the boss probably wasn't any good or I would have heard from her by now. I guess after being knocked down as many times as I have, I have to conclude that I can't do anything right. I think maybe the boss is avoiding me. What else did I do wrong? I'm such an ignoramus. I should have spent more time on that report. It's all my fault that the boss doesn't like it.

Strategy

Your goal is to salvage good workers by helping Self-Beraters become more emotionally mature. Once they gain confidence they'll stop the annoying habit of putting themselves down.

(1) *Continue giving them assignments they do well.* Offer help if they need it and leave them alone if they don't. Allow them to experience a lot of little successes to feel more secure and bolster their self-confidence in the good work they are capable of performing.

(2) *Get them to talk about their concerns.* Once they can discuss what's making them feel anxious and look at it for what it is, they can deal with it. But as long as they cover up their fears with self-incrimination they'll keep depreciating themselves to counteract anticipated criticism.

(3) *Explain the cost of begging for reassurance.* Recognize good work, but don't reinforce their habit by pumping out reassurance upon request. Make clear the negative effect this has on others.

Tactical Talk

Doug: "I GUESS MY REPORT WAS PRETTY BAD."

You: "DOUG, WAIT UNTIL YOU'VE GOOFED UP AS MANY TIMES AS I HAVE BEFORE YOU START PUTTING YOURSELF DOWN. ACTUALLY, THE REPORT WAS SHARP AND INCISIVE."

Doug: "YOU'RE JUST SAYING THAT TO BE NICE. YOU DON'T REALLY MEAN IT, DO YOU?"

You: "I DON'T SAY THINGS I DON'T MEAN AND I FIND IT UPSETTING WHEN SOMEONE DOUBTS

MY WORD. ON TUESDAY, I'D LIKE YOU TO PRESENT TO MY MANAGEMENT COMMITTEE EXCERPTS THAT YOU CAN HIGHLIGHT."

Doug: "YOU REALLY WANT ME TO DO THAT? I DON'T KNOW IF I CAN—"

You: "I KNOW YOU CAN, SO SUPPOSE YOU TELL ME WHAT YOU'RE REALLY CONCERNED ABOUT... I'M GLAD WE HAD THIS TALK, DOUG. IF YOU WAIT TO BE PROPPED UP BY CONSTANT REASSURANCE, YOU'LL LOSE OUT ON MANY GOOD OPPORTUNITIES. BUT YOU DECIDE AND LET ME KNOW TOMORROW."

Tip: Don't baby the Self-Beraters by spoon-feeding them compliments upon demand. You stunt their growth if you pay their emotional blackmail. When they cry for reassurance, give them the jobs they can handle and the recognition they deserve. Do what's reasonable to help them build self-confidence, and get them to identify and deal with their real concerns.

30.4 MARTYRS

Martyrs complain how they've sacrificed when you never even asked for their help.

These workhorses create resentment because they gripe about being overworked but won't accept help. They want you to feel dependent upon them. If they accept the offers of assistance, others workers might pick up their skills and the Martyrs might find themselves out in the cold.

They are obsessive workaholics who use work to smother some personal problem. When they fail, the fault is never theirs. Martyrs are indeed exploited because they volunteer their slave labor. While they complain about unfair distribution of assignments, they really enjoy their suffering as they watch others fail to meet their exhaustingly high level of performance.

What You're Thinking

Joe doesn't fool anyone but himself. He insists on taking the hardest cases. Then they pile up and he won't accept a lift with the load. It's pretty obvious to me that he resents his peers because he's doing some of their work. Although he tries to suppress the resentment, they see it also. And, because he refuses their help, they feel angry instead of grateful to him. Joe's frantic pace and antagonistic attitude is making everyone tense. How can I stop this merry-go-round?

A Martyr's Thoughts

They are all a bunch of ingrates. I stay late every night to clean up the worst cases and they don't appreciate what I'm doing for them. Don't they know if I didn't do it, it wouldn't get done. At least, it wouldn't get done as well. Yet nobody gives a darn how great my work is. I don't get the right recognition from the boss or anyone else. But I'll be the good little team player and not say anything.

Strategy

Your goal is to stop unnecessary tension by resolving legitimate criticism—an imbalance in the workload. By controlling the Martyrs, everyone can resume working at a reasonable rate.

(1) *Produce a plan to redistribute the work.* When Martyrs protect their workload like mother hens, scratching everyone else in the processs, it's time to change the mix. Giving each worker new assignments will prevent overburdening. It also loosens the Martyrs' grip and dispels the reason for resentment.

(2) *Politely refuse excessive help.* Within seconds, the compulsive Martyrs will again be volunteering. Don't accept. Keep their assignments within the limits you set. Martyrs have a personal problem and they'll have to find some way to deal with it other than running everybody in the office crazy.

(3) *Be more generous with recognition.* Utilize the talent of the Martyrs by recognizing their excellence and persuading them to help you coach others.

Tactical Talk

"WE'RE MAKING SOME NEEDED CHANGES AROUND HERE SO THAT THERE'S A MORE EQUITABLE WORK-LOAD. THIS NEW ASSIGNMENT SHEET..."

"THANKS, JOE, I APPRECIATE YOUR WANTING TO TAKE ON MORE WORK, BUT I HAVE SOMETHING MORE IMPORTANT FOR YOU TO DO. YOU'LL NOTICE THAT YOU'RE DOWN FOR A PLANNING SESSION WITH ME. I WANT YOU TO HEAD A NEW UNIT BE-CAUSE I NEED YOUR SPECIAL EXPERTISE TO HELP ME TRAIN..."

Tip: Hold fast to limiting the amount of work you let the Martyrs do. Give them more recognition for their dedicated performance. This won't make them less compulsive, but it should produce a happier atmosphere in your office.

Subordinate griping is good when it forces you to stop going around in circles and start moving forward toward improved performance. Help your workers develop by allowing them to be responsible for their own actions. Show them how to convert their anger into new energy and new answers.

Sometimes you need private conversations to uncover the source of frustration, and talking it through points the way to go. However, if clashes emanate from poor rules or directives, you can utilize buzz groups, staff meetings, and other brainstorming sessions to throw some problems back at your people. Then consider their recommendations. Talking to each other—listening and responding—and finally resolving the criticism leads to increased loyalty and productivity.

SUMMING IT UP

How you deal with a specific boss, colleague, or subordinate who's currently making your life miserable depends on the outcome you want to accomplish. However, several general guidelines also can help you.

1. *Put Problem People in Proper Perspective.* You're nothing but an afterthought to them, so don't take their antics personally. They're not concerned about you because they're too busy worrying about themselves. You just happen to be either an obstacle or an essential ingredient to their getting what they want. You have to figure out how to break free of their control.

2. *Take Your Pick—Positive or Negative.* You can't concentrate on constructive, creative alternatives while you cling to negative feelings. Go somewhere to vent your emotions and cool off. Think about the result you really want, the consequence or outcome that most benefits you. That will help you let go of the hurt.

3. *Don't Expect Difficult People to Change.* They won't. And in one way that's good. Because their behavior is often predictable, this enables you to plan ahead, plotting the tactics you'll use next time. Troublemakers may not change, but by choosing a better approach *you* can change the outcome.

4. *Learn to Respond as Well as to Listen.* Come forward and state that you feel annoyed, upset, enraged. No one can read your mind. Sometimes the offense was totally unintentional and can be easily resolved if allowed to surface. Ask questions instead of making accusations. If you

let others save face, you give them room to change their minds.

5. *Give and Request Frequent Feedback.* Regardless of your position in the organization, you need to know the perceptions of your boss, peers, and workers. Don't stew about what someone else may be thinking—ask! Use open-ended questions to let emotional people vent their feelings before you try to reason with them and explore options. When you link your objectives with another's wants, not only do you have his attention, but also you both win something.

6. *Look First at Policies and Procedures.* That starts the disagreement on a high professional level and prevents blaming a person's distasteful attitude or sinister motive. Don't place blame unless *you* made a mistake for which you apologize quickly and move on. If you both pay attention to each other's needs when identifying options—your stand may depend on which side of the desk you sit—each of you can feel you are exercising some control. At times all that's needed is a simple change in the system.

7. *Deal Directly and Discreetly.* Choose face-to-face talks over memos that can be misconstrued, phone calls that can conceal facial reactions, or ambassadors who do the talking for you. You don't want an audience for personal disagreements. Confront your accusers, tactfully putting your foot down when others are walking over you. Get right to the point because a preamble of excuses or warm-ups robs your effectiveness.

8. *Document for Self-Protection.* Get potentially troublesome verbal agreements in writing to prevent the other party from reneging. For assignments you fear may be hazardous to the health of your career, keep your boss informed with periodic progress reports. Send copies to anyone affected, as evidence, in case a misunderstanding should occur.

9. *Be Straightforward and Unemotional.* The more you remain calm and matter-of-fact, the sooner you gain

another's confidence. People want to feel you're leveling with them, that they can trust you. Remember that respect from others begins with self-respect. Don't continue a conversation with anyone, even your boss, who refuses to give you the courtesy you deserve. You have options, such as asking for politeness or leaving the room.

10. *Be Gracious.* Someone else's rudeness doesn't give you the right to be rude. Turn a bad situation to your advantage by disarming the offenders, treating them with the kindness you'd like to be shown, sharing credit, and allowing others to feel important. Make friends with your enemies—you never know when you'll need them. Others won't have to run you down to build themselves up if you're gracious in showing appreciation and giving recognition. When your own ego is healthy, you are rich. You can afford to be generous.

INDEX